Women of the
American Circus,
1880–1940

# Women of the American Circus, 1880–1940

KATHERINE H. ADAMS *and*
MICHAEL L. KEENE

McFarland & Company, Inc., Publishers
*Jefferson, North Carolina, and London*

LIBRARY OF CONGRESS CATALOGUING-IN-PUBLICATION DATA

Adams, Katherine H., 1954–
Women of the American circus, 1880–1940 /
Katherine H. Adams and Michael L. Keene.
p.    cm.
Includes bibliographical references and index.

ISBN 978-0-7864-7228-4
softcover : acid free paper ∞

1. Women circus performers — United States.    2. Circus performers — United
States — Biography.    3. Circus — United States.    I. Keene, Michael L.    II. Title.
GV1811.A1A33 2012        791.3092—dc23        [B]        2012035866

BRITISH LIBRARY CATALOGUING DATA ARE AVAILABLE

On the cover: untitled photograph of Bird Millman, no date
(color enhanced from original image) Harry A. Atwell, Allen Lester,
Black & White Photo Print, 10 × 8⅛ inch ht000430 (collection of the
John and Mable Ringling Museum of Art Tibbals Digital Collection);
background images © 2012 Shutterstock

Manufactured in the United States of America

*McFarland & Company, Inc., Publishers
Box 611, Jefferson, North Carolina 28640
www.mcfarlandpub.com*

For Claire
— MLK

For Chris, Bill, and Margaret
— KHA

# Acknowledgments

We would like to thank Rob Richards and especially Pete Shrake at Circus World's Robert L. Parkinson Library and Research Center in Baraboo, Wisconsin, for all of their help. At Feld Entertainment, we thank Peggy Williams and Julie Alexa Strauss, Vice President and Deputy General Counsel, for prompt assistance regarding circus art. We also thank Heidi Taylor of the John and Mable Ringling Museum of Art and Sean Campbell of the Buffalo Bill Historical Center for similar assistance. Moira Harrington at Pearce Wireless in Hayward, Wisconsin, provided critical technical support at a crucial moment, as did Ben Hall of Green Tea Digital in Asheville, North Carolina. And we additionally thank Pat Doran, astounding interlibrary loan officer at Loyola University, and Jim Hobbs, the finest of reference librarians. Special thanks to Claire Keene for careful reading of critical parts of the manuscript and for assistance with research materials as well as to Willie Wax for all his help with images and permissions. Special thanks also to the students in Mike's Fall 2011 Professional Writing class for suggestions on how to write about circus posters.

# Contents

# Preface

In four earlier books (*Controlling Representations: Depictions of Women in a Mainstream Newspaper, 1900–1950* with Melanie McKay; *Alice Paul: The Campaign for Suffrage*; *After the Vote Was Won: The Later Achievements of Fifteen Suffragists*; and *Seeing the American Woman, 1880–1920* with Jennifer C. Koella), we have explored the interaction between the visual culture of the United States in the critical period of 1880 to 1940 and the available and emerging roles for women at that time. By "visual culture," we mean the dominant pictorial images occurring in that particular time and place (although complications with that definition will arrive almost immediately). We generally ask "what images of women are available?" and "how are they evolving and changing?" But we also try to go deeper and investigate what arguments those images and that culture are making, to whom, and to what effect. In particular, we look at the interplay between that culture's pictorial images and the available and evolving roles for women.

To draw our particular interest, these roles need to be more than just indexed categories — "women in factories," "women in offices," "women in educational settings," and so on (although these indexed categories could fruitfully be examined). By "roles for women" we mean more than that; for example, we track categories of images like "the vamp" or "the crusading reporter" or "the Gibson girl," categories that for whatever reason have acquired some sort of *iconic* or *symbolic* status. Through their repeated and striking appearances in all kinds of public discourse (including experiences such as performance), these images become something more, recalling the phenomenon Kenneth Burke calls a "representative anecdote" (324). As powerful icons in their own right, these roles, tied to visual images, not only spring from the visual culture, but they come to shape the larger culture in ways both trivial and important.

We could, for example, look at such images from *Godey's Lady's Book*, or period cookbooks, or almanacs, and sort out the images' big characteristics, wondering whether and how they may have contributed to and/or shaped a visual culture for the country. Following that, we could ask what kind of argument these images and that culture make — such as "Women should be…" or "Women shall do…" (or "not do…").

Instead, our particular interest here is rather more focused — on the circus, specifically on women in the American circus. But we hope it will reach to a much larger argument concerning the interaction between the lives and careers of circus women and the lives and careers of all women, between women's history and their evolving choices as American workers.

# Introduction

*At present, I am courting death each day in La Tourbillon De La Mort, the supposed limit of human daring.... The game is one of mettle, not of death. So get your minds fermenting; give your imagination free play; and invent the real limit of human daring. Show us how to fly to the moon; direct the way to Mars; point the signboards down the roads of human daring. And I for one will go.* — Mademoiselle Octavie LaTour, aka Mademoiselle Mauricia De Tiers (quoted in Culhane 160)

Imagine being a child in Zanesville, Ohio, in 1900, when this town on the Muskingum and Licking rivers, fifty-five miles east of Columbus and seventy-three miles west of Wheeling, West Virginia, had a population of 23,000 (*United States Census of 1900* 50). Your father might work in a factory, such as the Schultz and Company Soap Factory or the New Granite Glass Company, at the Hook Brothers and Aston Mill, on a farm, or in a coal mine (Iwen). Your parents would shop downtown at Clossman Hardware Company, F.M. Kirby's 5 and 10 Cent Store, and Sturtevant and Martin Boston One Price Dry Goods House, known as Sturtevants. You would have been warned not to play near the railroad tracks, serving seven different lines and primarily used for shipping, though sometimes a passenger disembarked downtown (Lynch and Sims 35–73).

In a town like Zanesville, life might seem repetitive, a thing of school and hard work, of small-town commerce and family life, for town residents as well as those in rural communities nearby, such as Frazeysburg, Uniontown, and Adamsville, each with a population of 500 or less.

Citizens did have access to a few sources of information and entertainment. Those with the money to buy a piano might entertain friends by singing popular songs from sheet music. For the Fourth of July, civic groups put on plays around town and on the Y-shaped bridge spanning both rivers. Zanesville also had a newspaper, the *Zanesville Times Recorder,* which featured mostly local news. And it had a theatre, the Schultz Opera House, which opened in 1880, where more affluent adults saw plays and vaudeville.

For the child in Zanesville or anywhere else, as for the largest number of adults in the United States, "the major holidays ... were the Fourth of July, Christmas, and the day the circus came to town" ("Circus Poster"). Indeed, the most exciting live entertainment possibility, the one anxiously awaited and discussed long afterwards, the very best break from

**Bird's eye view of Zanesville, Ohio, 1913. Fuller & Harmount (Library of Congress Prints and Photographs Division).**

small-town life, was not the occasional play or town pageant but the circus, which came regularly, six to ten times a year, by wagon and by rail.

These circuses included small "dog and pony shows" that performed outdoors, including Sipe & Dolman, the Harper Brothers, and Stull & Miller, who all traveled the Middle West, running on a shoestring, with no more than a band and a ringmaster as well as the trained dogs and ponies of their circus type. The regularly arriving shows also included small one- or two-ring tented circuses traveling regionally, such as Sun Brothers, Campbell-Bailey-Hutchinson, and Downie Bros. And locals also got to see larger, national, three-ring shows, such as Barnum & Bailey. Since advance men brought huge numbers of colorful posters and left them pasted to fences and buildings, both in town and on rural roads, each circus created a presence in a town like Zanesville not just for a day in the spring, summer, or fall, but for weeks before and months thereafter.

As shown in the posters, and as people actually saw on "circus day," nothing else resembled a traveling circus: wild animals on exhibit well before the nation had zoos, an orchestra and calliope (pronounced "*ca*lley-ope" in circus lingo), equestrians, trapeze artists, clowns, freaks, lion tamers, and countless other acts small and large. Going to the railroad siding for the unloading, to downtown streets for the morning parade, and to a vacant lot near the railroad tracks for the show—these steps in an adventure marked an entrance into another world, one where the colors were brighter, the men stronger, and the women more beautiful and exotic. For our child in Zanesville, this special day had to be both scary and fascinating. And therein lay the source of its attractiveness.

The child in Zanesville in 1900 certainly encountered women each day—mothers and aunts, women in the neighborhood, the schoolteacher, and maybe a female shop clerk. Statistics show that at this time in the United States women were moving out of the home and into professional life, a movement that had its roots in the Civil War, with more and more women leaving home, getting educations, and taking jobs in other people's homes, schools, shops, offices, and factories. But in Zanesville, as in much of the country, the cult of true womanhood and the pictures from *Godey's Lady's Book*—along with Mom, Sis, and the schoolmarm—still controlled the visual culture of women.

And then came the circus.

Overnight, 5000 or more full color posters would appear, covering seemingly every flat surface in town and way out into the countryside with images of all kinds of exotica—elephants, tigers, aerialists, rough riders, clowns, gypsies, gorillas—the full panoply that would soon be pouring out of maybe a hundred specially built railroad cars and coming

Carson and Barnes Circus poster, as displayed in Zanesville, Ohio (John and Mable Ringling Museum of Art).

right down through the middle of town. And, especially, there were pictures of women: women in ballet costumes, women in tights, women riding bareback, women in what were supposed to look like Arabian Nights costumes.

Imagine the impact in a small town of these 5000 posters, in full color, and chock full of these images, posters anywhere from 28 by 42 inches to twenty times that, posters that appeared seemingly overnight. These posters were often renewed or pasted over five or six times a year, not just by the original show that put them up, but also by competitors.

The big show itself presented all kinds of visions of women that also challenged the daily norms of our notional Zanesville (or Manhattan or Denver). Women appeared as up to half of the cast: as dancers, equestrians, aerialists, lion tamers, clowns, sharpshooters, and ringmasters, as well as the sideshow's Johanna the Gorilla, the world's smallest and biggest woman, and the woman wrapped in snakes. This other world of the circus, as manifested in both the big and small shows that appeared regularly across the United States, had a tremendous power, not just to draw in spectators, but to bring what had been the exotic and transgressive into what could now perhaps be seen as acceptable routine. And that routine involved women quite visibly at work.

## Circus History

This other world of the circus started in England in the late eighteenth century, centered around the all important horse. In 1768, Englishman Philip Astley, a skilled equestrian with cavalry experience, trained a horse to canter in a tight circle forty-two feet in diameter. Maintaining a constant speed around this circle and leaning inward enabled centrifugal force to keep him standing on a horse's back and thus created a dramatic demonstration of equestrian ability for an audience of horse buyers and owners. Another rider, dubbed "La Fille de l'Air," was Astley's wife, Petsy, who danced on a horse's back as it circled the ring (May, *The Circus from Rome* 265). In Islington, a popular rural resort area, the Astleys created a full show by adding tumbling, juggling, rope dancing, and dog acts (McConnell 11). In 1769, they erected a more permanent structure, with bleachers, at the south end of Westminster Bridge, enabling large crowds of spectators to see the performance. One of the riders, Charles Hughes, started a competing arena in 1782, and used the word "circus," from the Roman tradition, to describe it. Equestrian acts had been popular in ancient Greece and Rome, but interspersing physical feats on horseback with rope dancers, tumbling, and clown performances, as both Hughes and the Astleys did, was new (Culhane 1).

Almost immediately, this popular entertainment came to the United States. As early as November 1771, equestrian John Sharp offered performances in Boston (Moy 187). By 1786, Thomas Pool owned circuses in Boston and New York, where clowns entertained between equestrian feats (Thayer, *Annals* 4). In 1793, in Philadelphia, John Bill Ricketts opened an indoor ring, with equestrians, clowns, an acrobat, and a ropewalker. He appeared along with Mrs. Spinacuta, her first name not recorded on programs or in circus histories, who rode two horses at full gallop. She appeared with her husband, Seignoir Spinacuta, perhaps the same Laurent Spinacuta who earlier had worked in a London menagerie. Ricketts prospered and took his show on a wagon tour from Boston to Baltimore and then opened a second amphitheatre, in New York, where he added a pantomime and a dramatic entertainment based on George Washington's suppression of the Whiskey Rebellion in 1794 (Huey). In a depiction of the life of Don Juan, with hell's fires burning this profligate, Ricketts accidentally ignited his amphitheatre and thus ended his career in the United States (Smith, "Spec-ology" 51).

At the beginning of the 1800s, circuses played in large eastern population centers like Philadelphia and New York for runs of up to three months. Only at the end of a long stand did they take to the roads in wagons ("mud-wagons") to earn additional money. In the next decades, with improving roads and a burgeoning population throughout the country, the balance shifted to long periods spent touring, with tents put up along the way. By 1836, the twelve circus companies then operating used tents instead of permanent pavilions for their shows, and they averaged 150 locations annually.

Beginning that year, P.T. Barnum began traveling with a small variety show, including Signor Antonio Vivalla, a juggler; Joe Pentland, a clown and magician; and John Diamond, a specialist in "Ethiopian breakdowns," who "sang and danced with wild twisting of the feet and legs" (Saxon 77–79). The Seeley Circus of 1840 was the first wagon show to exhibit west of St. Louis. By 1856, ten different circuses followed the route Seeley had taken. In 1857, Rowe and Co.'s Pioneer Circus of California toured the mining districts of that state (Culhane 79–81).

With scantily dressed women, galloping equestrians, games of chance on the Midway, and a mysterious power to enthrall spectators, these traveling circuses faced hostility from clergy, before the Civil War especially, who depicted them as immoral dens that could taint the soul. In the colonial era, laws had forbidden the performance of plays in Massachusetts, Pennsylvania, and Rhode Island. Timothy Dwight IV, Congregationalist minister and president of Yale College from 1795 to 1817, spoke of churchgoers as properly working to "save the world from absolute ruin" by re-establishing a religious life in the United States, from which the worst elements of corruption would be eliminated: "The Theatre will cease to entice, corrupt, and destroy the thoughtless crowd of victims to sense and sin" (226, 236). And if a three-act play could seem questionable, so much more so the circus.

In 1815, the *Chillicothe Weekly Recorder*, in Chillicothe, Ohio, condemned a traveling circus for "prosecuting an unlawful calling — one that can not be defended on Scriptural ground, or on principles of sound reason and good policy" (Chindahl 21; Dickinson 7). In 1826, authorities in Sudbury, Pennsylvania, arrested a circus troupe for witchcraft (Thayer, *Annals* 14). In 1844, the Rev. Henry Ward Beecher described both circus performers and their audiences as the worst of the irreligious: "the idle, dissipated, the rogues, the licentious, the epicures, the gluttons, the artful jades, the immodest prudes, the joyous, the worthless, the refuse" (187–88). Such "corrupters of youth," he argued, "have no mitigation of their baseness" (194). Sermons by men like Dwight and Beecher, as well as newspaper coverage of them, could hurt circus business at any local site, as circus equestrian Balinda Merriam Spencer noted in her journal on October 9, 1889, while on tour with John Robinson's Ten Big Shows Combined in Rock Hill, South Carolina: "Poor business on account of big revival meetings in this place. Prayers from eleven till twelve for the poor sinful showmen" (28).

As negative press dogged the circus, managers did whatever they could to improve their reputations and thus increase the size of the house. Higher revenues came from incorporating acts that had begun as separate entertainment industries, some of them judged more morally uplifting than the antics of equestrians and clowns.

## Menageries

Menageries had started as separate stationary exhibits and then became wagon shows, usually touring only through a small area: the site where many Americans first saw exotic animals in an era before public zoos (Kisling). In the nineteenth century, menageries were accorded a tolerance not always given to circuses. They brought with them informative souvenir booklets referring, often vaguely, to scientists and explorers; their exhibition of animals thus seemed more educational (and thus morally acceptable) than circus acts. These menageries began with exhibits of native animals, like bears, and then added more exotic species, with a lion coming to the United States for exhibition in 1720, a camel in 1721, a polar bear in 1733, a leopard in 1768, and an elephant in 1796. In the early 1820s, thirty or more menageries with various combinations of these animals toured the eastern part of the country (Culhane 17). In 1834, the New York Menagerie featured an elephant and a rhinoceros, its biggest draws and most expensive animals, along with a camel, zebra, gnu, two tigers, a polar bear, monkeys, and parrots (Flint 98).

As excitement for these traveling exhibits began to wane, their novelty wearing off, owners created trained animal acts to extend their audience. In 1833, to augment his earnings, Isaac Van Amburgh, "The Lion King," began entering the cage during each show and putting his head in a lion's mouth (Culhane 21; Dickinson 3). As menagerie owners then began engaging clowns and acrobats and as circuses added animal acts, the distinction between circuses and menageries began to disappear.

## Museum Shows

It was P.T. Barnum who helped lead another merger, this one of circuses with privately owned city museums. In the mid-nineteenth century, these museums appeared in cities around the country. Like menageries, they were deemed acceptable to a wide audience for their supposed educational content (Saxon 90). These sites, as Artemus Ward, a visitor from England, noted in 1870, provided a jumble of attractions divorced from what might be found at the Louvre, the British Museum, or any other European institution:

> A "museum" in the American sense of the word means a place of amusement, wherein there shall be a theatre, some wax figures, a giant and a dwarf or two, a jumble of pictures, and a few live snakes. In order that there may be some excuse for the use of the word, there is, in most instances a collection of stuffed birds, a few preserved animals, and a stock of oddly assorted and very dubitable curiosities; but the mainstay of the "Museum" is the "live art," that is, the theatrical performance, the precocious mannikins, or the intellectual dogs and monkeys [Hingston 16].

The Ninth and Arch Street Museum in Philadelphia, typical of these American institutions, stayed in business from 1883 to 1910. By the late 1880s, the first floor had distorting mirrors, a penny arcade, and penny-in-the-slot peep shows; the second floor housed a menagerie; and the third floor contained a Curio Hall, a room in which people designated as "freaks" stood along the walls in niches.

P.T. Barnum, better than anyone else, knew how to create what historian Brooks McNamara labeled as "the complex mixture of novelty, piety, pedantry, and outright fraud that spelled spectacular success in the museum business" (219). In 1841, after Barnum purchased Scudder's American Museum, he exhibited stuffed animals, wax figures, trick mirrors, optical instruments, a large magnet, suits of armor, the mummified body of an Indian found at Mammoth Cave, insects and butterflies, minerals and crystals, and Roman, Asian, and Indian artifacts. His museum also contained a menagerie of living animals, including the first hippopotamus and the first public aquarium in America.

On the stage of his "so-called lecture room," in McNamara's terminology, Barnum offered "educated dogs, industrious fleas, automatons, jugglers, ventriloquists, living statuary, tableaux" along with vocal and instrumental music, pantomime, dioramas and panoramas, comics, rope dancers, puppet shows, Indian war dances featuring scantily clothed maids and braves, and pious theatrical favorites such as W.H. Smith's *The Drunkard, or the Fallen Saved*. At this site, Barnum thus created entertainments "on a scale undreamt of by earlier operators" (McNamara 219). It was a complex mix, one that placed side by side (purportedly) uplifting educational exhibits and exotic, sexually titillating ones.

At museums also, freaks were exhibited in niches along the wall of an exhibit room. This group included "born freaks," such as midgets, giants, or persons with other physical differences, and "made freaks," like tattooed people or fat people. Barnum, for example, presented fat ladies, dwarfs, and other "Vagaries of Nature in the human family," as his catalogue stated. For variety, the niches also contained "working acts," featuring people who swallowed swords or lay on nails. In addition, performers sold souvenirs like autographed pictures, "giant's rings," and pamphlets with astounding life stories.

Over time, as even this combination of entertainments failed to lure enough customers, especially in large cities like New York where citizens could visit several museums open day and night, operators turned to stunts that provided something extra to advertise and thus increase interest. The manager of New York's Huber's Museum, for example, asked his fat man and fat lady, Chauncey Morlan and Annie Bell, to get married on the museum stage in November 1892 in front of a capacity crowd, with hundreds turned away, an event that circus historian William G. FitzGerald described as "a masterstroke of showmanship." The "newlyweds," also advertised as a "colossal couple," then held daily receptions for six weeks to packed houses (521).

By the end of the century, a new site for museum revenue occurred through affiliation with the circus. In April of 1871, Barnum went into business with circus men Coup and Costello; Barnum's museum acts, including the Cardiff Giant and a family of Fiji cannibals, formed the circus's sideshow. Making such additions to the circus more acceptable, more appropriate for women and children, were pamphlets and "professors" associating sideshow acts with world geography, distant cultures, and physical anomalies in a supposedly arcane manner.

## The Wild West Show

While some circuses increased their audiences by adding menagerie and museum exhibits, another enlargement through merger occurred with Wild West shows. Buffalo Bill Cody spurred their popularity, his own performances shaped from real and exaggerated moments of his life: working as a young boy for the Pony Express and then for the cavalry, killing two Indians at a time while they attempted to escape by fleeing on the same horse, freeing a captured white woman, and being saved by Sioux after breaking his leg out alone on the Plains (McMurtry 59). On the Fourth of July, 1882, Cody organized a rodeo, the Old Glory Blow Out. At age thirty-one, he labeled his inaugural show as his "farewell tour," a promotional technique that he repeated frequently. Against advice, he then embarked on a very successful tour around the West, perceiving that residents there might prefer the fantasy of his show to the reality in which they lived. He soon got Native Americans of several tribes to join him, paying a bond to the government to hire them.

Cody's Wild West went to England in 1887 for part of Queen Victoria's Jubilee Year, with Annie Oakley among the trick shooters. His group at first provided the entertainment at a trade show but then, as it grew in popularity, became a separate entity. With ninety-seven Native Americans, scores of other performers and stagehands, 160 horses, sixteen buffalo, and bears, elk, and deer, Cody played in England to two and a half million people (McMurtry 157). In 1893, he set up shop with a similarly large group right outside the World's Fair in Chicago, in two large lots across from the main entrance, where many visitors paid admission to his show and thought they had entered the actual fair.

After Cody launched his Wild West show, dozens of others shortly followed, started by men who took flamboyant names like Pawnee Bill, Buckskin Joe, and Mexican Joe. Major Gordon W. Lillie, who performed as Pawnee Bill, and his wife May Manning launched a show involving "kinfolk and old friends, a huge troop of cowboys, Mexican riders, scouts, and Indians from five tribes," with which they toured around the United States and Europe (Wallis 269). José Barrera, who began with Lillie as Mexican Joe, formed his own smaller show. Joe Miller and his brothers, who operated their 101 Ranch in Oklahoma as a spot where visitors could see a western show in a western setting, began touring in 1906 (Wallis 276–77). Over the course of the show's history, which stretched to 1927, the cast included cowboy movie stars like Hoot Gibson and Tom Mix, who appeared in many films made at the ranch, as well as Buffalo Bill himself.

Some of these organizations, like the touring version of the 101 Ranch, continued into the 1920s, but with hard economic times after the Depression of 1893, as well as competition from circuses and early western films, many of the Wild West shows began to constrict into rodeos, to close altogether, or to join with circuses. Cody himself, having trouble funding a large show in an ailing economy, began touring with the Sells-Floto Circus in 1894. Similarly, after leaving the 101 Ranch show for a long film career, Tom Mix appeared with the Sells-Floto Circus from 1929 to 1931 and then with the Sam B. Dill Circus. To draw in the audiences of Wild West shows, circuses incorporated western costumes in their morning parades and opening processions; their equestrian acts often involved western garb and scenarios; and they included sharpshooting acts in their programs.

## Circus Geography

With their own menageries, museum freaks, and sharpshooters as well as equestrians, clowns, and tightrope walkers, circuses swelled in popularity toward the end of the nineteenth century. In 1884, fourteen shows traveled nationally; in 1889, twenty-two (Culhane 150). The larger, three-ring circus, invented in the United States, became a phenomenon around 1890. The three-ringed tent eventually used by the Ringling Brothers, who began touring in 1884, seated 12,000 people. Barnum & Bailey's Greatest Show on Earth commonly spent its first month at Madison Square Garden before heading to Brooklyn and then out to sites around the country on a tour that would last until November, as the 1895 *Route Book* shows, a year in which its performance on May 24 was in Zanesville:

MARCH/APRIL: Mar. 28–Apr. 17 New York, Madison Square Garden; Apr. 29–May 4 Brooklyn, N.Y.

MAY: 6 Jersey City, N.J.; 7 Paterson, N.J.; 8 Morristown, N.J.; 9 Orange, N.J.; 10 Newark, N.J.; 11 Trenton, N.J.; 13 Lancaster, Pa.; 14 York, Pa.; 15–16 Baltimore, Md.; 17–18 Washington, D.C.; 20–21 Pittsburgh, Pa.; 22 Steubenville, O.; 23 Wheeling, W.Va.; 24 Zanesville, O.; 25 Newark, O.; 27 Columbus, O.; 28 Springfield, O.; 29 Dayton, O.; 30 Richmond, Ind.; 31 Indianapolis, Ind.

JUNE: 1 Brazil, Ind.; 3–8 St. Louis, Mo.; 10 Springfield, Ill.; 11 Jacksonville, Ill.; 12 Decatur, Ill.;

13 Bloomington, Ill.; 14 Champaign, Ill.; 15 Kankakee, Ill.; 17 Centralia, Ill.; 18 Carbondale, Ill.; 19 Cairo, Ill.; 20 Carmi, Ill.; 21 Vincennes, Ind.; 22 Worthington, Ind.; 24 Frankfort, Ind.; 25 Kokomo, Ind.; 26 Muncie, Ind.; 27 Celina, O.; 28 Lima, O.; 29 Findlay, O.

JULY: 1 Cleveland, O.; 2 Ashtabula, O.; 3 Greenville, O.; 4 Warren, O.; 5 Alliance, O.; 6 Massillon, O.; 8 Bucyrus, O.; 9 Sandusky, O.; 10 Toledo, O.; 11 Defiance, O.; 12 Butler, Ind.; 13 Adrian, Mich.; 15 Detroit, Mich.; 16 Chatham, Ont.; 17 St. Thomas, Ont.; 18 Brantford, Ont.; 19 Hamilton, Ont.; 20 Port Hope, Ont.; 22–23 Montreal, Que.; 24 Ottawa, Ont.; 25 Cornwall, Ont.; 26 Kingston, Ont.; 27 Belleville, Ont.; 29 Toronto, Ont.; 30 Stratford, Ont.; 31 London, Ont.

AUGUST: 1 Port Huron, Mich.; 2 Saginaw, Mich.; 3 Flint, Mich.; 5 Elkhart, Ind.; 6 Valparaiso, Ind.; 7 Plymouth, Ind.; 8 Wabash, Ind.; 9 Bluffton, Ind.; 10 Connersville, Ind.; 12 Shelbyville, Ind.; 13 Seymour, Ind.; 14 New Albany, Ind.; 15 Bedford, Ind.; 16 Crawfordsville, Ind.; 17 Logansport, Ind.; 19 Lafayette, Ind.; 20 Hoopeston, Ill.; 21 Paris, Ill.; 22 Mattoon, Ill.; 23 Lincoln, Ill.; 24 Canton, Ill.; 26 Peoria, Ill.; 27 Streator, Ill.; 28 Joliet, Ill.; 29 Aurora, Ill.; 30 Elgin, Ill.; 31 Rockford, Ill.

SEPTEMBER: 2–14 Chicago, Ill.; 16 Milwaukee, Wis.; 17 Madison, Wis.; 18 Freeport. Ill.; 19 Dixon, Ill.; 20 Clinton, Ia.; 21 Davenport, Ia.; 23 Galesburg, Ill.; 24 Quincy, Ill.; 25 Burlington, Ia.; 26 Ottumwa, Ia.; 27 Des Moines, Ia.; 28 Council Bluffs, Ia.; 30 Cheyenne, Wyo.

OCTOBER: 1–2 Denver, Colo.; 3 Colorado Springs, Colo.; 4 Pueblo, Colo.; 5 Trinidad, Colo.; 7 Wichita Falls, Tex.; 8 Ft. Worth, Tex.; 9 Weatherford, Tex.; 10 Cleburne, Tex.; 11 Dallas, Tex.; 12 Paris, Tex.; 14 Gainesville, Tex.; 15 Denison, Tex.; 16 Sulphur Springs, Tex.; 17 McKinney, Tex.; 18 Greenville, Tex.; 19 Waxahachie, Tex.; 21 Hillsboro, Tex.; 22 Corsicana, Tex.; 23 Waco, Tex.; 24 Temple, Tex.; 25 Austin, Tex.; 26 San Antonio, Tex.; 28 Galveston, Tex.; 29 Houston, Tex.; 30 Palestine, Tex.; 31 Tyler, Tex.

NOVEMBER: 1 Marshall, Tex.; 2 Shreveport, La.; 4–5 New Orleans, La.; 6 Baton Rouge, La.; 7 Natchez, Miss.; 8 Jackson, Miss.; 9 Meridian, Miss.; End of season, winter quarters Bridgeport, Conn.

As this season-long schedule makes clear, circus owners incorporated into their runs any city of 2000 or more near which a crowd might gather. Coming to the showgrounds in wagons and later in cars, rural residents could swell a circus crowd. As a Ringling Bros. manager commented in 1919, "One place in Kansas where we give our performance has a population of about 8,000, yet we get an audience of over 30,000. The automobiles stand around the tent as thick as flies" ("Horseback").

Small southern towns, as circus historian Earl Chapin May wrote in 1926, generated especially good business: the Sparks Circus played small towns in Mississippi that year, such as Yazoo City, Cleveland, and Okolona, where they "cleaned up." To get to Plainview, Texas, a town of 4000, in 1926, the Sells-Floto Circus traveled 281 miles because the owners expected a crowd of 10,000 to attend ( "Keeping the Circus" 389). In these Southern locations, white and African American customers might have separate entrances and seating areas as well as separate streets for viewing the parade. In Waco, Texas, in October 1904, police arrested three "well dressed" white women when they sat in the white seating area with three African American children that they had taken on a "sightseeing expedition" ("Race Issue").

The circus, some owners argued, especially interested citizens of the Great Plains because of the contrast to their own lives: "The color, the glitter, the grace of gesture, the precision of movement, all so alien to the Plains — so different from the slow movement of stiffened old farmers and faded and angular women" (Sutherland 257). Some areas of the country, owners also knew, rarely led to profit: many New England towns dominated by disapproving members of the clergy, circus historian Earl Chapin May claimed, generated crowds of an insignificant size ("Keeping the Circus" 389). Along with studying towns and states, tour organizers tried to analyze temporary conditions: they knew when a good harvest or new factory might provide extra spending money.

## The Golden Age

By 1905, at the "height of the circus' golden age," as circus historian Linda Granfield has written, "there were nearly 100 circuses and menageries, each playing to mesmerized audiences of between several hundred to over 20,000 a day all over the country. Well before the advent of film, radio, and television, the circus was the largest entertainment industry the world had ever seen" (25). In 1910, Barnum & Bailey toured with eighty-four railroad cars, Ringling Brothers with eighty-four, Forepaugh-Sells with forty-seven, and Hagen-beck-Wallace with forty-five (Chindahl 150). In 1917, right before the war began, Ringling had more than a thousand personnel, 335 horses, and a huge menagerie; the show traveled in ninety-two rail cars (Culhane 177; Dickinson 4). Carnivals also brought shows to small rural towns, adding to the circus impact: in 1902 seventeen organized carnivals toured regionally and nationally ; by 1905 there were forty six (Bogdan, *Freak Show* 59). As circus historian Kenneth Dickinson commented, from 1880 to 1940 circuses "were the main form of entertainment for the people of the United States" and certainly the most common live form, the only live entertainment seen by American men, women, and children of all classes, on the street as well as under the tents. The presence of posters as well as newspaper and magazine publicity, along with the shows themselves, brought a circus presence to towns everywhere, not just to the upper class or to residents of larger cities (84). As circus historian Janet M. Davis has claimed, at the beginning of the twentieth century circuses reached virtually all Americans (13).

This success occurred as circuses shed much of their earlier association with the tawdry and immoral. After the Civil War especially, circus managers used the media, as well as the addition of more "wholesome" acts, to alter this reputation and thus expand their potential audience. Press agents placed stories in small-town papers, as novelist Mary S. Deering wrote in 1876, to construct the circus as "by far the most respectably conducted and universally popular first class amusement now before the public. Entirely unexceptionable and such as heads of the most respectable families, and seminaries for youth, will not hesitate to encourage those under their charge to attend." As she noted, this effort had started to work, changing the group that entered the tents: "The canvas had been overflowing everywhere with literary men, clergymen, artisans, shopkeepers and laborers — all with their respectable and delighted families" (115–17). (See C-6.) Into the twentieth century, especially the Ringling Brothers stressed in their ads and on their grounds that the circus provided good, clean fun, more appropriate for a family than any other entertainment. In 1900, Alfred T. Ringling, the middle brother of five, wrote in his *Life Story of the Ringling Brothers* of the changes that his brothers thus created: "Formerly these circuses were severely censured by moralists. These brothers have created a style, a moral tone, and a character for their show which have changed this censure into warmest praise" (14). As Janet M. Davis wrote concerning the last decades of the nineteenth century and the beginning of the twentieth, the circus had "self-consciously defined itself as respectable and moral since the postbellum era"

May Wirth (standing) and Lillian Leitzel, two stars on the road, May 14, 1924 (Library of Congress Prints and Photographs Division).

and thus it was "not a target of purity reform during the Progressive era, despite its titillating bodily performances" (11).

With the first world war and the Depression, circuses began to change and then to consolidate. Ringling Bros. and Barnum & Bailey became a combined show in 1919, with great stars like Poodles Hanneford, Tiny Kline, Bird Millman, May Wirth, and Lillian Leitzel appearing throughout the 1920s. Ringling bought the American Circus Corporations holdings — Sells-Floto, Hagenbeck-Wallace, John Robinson, Sparks, and Al G. Barnes —

in September 1929, bad timing with the crash occurring in October and with circus attendance lowering in the 1930s (Kline 342). But circuses kept rolling during the Depression. The WPA helped to fund some shows, keeping stars and crews in front of audiences ("WPA Circus Performance"). Thirty circuses remained on the rails in 1933; even in difficult times, Americans continued to appreciate the magic of the big show and to attend if they could (May, "Bigger and Better").

## The Performance Situation

The big success of circus from 1880 to 1940 involved a unique type of performance and performer. In contrast to other entertainers, circus stars seemingly did not just play roles but performed as part of their own lives, right along with their parents, siblings, spouses, and children, a separate and itinerant group. Social critic Antony H. Coxe argues that "any performance presented on a stage, framed by a proscenium, is a spectacle based on an illusion," but in comparison, he continues, in the circus "there can be no illusion, for there are eyes all round to prove that there is no deception. The performers actually do exactly what they appear to do. Their feats of dexterity and balance and strength must never be confused with the make believe world of the actor … for while an actor says he will 'play his part,' the circus artiste tells you he will 'work his act.'" This "spectacle of actuality," Coxe argues further, thus contains an authenticity, integrity, vitality, and honesty that contrast with the theatre's implied artifice and effeteness. The circus performance may thus be labeled realism, in fact a "spectacular realism," quite unlike the set roles of a play or film or the set movements of a dance (24–25). As anthropologist Yoram Carmeli has written, the circus, different from any other art form, seemed to the public to "engulf the totality of performers' offstage lives," of women as well as men (158).

Performers also commented on the difference between the circus and other entertainments, especially on the primacy of real risk in the circus. Aerialist Fritzi Huber, speaking with interviewer Donnalee Frega, commented on the "intimate proximity" in the big top as a "real way of life":

> "The air fills with sawdust and your throat gets dry; that's when it starts to register that all this is *real.* There's an intimate proximity in the tent: You can make eye contact, feel the physical presence of people around you, gauge their emotional feedback. In a theatre, by contrast, you are in a dark cocoon."
>
> "But in a theater, you know that you are watching actors who are playing roles," I remind her. "Circus performers live their profession."
>
> "Yes, and that's part of the curiosity. You know that you are seeing the manifestation of a real way of life. It's not safe, either. The danger that you're witnessing is actual and immediate" [266].

This entertainment type — involving acts announced verbally but performed only to music — directs the eyes to and places strong emphasis on the body. As Antonin Artaud, French playwright and director, commented in 1931 on Balinese dance and other highly symbolic visual performances, such forms of art offer "the sense of a new physical language based on signs rather than words" through which performers "demonstrate the power and the supremely effective force of a certain number of conventions that are well learned and above all masterfully executed … a superabundance of impressions, each richer than the last" (Artaud 215–18; Savarese and Fowler 51).

In this sphere of real bodies placed at real risk, the proceedings also involved the audience. In comparison to the theatre, occurring within the bounds of a proscenium arch to which audiences remained at a distance, circuses presented an interactive art form, with spectators switching their attention from outside the tents to inside and from one ring to another, their participation invited in various ways. Ringmasters called out for spectators to make noise and then be silent as though the tricks could not be done without the appropriate responses. Clowns entered the audience to recruit participants for their tricks. And sometimes apparent audience members (actually thinly disguised circus workers, a practice called "duping") were riled up, almost to violence, to heighten the impact, as is recorded about a common type of equestrian act that Huck Finn witnesses:

> And by and by a drunken man tried to get into the ring — said he wanted to ride; said he could ride as well as anybody that ever was. They argued and tried to keep him out, but he wouldn't listen, and the whole show come to a standstill. Then the people begun to holler at him and make fun of him, and that made him mad, and he begun to rip and tear; so that stirred up the people, and a lot of men begun to pile down off of the benches and swarm toward the ring, saying, "Knock him down! throw him out!" and one or two women begun to scream. So, then, the ringmaster he made a little speech, and said he hoped there wouldn't be no disturbance, and if the man would promise he wouldn't make no more trouble he would let him ride if he thought he could stay on the horse. So everybody laughed and said all right, and the man got on. The minute he was on, the horse begun to rip and tear and jump and cavort around, with two circus men hanging on to his bridle trying to hold him, and the drunken man hanging on to his neck, and his heels flying in the air every jump, and the whole crowd of people standing up shouting and laughing till tears rolled down.... But pretty soon he struggled up astraddle and grabbed the bridle, a-reeling this way and that; and the next minute he sprung up and dropped the bridle and stood! and the horse a-going like a house afire, too. He just stood up there, a-sailing around as easy and comfortable as if he warn't ever drunk in his life [222–24].

## Women and the Big Top

"Real" circus entertainments, with real performers acting and reacting with a live audience, increasingly involved women both in the audience and in the show. Especially with an improving reputation after the Civil War, the circus drew greater numbers of women to its audience. In fact, matinees would commonly be filled with more women than men, there with their children for a day of family entertainment.

Along with more women in the audience came more women in circus casts. Whereas the ratio of women to men in circus troupes was about one to fifty in 1880, those percentages changed dramatically afterwards, from the earlier two percent to a third or more after 1910. As retired clown Charles I. Willey commented in 1924 in a *New York Times* interview, women moved up in their responsibilities as well as their numbers: "In the old days women were a decoration. They didn't do much but trim up the acts. Now they are the headliners" ("Old Circus Clown"). A *Nation* article from that same month included the following comment on a star trapeze performer and an equestrian, the two performing "heroic feats, unrivaled world-heralded, unique" under the spotlight in the center ring: "they are both women; feminism has entered the sawdust ring, and mere males are allowed to lead in the horse, or hand the lady the proper rope" ("In the Driftway" Apr. 1924). Audiences thrilled to risks taken by incredibly skilled women, who might seem more vulnerable than men to possible injury and more shocking in their risks and their costuming. By 1900, as Kenneth Dickinson has written, "Any act commonly performed by a man became a much greater draw with a woman performing it" (10).

Some of these women were actually female impersonators. For example "Barbette," his birth name cited as Vander Clyde and Vander Clyde Broadway, born in Round Rock, Texas, answered an ad in *Billboard* after high school and joined the Alfaretta Sisters World-Famous Aerial Queens. As he recalled, his new boss wanted women on the high wire: "She told me that women's clothes always make a wire act more impressive — the plunging and gyrating more dramatic in a woman — and asked me if I would mind dressing as a girl." Barbette then developed his solo act, performing trapeze and wire stunts in full drag, maintaining the illusion until the end of the act when he would pull off his wig and strike exaggerated masculine poses — "an exercise in mystification and a play on masculine-feminine contrast" (Steegmuller 132). Barbette made his European debut in 1923 and returned to the United States in 1924 as a featured attraction with the Ringling Bros. and Barnum & Bailey Circus. Other female impersonators included bareback riders Ella Zoyara (Omar Kingsley) and Albert Hodgini and wire walker Berta "Slats" Beeson, who as "Julian Eltinge of the Wire" paid homage to Lillian Leitzel (Frank 111).

Such impersonators toured with many circuses, but almost all of the women creating the third to half of the cast by 1910 were actually women. Their numbers increased even further for special shows. In 1895 and 1896, taking advantage of publicity about a more modern, independent woman in the United States, Barnum & Bailey featured the gimmick of a separate ring populated by "New Women," as newspaper articles noted: "The circus has this year followed the lead of every other up-to-date enterprise and made room for the new woman" ("The Latest New Woman"). For those years, this circus included a separate ring in which the ringmaster, equestrians, trapeze artists, and clowns were all women, providing a chance for training and employment that allowed many young women to launch circus careers ("The Tank's"). As publicity for the New Woman Show of 1896 indicated, "there is no costume, no phase, no degree of New Womanhood that is not represented in the big show." This innovation proved popular in the two years in which it was employed: "Mr. Bailey counts the scheme a grand success, and judging from the applause of the chappies and the sisters in the cause the stamp of public approval is guaranteed" ("The Latest New Woman").

In contrast to theatre and film, which seemed to hire only beautiful young women, the circus had to place emphasis on very particular skills, as the *New York Times* noted: "Unlike the more pretentious musical shows along Broadway where beauty is a prerequisite for admittance to the chorus, the Ringling Brothers-Barnum & Bailey circus, now preparing for its last week at the new Madison Square Garden, does not demand pulchritude in its women performers. For skill is what the circus demands — skill at tumbling, trapeze flying, horsewomanship, and even skill at clowning, just as among the animals it demands either rarity or intelligence" ("Circus Combines"). Circus writer Charles T. Murray stated this point about equestrian acts and the concentration on skill much more bluntly: some of the riders "though elaborately rouged, would scarcely bear favorable daylight inspection. They were evidently hired for what they could do, and not for their personal appearance" (21).

The combination of female skill and beauty however, even if not required, could certainly rivet the audience's attention. Charles T. Murray, in fact, argued that the best effect occurred when beautiful horses had beautiful, skilled women astride them: "A pudgy woman on horseback excites only laughter, however clever a horsewoman she may be. She breaks the rhythm" (23). And the *New York Times* article that made the claim about skill and not pulchritude commented at length about the women in the Ringling Bros. and Barnum & Bailey Circus, such as Jennie Rooney, Cinderella of the opening pageant, who combined both ("Circus Combines"). Certainly sex appeal, best observed in a scanty costume, could help a woman land the first job and get opportunities to improve her skills. In one of her poems, acrobatic performer Marjorie Hackett recreated the young female cast on the Lewis Brothers Circus, focusing on their sexual looks and dress: Adaline and Cherie, who are "dolled up fit to kill" to "bring money into the till"; Lola Bell and Elsie May, who dance to "keep the audience in a trance"; and trapeze artists Adeline and Virginia, who "hanging by their knees ... will lose their clothes if they ever sneeze" (np).

For these women in the circus, a clear hierarchy existed. It started with the chorus, a large number of women with the least skill and the least salary: a job from which to launch a career. In the Kiralfy circus, as an article in the *New York Sun* claimed in March of 1903, backstage waiting to enter might be "a hundred girls" along with "nearly a hundred men, four chariots, a hundred horses and ten camels" ("The Ballet at the Circus").

Above these women in stature were acrobats, dog and elephant trainers, equestrians, big cat trainers, aerialists, and clowns. Animal trainers ranked above those who just performed with animals though the difference might not be clear to the viewer; those that trained dangerous cats ranked above those working with dogs or elephants. And for each skill well-known stars ranked above all others, this complex order determining place in the dressing tent and train car, salary, and performance time and placement in the big top.

## A National — Visual — Culture of Work

As the pervasive American entertainment form, reaching many more people than magazines or plays, the circus created the first truly national visual depiction of women at work — seen by an audience of women as well as men and children. Most of these women performed unnamed, in huge casts, but there were also stars with very well-known names. As Janet M. Davis commented, well before film and with a realism it couldn't possess, circuses thus "celebrated female power" and expanded notions of a women's capabilities and appropriate work (83). For women especially, the "bodily language" of the circus offered, as Davis argued, "a startling alternative to contemporary social norms" (83).

In an array of acts, circus women did not just startle the audience because of skill, beauty, and small costumes. In the narrative arc of the circus trick, women performers took on the role of hero as they rarely did in American culture and art. Critic Paul Bouissac described the circus trick as generally following a narrative structure that involves "a person (or group of persons) who survives several obstacles, followed by a crucial test that gives the person (or a group of persons) hero status, which is confirmed through further action" (70). Bouissac commented that the circus act thus conforms to the structure of many novels and folktales, but in those genres the conquering hero was generally a man. Increasingly in the circus, this hero, seen working in the most dramatic of costumes, was a woman.

In this depiction of women's physical strength, risk, and sexuality, such elements were constructed as part of circus women's lives, not just of roles they might play. Here we can see feminism not as a theory, but as a daily practice and profession. Even more than the stage studied by Susan Glenn in *The Female Spectacle*, the circus "was practically the only place where a woman could be rewarded in spite of, or even because of, her transgressiveness" (7). In encouraging women to cultivate their strength, skill, and uniqueness, this national entertainment form contributed to changing ideas about female identity and work. As discussed by Laura Lengel and John T. Warren in *Casting Gender: Women and Performance in Intercultural Contexts*, with the circus, much more than the theatre, we can consider "how gender is put on stage — that is, strategic, crafted, and (re)iterated as a meaningful communicative act" as well as "the effects of these repetitive acts on our social lives" (13–14). And certainly such pervasive performances of gender mattered. As Judith Butler claimed in *Bodies That Matter*, "power relations work in the very formation of 'sex,'" and a change in regularly viewed power relations, as occurred at the circus, could change what gender restrictions would prevail and thus what women could be and do in the larger society (16). In the "spectacular realism" at the circus, women took on new roles and capabilities, made pervasive through media representations as well as the shows themselves. These circus roles for women became an American presence, one often shocking and placed within a category of Other, but also one that was influential to a changing evaluation of American women and their work.

In this book, we want to look at the circus as it evolved in the U.S. from 1880 to 1940 and pay particular attention to the corresponding growth and changes in work roles for women. Part One begins by considering the depiction of these circus performers in popular culture — to see how a particular myth or depiction of the circus, and especially of circus women, became an essential element of American life. This depiction, iterated in novels, articles, and film, juxtaposed extreme sordidness with exhilarating freedom, an exaggerated means of both blaming and praising the circus' working women.

In the second part, we turn to depictions of the experience created by women performers themselves, by which they provided commentary on their status as exotic outsiders. In their writing, they both reiterated and rejected common constructions of circus women, enriching the public understanding of this work world.

Then in part three we move to the circus experience itself, to the rhythm of the circus day as experienced across the United States. A special power of space and place occurred in the parade, menagerie, games of skill and chance, visits to the dressing tents, sideshows, and tent show, creating an intense sense of involvement. The impact of the long circus day greatly depended on its repeated presentation of highly decorated and skillful women, on the streets and then in three rings, in close relationship with the audience, creating a unique form of interaction between worker and customer.

In part four we turn to the particular occupations of these women performers — to look at the meaning constructed through their individual acts: by equestrians, trapeze artists, lion and tiger trainers, sharpshooters, dancers, the few women allowed to appear as clowns, and the women appearing under the appellation of "freak."

In the concluding section, we further consider what it meant from 1880 to 1940 for the circus to come to town — and how that meaning changed cultural roles and opportunities for women. Through its visual representations, the continuously returning circus indicated that women could do amazing work and live incredibly different lives, out beyond what American culture coded as normal, a possibility that might be intimidating but could also be glorious. Though historians have looked at many careers that women began entering in the late nineteenth and early twentieth century, such as teaching, nursing, social work, law, business and acting, they have not examined the history of women's work at the circus, a more shocking choice of work perhaps, but an influential one, as Americans across the country regularly interacted with these women and with the media's constructions of them.*

Social historian Marcello Truzzi has noted that the literature of the circus has "largely been written by circus fans who have romanticized circus life" (533). Similarly Yoram Carmeli has noted that the aura of the circus, as bigger than life, has led to an exaggerated style of writing in all types of books about it: "People write about the circus (in local newspapers, children's books, fans' books) in a style which discloses its own exaggerations, a writing that represents yet plays its own signs, a writing that clowns, that plays signification itself" (162). Here we hope not to romanticize or exaggerate too much as we tell a circus story.

*This historical study of American women's work appears in Joel Perlmann and Robert A. Margo's *Women's Work?: American Schoolteachers, 1650–1920*; Susan McGann's *The Battle of the Nurses: A Study of Eight Women Who Influenced the Development of Professional Nursing, 1880–1930;* Winifred D. Bolin's *Feminism, Reform and Social Service : A History of Women in Social Work*; Karen Morello's *The Invisible Bar: The Woman Lawyer in America, 1638–1986*; Barbara M. Wertheimer's *We Were There: The Story of Working Women in America;* Caroline Bird's *Enterprising Women,* and Faye E. Dudden's *Women in the American Theatre: Actresses and Audiences, 1790–1870.*

# PART ONE

# Media Depictions: The Stories Told About Circus People

As the most prevalent form of entertainment in the United States from 1880 to 1940, the circus appeared in constant media depictions, across the country taking on a reality constructed by those depictions. The circus often appeared as a fun site for children, where boys might have an adventure and girls might long to have one. But it also took on a more complex meaning for adults, especially for women. In newspapers, magazines, fiction, and film, the circus became a well-known thing of extremes, of what to seek to be or seek to avoid, way beyond the realm of the American normal. In these depictions, circus work could be scandalous or even frightening (though certainly intriguing, either way).

Conversely, circus could also represent a romantic dream for women who could thus shed the restrictions of small-town life for an exciting world of love and career. Women moved into many working roles, their workplace participation going from 14.7 percent of women in 1880 to 25.4 percent in 1940 and from 2.6 million to 12.8 million, a huge increase in numbers with a growing population, even more dramatic in some age groups: a 41 percent increase in numbers of women working from the age of 16 to 19; over twice as many for 20 to 24 and 65 and over; and over four times as many for 25 to 44 and 45 to 64. Additionally, while 13.9 percent of those women who worked in 1890 were married, 35.9 percent were in 1900, a labor group that many Americans found more controversial than single women. And women also entered many different professions in large numbers: twice as many in factory jobs between 1900 and 1940, three times as many in sales, five times as many in white-collar professions, not just in teaching but also in health care and other industries, and ten times as many in clerical jobs (*Historical Statistics* 128–34). In this rapidly changing work environment, involving greater percentages and numbers of women with each decade, the circus dramatized the best and worst of what women entering an outside or public world could come to mean.

In journals and novels and films, when writers re-created circus, they were participating in the oldest type of writing about art in the West. Called ekphrasis, this literary form, a description of a visual work of art, "makes the reader envision the thing described as if it were physically present," but not as a mirror image of the original. Indeed, this description of art, either actual or imagined or somewhere in between, seeks to engage the imagination in a quasi-realness and thus accomplish the rhetorical purposes of the author of the description (Munsterberg). What literary critic Timothy Morton has written about this artistic tradition aptly applies to the extreme renderings of circus across fiction and nonfiction: "everything is seen from the outside and exoticized, in the very gesture of embedding us in a deep, dark inside" (145).

# CHAPTER 1

---

# Circus in the Established Media:
# Unnatural, Scandalous, Perilous

In the early twentieth century, much of the writing about the circus continued the negative judgments voiced in the nineteenth century. While some regularly appearing circus articles, as in the *New York Times,* contained actual news, others didn't seem to convey any news at all: from the bold headlines onward, they simply enveloped readers in the bodily details of a world that might fascinate but that certainly should be avoided. In this frequently reiterated description, interaction with such a world was always dangerous and often deadly. Such depictions often focused on circus women, on the inappropriateness of their involvement as performers, and on the scandals that engulfed them. Newspapers also stressed the hazards posed to "women and children" in the audience, a group envisioned as entirely separate, in their morality and worth, from those who performed. These dire depictions warned of the calamity of this career — but they also rendered it quite fascinating.

## Fear of Freaks

Many newspaper articles focused on weird physical details that separated circus women, especially those seen in freak shows, from all others. A frightening mishmash of headlines and paragraphs reminded readers that such circus performers were perhaps dangerous and certainly disgusting. When Jolly Irene (Amanda Siebert) died in 1940 of a heart attack, an article concerning her death began with the headline, "Fat Lady Is Dead at Coney Island." She performed with Ringling Bros. and Barnum & Bailey in Madison Square Garden, and they wanted her to tour with them, but the article tells readers totally unnecessarily, "her bulk was too large to pass through the doors of a regular railway car and she refused to ride in a freight car." When Madame Victoria, or Emma Markey, a well-known fat woman who began exhibiting in 1876, died in September 1885, the obituary's many details concerned what happened after her death: getting her out of the house in front of a large group of onlookers, making the special coffin, trying to find a large enough hearse ("Madame Victoria"). When fat lady Lizzie Whitlock died in August of 1899, the obituary in the *Coldwater Courier* in Ontario discussed the size of the casket and its weight that might crack the floor ("Lizzie Whitlock").

Many articles reported weird news along with weird body details, with the headline involving readers in the most bizarre, as in "Legless Woman Gone. Husband Mystified. Circus Performer Left with Man in Taxi, Janitor Says, as Mate Sought Job for Her." The article concerns "Gabrielle, the only living half woman in the world," whose disappearance had been reported to the police the night before. The husband insisted that his legless wife had not eloped with another man, with whom she had been seen getting into a taxi, but that she must have known him: "Whoever took her from the apartment, he said, had to carry her, and if she had been carried out against her will she would certainly have screamed for help." In "Noted Woman Midget Ends Life by Hanging" in 1940, the story focuses on a suicide in Rye, New York, of a performing little person who had retired from the circus and was selling hotdogs. The details in the story concern the small sizes of everything involved when she "made a noose with a clothes rope, attached it to a hook and kicked a chair from under herself." Other suspicious deaths of circus freaks also merited long head-lines, as in "'Elastic Skin Joe' Takes His Life at Circus because the Tattooed Woman Jilted Him" from 1927, concerning "the boy with the elastic skin" who took strychnine because he was "recently jilted by the tattooed woman and the matter had preyed upon his mind for several days."

Some pieces, not about death or abduction or any other type of actual news, seemed to be presented just to engage readers in inappropriateness, as in the following series of headlines from a *New York Times* article in 1929:

HOMELIEST WOMAN RISKS CIRCUS FAME

MARY ANN BEVAN, ENSNARED BY CUPID, TRIES FULL MENU OF BEAUTY PARLOR
BUT SHE STILL HOLDS TITLE

ANDREW, THE GIRAFFE KEEPER, MAY LIKE THE CHANGES,
BUT THEY DON'T DISQUALIFY HER FOR JOB

As the detailed bodily discussion that followed these headlines makes clear, Bevan exhibited in the sideshow area of Madison Square Garden as the world's homeliest woman. She was said to have faced the dilemma of choosing between love and her job, with the fun here for the reader of the world's homeliest woman trying to make herself pretty to get her man; this fascination with physical details thus involved Bevan's desire for normality:

> The time had come for her to choose, as so many women are forced to choose, between romance and a career. She decided in the old-fashioned way in favor of romance and yesterday she betook herself to a beauty shop in the Hotel Pennsylvania and ordered everything on the menu. Legions of beauty experts went to work on her. Batteries of mechanical contrivances were brought into play. She was permanently waved, manicured and massaged.

But all that work, the long article continues, can't make Mary Ann into an attractive woman: she is forever separate from normal, forever relegated to the freak show. To make this point, the reporter provides her with dialogue and gesture: "'I guess I'll be getting back to work,' she said, adjusting her bonnet with two antler-like horns protruding above the crown."

## Schools for Scandal

Circus stories involving various sorts of scandal also filled newspapers, giving readers another type of warning about this bizarre, unnatural career. Any weird and sexual detail seemed worthy of report in order to further shock (and enthrall) readers with the seediness of it all.

Especially about the biggest stars, readers seemed to enjoy the wildest of tales. In 1903, William Randolph Hearst sold copies of his *San Francisco Examiner, Los Angeles Examiner, Chicago American,* and *New York Morning Journal* by reporting that sharpshooter Annie Oakley was in prison, sentenced for "stealing the trousers of a negro in order to get money with which to buy cocaine" (McMurtry 197). Though completely false, the story was immediately picked up by other newspapers from coast to coast (G. Riley 76). Oakley demanded retractions, and even though most newspapers complied, she ended up filing fifty-five libel suits. The legal battles continued until 1910, with Oakley traveling the country to testify in various courtrooms. To keep from having to pay the fines, Hearst hired a detective to travel to Oakley's hometown in Ohio and attempt to dig up additional, supposedly true dirt about her.

While some stories involved completely made-up scandals to shock readers with what circus stars would be willing to do, others took advantage of titillating facts. Dramatic stories covered the death of aerialist Lillian Leitzel, caused by a fall during her act at a Copenhagen circus in 1931. As the *National Geographic* commented, "part of her trapeze rigging gave way and she was hurled to the sawdust ring from which she had rocketed to fame" (Kelley, "The Land of Sawdust" 516).

Lillian Leitzel and Alfredo Codona, star-crossed lovers, on the Ringling Bros. and Barnum & Bailey Circus, 1928. Photograph by H.A. Atwell (Circus World Museum, Baraboo, Wisconsin).

But newspapers and magazines gave even more attention to the piteous grief of her husband, Alfredo Codona, one of the greatest of flyers. In many interviews and articles before Leitzel's death, as in one with the *Saturday Evening Post* in December of 1930, he had spoken of the terrifying possibility of death that often inhabited her mind and always attended each swing-over in her act: "If in that hundredth of an instant the hands would fail to grip, there would be little left of Lillian Leitzel" ("Split Seconds" 76). His return to the United States with her ashes in April of 1931 was widely covered, with stirring headlines such as the *New York Times'* 'Liner Brings Ashes of Lillian Leitzel; Plane Circles Over Mauretania and Drops Wreaths in Tribute to Circus Star." The repeated stories of his complete devotion and of his devastation after her death continued when he had a career-ending accident, seemingly as a result of his inability to soar without her.

Then, in July 1937, he killed competing aerialist Vera Bruce, the woman that he had married and divorced after losing Leitzel, and then he killed himself. As a long series of headlines in the *New York Times* and other newspapers told this part of his story: "Codona Kills Self, Shooting Ex-Wife; Vera Bruce, Also Aerialist, Who Divorced Him July 1, Is in Grave Condition. Met in Lawyer's Office, Two Were Discussing Property—Circus Artist, Hurt in Fall Here, Had Failed in Comeback, Tried Comeback After Injury, Began at 4 to Learn His Art." The *Los Angeles Times* featured large pictures of Codona and Bruce with the headline "Codonas in Dual Tragedy" and the subheading "Death Writes Sequel to Divorce." In the next days, the *Times* dramatically announced Bruce's death from gunshot wounds: "Bullets of Codona Fatal to His Ex-Wife; The *Los Angeles Times* featured a large painting of the couple looking at a picture of Codona on the high wire during his glory years ("Shots Kill Mrs. Codona"). On both coasts, the story had much to offer: the adored wife who died from an injury and then the rejected second wife whom the fallen star murdered in a lawyer's office in front of her mother.

## Danger for the Audience, Especially for Women

Newspapers frequently offered scandals involving circus performers, with extreme depictions that might rely on fact or fiction and that warned readers about extremes and dangers. Many other stories engaged readers with perils that occurred under the big top during performances, perils made so much worse by the presence of normal, non-circus audience members, especially "women and children." Scandal stories posited newspaper readers as outsiders, perusing stories about "them" (circus people) from a certain amount of distance. These injury stories, on the other hand, might cause more anxiety because they involve "regular" Americans who find themselves engulfed in the circus's potential for sudden violence and death. Their physical vulnerability is often described before the bodily details of the accident, their ruination having been made possible or even likely when they entered the big top, clearly a dangerous site for a visit and thus even more dangerous as a potential site for work.

In trapeze and other death stories, the emphasis is first on the size of the crowd that saw the accident, much more than on the death itself, though explicit injury details usually end these reports. An article entitled "10,000 See Woman Die in Detroit Circus Trapeze Act" in 1931, concerning a trapeze artist who died at the Shriners' circus in Detroit, focuses in the first paragraph on the confusion within the audience: "The 10,000 spectators did not realize that she was mortally wounded." Not until the second paragraph does the writer give the performer's name. There readers learn that she is Catherine Solt, in the circus business for twelve years with her husband, and they then get to read the violent details of her fall: "The timing was faulty and, missing her wrists, he seized her fingers. The hold broke and she fell thirty feet, fracturing her skull."

This article follows an outline that many others employed. "Fall from Trapeze Kills Girl in Circus," from 1932, concerns two women who fell in Atlantic City while performing. Again in the first paragraph the details describe those who see the disaster, both the 2500 in the audience and the larger group that amasses as news of tragedy spreads: "More than 10,000 persons milled around the pier as an ambulance from the Atlantic City Hospital rushed them to the hospital." Then the next paragraphs give the victims' names and move to the gory details of what happened: "Miss LaRose swung toward Miss Berger, who had braced herself in readiness to catch the girl. As her partner swung in preparation for her flight through the air, Miss Berger's knees slipped from the trapeze. As she fell, several guide wires were broken, lowering the apparatus. Miss La Rose also lost her hold and plunged toward the floor after her partner."

Similarly, "5,000 See Acrobat Injured at Circus," from 1935, immediately concerns what the audience members saw and how they reacted to the severe injury of trapeze artist America Olvera at Madison Square Garden: "Five thousand spectators, in the midst of applauding her, gasped when they saw her fall." The requisite details of pain follow: "She let go the trapeze and caught at the rope lower down but apparently missed. Her body swung downward and she landed hard on her face and arms on the wooden stage. She always had refused to use a net." When Olvera returned to New York in 1936, the articles concentrated not on her new act but on the fall from the year before, made more dramatic by again citing the number of New Yorkers who saw the accident, who thus participated in near death: "Last April 12, 5,000 spectators in Madison Square Garden saw Miss Olvera fall at the end of her afternoon performance" ("Woman, Undeterred by Fall").

Many of these front-page articles especially emphasize the danger and possibility of death for women in the audience, who presumably would not be able to handle themselves in a crisis and who thus put themselves and their children at risk by going to the show. A headline emphasizing such facts appeared, for example, on the front page of the *New York Times* in 1906:

> Circus Crowd Flees While the Tent Burns. New Rochelle Crowd Panic-Stricken by Gasoline Explosion. Women Were Trampled On. Some Burned by Splattering Gasoline — Mayor Helps Calm Crowd — No One Badly Hurt.

As the article describes, when a tank exploded at the Frank A. Robbins Circus during the Dip of Death act, in which a car turned upside down on a looped track, "The 2,000 persons arose as one. A deep murmur swelled into a roar of terror, and within two seconds the scene was one of confusion." The mayor took center stage, and men ripped exits in the canvas tent with their knives, enabling the women and children to make it out of this dangerous site alive, rescued by the efforts of courageous men from a place where these vulnerable visitors probably should not have been. Concerning another accident that August, the *Times* led with the number of those hurt and also announced that they were posh summer vacationers, as the headline makes clear: "Circus Seats Fall and 100 Are Hurt. Panic in Far Rockaway Tent after the Collapse. 500 Go Down in Wreckage. Men Fight Women to Get Free — Cottagers from Cedarhurst, Woodmere, and Lawrence in the Crash." To free themselves from this dangerous space, this time men do not save the vulnerable but instead trample over women and children and even "nursegirls with babies in their arms." Here their actions seem appropriate during a crisis in which they have to save themselves: women and children had risked their own lives, and perhaps their own definitions as respected and protected "cottagers," by being in this place.

Many other articles emphasized women's inability to survive the circus. On the first page of the *New York Times* on April 30, 1907, for example, under the headline of "Seats Fall at a Circus: Woman Badly Crushed and 50 Other Persons Hurt at White Plains," appeared the following dramatic description, again featuring passive women from the audience and active men: "While the trick elephants were performing there was heard the crunching of wood, and the whole reserved seat section seemed to move forward toward the arena and then collapsed. About five hundred persons were thrown in a heap. Women screamed and men fought to escape, and the rest of the audience rushed into the ring and then out of the tent."

Besides falling performers and seats, another common theme was severe weather that caused circus accidents, again with the emphasis on the audience and especially on vulnerable "women and children." A headline like "Storm Hits Circus; Audience in a Panic" reflects this concentration on circus danger: "One woman was so badly hurt that there is little hope of saving her life, two or three more persons are believed to have been injured, but not seriously, and nearly 4,000 people were thrown into a panic yesterday afternoon when the Forepaugh & Sells Brothers' circus, which was exhibiting under canvass at 155th Street and Eighth Avenue, was hit by the storm that swept the city in the middle of the afternoon." Even though only one person seemed to be seriously injured, and the next day's paper listed her as recovered, the *Times* made the most of what women did in an out-of-control circus scene: "Women and children cried aloud as the tent darkened and the howling of the wind came as an accompaniment. Some spectators started in a rush for the exits, but a feeling of terror kept most of them in their seats, which seemed providential, for a stampede must have resulted in death."

Newspaper accounts of howling winds and "a feeling of terror" repeatedly signaled danger. So too did the depiction of the circus star as someone who lived for risk. It seemed the circus star was one who almost sought to be hurt: not a professional doing a dangerous job as carefully as possible, but an irresponsible thrill-seeker. Thus the circus star was not worthy of concern and protection as were normal women and children. Articles about trapeze star America Olvera, for example, separated the star and family from the realm of the normal: "Apparently, neither her aunt's death, nor the experience of her brother, Julio, who fell in 1933 in Philadelphia, nor her own serious fall, affected her nerves. Such things are only to be expected when destiny has marked one for the circus" ("Woman, Undeterred by Fall"). Many other articles focused on the circus star as reveling in risk, as other women would not do, as living for the moment of near death.

In regularly appearing articles, newspaper readers encountered the unnatural bodies of freakish women, with husbands like Alfredo Codona who might seem devoted but could also be violent, and with every sort of highly dramatized injury, fire, and weather crisis that could be avoided by remaining at home. Though this repeatedly appearing literature did not so openly declare the circus to be immoral as had articles and sermons in the nineteenth century, it did cast an aura of seediness and danger over the circus, showing it to be a world in which "women and children," normal and law abiding as they were, should not be embroiled, not even as audience members and certainly not as cast members. This negative literature about circus issued a severe, often repeated warning that this entertainment could lead to the worst of consequences, for the viewer as well as the viewed, that circus was a space only appropriate for the most unnatural of risk takers, whether in the audience or within the three rings. And with this one employment type so much under discussion, the rhetoric used to describe it seemed to imply a general distrust of women who were out and about, as consumers and as workers, risking health and reputation in ways they would not be within their homes. Of course, like any literature of negativity and evil, this regularly repeating genre could entice as well as repulse as it riveted attention to a shocking American occupation.

# CHAPTER 2

# Circus by Press Agents: Contradictory Extremes

Many newspaper accounts of the circus in the late nineteenth and early twentieth century fostered associations with frightening visions of abnormality, scandal, and danger, simultaneously drawing curious readers in while warning them repeatedly to keep away. In these accounts, which continued a tradition of negative judgments about circus stretching back to the colonial period, the circus could cause men to run amok and leave women and children to their own meager devices. But by the end of the nineteenth century this fearsome depiction, even though it remained an intriguing and vibrant part of newspapers, was not the primary means of circus representation. Instead, there developed a very different circus myth, another extreme, in which the circus might still involve danger and difference, but instead of being a cesspool to avoid, it becomes a place to visit over and over, even with the youngest of children. Just as the circus could be a site of danger, conversely it now could also be an entrance into an enticing, separate realm of old-fashioned fun, one which involved young Americans, the parents who accompanied them, and the performers who worked to entertain them, in the best of cultural traditions.

## Circus as Made by Press Agents, Especially Tody Hamilton

One highly literary, positive depiction of circus, and thus of circus women, was to a great extent created by the circus's hard-working press agents, who were determined to expand the market for their product by making it seem more wholesome, acceptable, and fun. Many newspapers and magazines, in fact, referred to agents from the top shows as though their readers knew who they were — and knew that their electrifying stories had been concocted for effect, as part of a fun circus aura. Circus writer Charles Murray described such a powerful promoter in 1897:

> He was the general press-agent of the great show — a man who personally and professionally was better known among the newspaper offices and brethren of the journalistic world than any public man who ever lived. He knew every town in the country, its newspapers, their circulation and character, and about just how much per line, inch and column, they would charge for advertising matter — their liberality or illiberality to advance notices. He knew their business

managers, their editors, and their leading reporters — and, if they were not wholly new to the profession, they knew him, or of him. He was not merely an agent — he was to them "the" agent [185].

One such agent was Barnum & Bailey's Tody Hamilton, often referred to in magazine and newspaper articles without any need to note his profession. When P.T. Barnum lay dying of heart disease, Hamilton got Barnum's obituary printed in the local paper before Barnum died, so Hamilton could show it to Barnum and cheer him up. All through his career, Hamilton placed stories, mostly exaggerated if not completely make-believe, that pleased Barnum and marketed his circus.

Throughout the big, positive literature of circus around the turn of the century, writers seemed to enjoy admitting that Hamilton pulled the strings. In "New, Bigger Circus Thrills Garden Crowd," in 1905, the *New York Times* reporter writes about L'Auto-Bolide, the Dip of Death, in which Mademoiselle De Tiers of Paris looped a gap in an automobile. Here readers learn that Hamilton would have no trouble creating the rhetoric to depict this thrill; the journalist, in fact, enjoys repeating some of the alliterations that this well-known rhetorician had created: "an astounding and audaciously abysmal feat ... a peerless, pre-eminent, perilous, puzzling, prodigious plunge." The point here is that, in contrast to many other acts in the service of which Hamilton had employed such phrases, "Mlle. De Tier's feat deserved every word of it."

In 1903, in an article entitled "One Circus Afternoon," about the morning after a boy and girl go to the circus, a reporter again alludes to the control that Hamilton exercised: the children "begin a day of circus talk, which will undoubtedly continue for many days, while they shall be clowns, kings and queens, soldiers, and every one of the strange beings and animals that they saw in the wonderland of 'Tody' Hamilton." In his obituary in 1916, the *Times* calls Hamilton a "circus agent" in the title and "Barnum's Famed Writer" who "Jingled Words like Bells" in the sub-title. The writer here quotes one of his famed alliterations, "peerless prodigies of physical phenomenons," for circus freaks ("Tody Hamilton").

Other articles further delighted in Hamilton's rhetorical powers. His ability to use "the English language in Gargantuan epithets, and to match them like bells in a melodious series," a reporter claimed, had caused poets to give up alliteration because now "verbal tintinnabulations of all kinds belong exclusively to the circus." Hamilton even told the reporter that he had never seen the show, a false claim, but one that heightened appreciation of Hamilton's power to depict: "He would not allow his conception of it [the show] to be distorted by contact with the details." With "no rivals for the reputation of the greatest press agent who ever lived," the reporter admitted, Hamilton had gotten "miles of free press" from this and other newspapers from coast to coast. At a retirement dinner, Hamilton had uttered a line that the reporter enjoyed repeating: "I have grabbed more space for nothing than any other man you know" ("400 Entertain").

Though Hamilton was an early and well-known purveyor of the circus publicity trade, he was not the only one noted for his power over the public, nor the only one whose name readers know. When Lillian Leitzel died in 1931, the *New York Times* quoted the memorial elegy of Dexter Fellows, Barnum & Bailey agent, at length, referring to him as the "dean of circus exploitation men" ("Circus Fall Fatal"). In 1937, in "A Study in Concentration as Circus Opened in Garden," the highly wrought description of the effect of the circus's opening also includes what Fellows had to say about it:

> There was a fresh, new tingle to the air spreading through the city last night, starting from a corner on Eighth Avenue and reaching right out to the heart of every young boy or girl, or man

or woman. It was the final herald of Spring, the sparkling purveyor of youth. As Dexter Fellows would have said, it was "the greatest show on earth; the circus" and the first-night crowd was thrilled by it. Not that Mr. Fellows did not actually have things to say about the new Ringling Bros. & Barnum & Bailey show at Madison Square Garden. Asked how it compared with last year's, he pondered and said: "I can't answer that. I can tell you that we have more new and great acts than we have had in many years."

During World War II, one of the Liberty Ships of the Merchant Marine, a fleet named after prominent Americans, was given his name: the *Dexter W. Fellows* launched on June 16, 1944, and went into service in the North Atlantic ("Vessel Type").

Though Dexter Fellows died in 1937, his replacement seemed to immediately garnish as much attention from the public. In "Circus Remodels New Lady Clown," in 1939, the article purportedly concerns a "new lady clown" but gives more attention to Roland Butler, the publicist who depicts her act as brand new: "But Roland Butler, the big-hatted man with the free tickets in his pocket and a story about a lady clown on his mind, insisted that no one would be staler than a fresh-roasted peanut." Butler, the article continues, waits for the end of the press conference to involve reporters in a dramatic lie about women clowns that they will believe and repeat: "First time we've ever had one.... First time anybody's ever had one. First time there's ever been one, in fact."

## Circus as Part of a Time Gone By

The dramatic story created by powerful press agents such as Hamilton, Fellows, and Butler depicted the circus and the performers involved in it as an iconic part of American life, the embodiment of a myth of an eternal, unchanging presence occurring right outside of town. These stories situated the circus as old fashioned, as something about which Americans felt nostalgic, as Yoram Carmeli noted: "In their circus gaze the spectators thus conjure up a community of which the circus is a part, an illusion of history, of collective and personal biography." This "illusionary community and history," encouraged by press agents and show owners, lent a type of continuity and order during years of American life in which so much was changing: "It is not variety and uniqueness that the townsfolk look for in circus, but rather the experience of their own selves, their own time and biography which are conjured up by facing the played, unchanging 'always the same' circus" (158, 160). From 1880 to 1940, sixty years involving a world war, the invention of the plane and car, and so many changes in social life, there was an enlarging circus myth, depicting the big show and its performers as a wonder from times gone by.

Even from the early twentieth century, articles evidenced nostalgia for what the circus somehow used to be and might still be on any given sunny afternoon. A 1900 article in the *New York Times* quoted at length a manager for Forepaugh-Sells Circus, explaining the continuing attraction of the circus for boys and the "fond parents" who accompany them: "The small boy and the circus are two ideas so intimately associated that no modern writer has had the courage to divorce them." The manager claims that for older people the circus created a nostalgia for an earlier time, and especially for what a circus meant in older farming communities: it "revived a memory" of a "time before the day of trolley and suburbanite, when the circus was an educator, when the sole amusement of a whole countryside was annually compressed within the canvas confines of a circus tent." The article further discusses the circus day, for a young man taking a date there, as always a thing of reminiscence:

The early morning breakfast at the farm before the start of the circus, the new colt and the spick and span rig driven to her house, her fluttering appearance in a new gown that appeared divine, and the long jolting over country roads while holding her hand — all these come back to those who have lived in the country of years ago, at the crack of the ringmaster's whip or the kindly reminiscent joke of the clown, for it's the same joke, though uttered by a different clown ["Why They Go"].

Throughout the years, press agents and newspaper writers played variations on the idea that the circus harkened back to another time, and thus they depicted it a mythic presence in American life. In 1905, concerning Barnum & Bailey coming to Madison Square Garden, the *Times* declared that this circus joined the boy of 1905 to those of earlier times: "Without a vacant seat in the whole Madison Square Garden, Barnum & Bailey's 'greatest show on earth' opened last night with a blare of trumpets, a blaze of light and color, and all that is dear to the heart of a small boy of today and the small boy of yesterday" ("New, Bigger Circus").

In 1913, in a story about an opening performance, the *Times* commented that "Everything was new, of course, but in a deeper sense everything was satisfactorily old" ("Elephants, Peanuts"). In 1924, a *Nation* editorialist similarly emphasized that the circus was the art form, the part of American life, that did not change: "The Circus, of course, is unalterably conservative. The acrobats still wear bright pink tights, the lady performers, in spite of the bewildering skill at gymnastics, are adorned with long curls, the bucket of water still falls from above the clowns, the hair grower still produces luxuriant herbage on a bare head" ("In the Driftway" Apr. 1924).

Even as performers tried new and more dangerous tricks, as acts and stars came and went, the much heralded nature of this art form — "unalterably conservative" — made it something in which to trust. In a review of *Jumbo*, a circus musical that opened on Broadway in 1935, starring Jimmy Durante and circus performers, the *Times* reviewer called attention to this "idea of the circus": "If, in your middle years, you have been churlish enough to wish that the circus were as good-humored as your idea of the circus, 'Jumbo' deserves your fond attention" ("The Play"). *National Geographic* joined in the positive commentary about the fact that "time changes all things except circuses" in 1931: "The trend of the times leaves but a faint impression upon the land of the big tents" (Kelley, "The Land of Sawdust" 487).

Even in the new century, as theories of disability and genetics made sideshow exhibitions morally questionable, articles constructed freaks as part of what a circus always should be and argued that audiences complained if this essential element was removed. A *Times* reporter, in a story in 1913 about Claude Hamilton, a sideshow promoter working with Barnum & Bailey, described the Obongos, from near the equatorial line in Africa, as among the very lowest of the human race, not only in stature but in civilization: this ownership of human beings, the reporter argues, belongs to a venerable circus tradition "remembered by those of us who are out of youngsterhood" ("The Circus Freak"). Barnum & Bailey removed sideshow artists from 1908 to 1913, in response to protests that exhibitions of human beings with disabilities were cruel ("The Passing"). But people missed the freaks, as the *Times* reported — "it wasn't a complete, old-fashioned circus without them" — and they were brought back ("The Circus Freak"; "Elephants, Peanuts").

Though the *New York Times* may have featured more circus stories than other newspapers because circuses stayed the longest in New York City, publicity agents placed similar articles in newspapers across the country, filled with inflated rhetoric and thrilling action, reinforcing newspapers themselves as a site of mythic meanings of circus. When the Barnum & Bailey Circus came to Chicago in September 1895, a long article in the Sunday *Tribune* entitled "Giraffe, a Rarity in America" began with this wonder of the menagerie and went on to other "magnificent, stupendous and colossal exhibitions" that returned to Chicago each year. When the Al G. Barnes Circus came to the west coast in 1931, a *Los Angeles Times* article described the opening spectacle as "a blare of trumpets and a burst of splendor," in which "as in previous years, plumes waved, brilliants flashed, banners fluttered, the elephants lumbered by and crashing symbols rent the air" ("Boy, It's Grand"). As the New Orleans *Times-Picayune* reported in 1927, perhaps repeating the alliteration of a press agent, the Sells-Floto Circus had returned to town to again present "a monster maelstrom of amusement from the far corners of earth" ("Circus Arrival"). This powerful literature of an iconic American circus, part of a landscape not to be missed, also appeared regularly in American family magazines, such as *Colliers, Saturday Evening Post, Literary Digest,* and *Illustrated World.*

In positive and nostalgic terms, many evocative magazine articles introduced readers to the mechanical side of the circus, the insider details of how circuses continually crossed the country and engaged new acts. With encouragement and information from press agents, these magazines thus gave readers a "you are there" feeling, a sunny, insider approach with a general thesis of "let's put on a show!" L.B. Yates' "Troupin' with the Tents" in 1922 brought readers of the *Saturday Evening Post* into a cross-country trek. In 1926, *Popular Mechanics* featured Earl Chapin May's "Keeping the Circus in Motion"; in 1937, *Popular Science* added "Circus Scout Finds New Thrills for the Big Top" to involve readers in how a scout, Pat Valdo, went out "searching the four corners of the earth for new and sensational acts for American circuses" (38). The *National Geographic* also featured two long articles by Ringling publicist and circus writer Francis Beverly Kelley, in 1931 and 1948, that gave readers an inside look at the care and training of circus animals, the winter quarters, and the finances of the big show, with a large number of photographs making up a separate photo essay accompanying the 1948 article (Edgerton).

Circuses received attention not just through magazine articles about how a circus travels and books its acts, but through interview essays that provided a positive inside view of particular skills and performances. Profiling the Ringling management were many articles, such as J. Bryan III's "Big Shot of the Big Top," in the *Saturday Evening Post*, concerning John Ringling North and his single-handed work in maintaining a circus through the Depression. Articles also concerned circus stars, with many about the fierce lion tamer Clyde Beatty, such as the starkly titled "Cat Man: Clyde Beatty," discussed as "the most celebrated trainer of lions and tigers in the world" in *Time* in 1937 (29). Other articles present exciting profiles of less well-known performers whose specialties the article titles dramatically label: Courtney Ryley Cooper's "The Keeper of the Bulls," concerning work with elephants, in the *Saturday Evening Post* in 1922; Captain Charles F. Adams' "Trouping with Seals" in the *Saturday Evening Post* in 1930; and "Sword-Swallower X-Rayed," which showed x-ray scans of star Sebastian Montenero with "a blade jammed down his throat to the hilt," in *Popular Science* in 1938.

## Women and Men

In the voluminous number of articles about circuses in both magazines and newspapers, circus men, like Clyde Beatty, received much more attention than circus women, but readers did learn about the beauty and skill of women stars. Many articles concerned Dorothy Herbert's dramatic equestrian performance, focusing on bodily details, as when she jumped through a fire hoop, "her blonde hair all but trailing in the flames." Her act's finale provided a tense scene described in specifics: "In her magnum opus, the grand equestrian finale of the show, she rides a black stallion named Satan over the six-foot bar, wearing a blindfold, her body thrown backwards toward the horse's plunging withers, one small sandaled foot raised in the air" ("Circus's Valkyrie").

Another part of this publicity involved the creation of mystifying and thrilling biographical details that could be varied from town to town, a make-believe past about which readers were both tricked and not tricked. Writer L.B. Yates, in the *Saturday Evening Post* in 1920, described this publicity practice from the "good old days" that was still alive and well, by using the example of trapeze artist Lucy Lightfoot. To stir interest, she chose to take the name of a child who had disappeared mysteriously during an eclipse of the sun on the Isle of Wight in 1831. As Yates enjoyed revealing to his readers, described as "in the know," the press agent might take a story to a local paper about how this circus star was the original English Lightfoot appearing by time travel. In the next town, she might abandon the Isle of Wight theme and instead appear as someone whose family intended for her to marry nobility but who had disobeyed and left for the alliteration of "the scintillating seduction of sawdust and spangles." In another town, Yates continued, Lightfoot might be transformed into the "poor little waif, rescued in childhood from the slums of a big city and adopted by the kind-hearted circus people" ("The Circus Girl" 30).

As years went by, readers enjoyed many stories about supposedly exotic performers involved in an iconic American entertainment. These articles expanded the circus audience, as did another type of article about women performers, placed on the women's page of newspapers, in women's magazines, and even in magazines commonly read by men. These pieces asserted, a bit ironically perhaps, that circus women, who generally toured from March through November, actually cared about nothing but traditional domestic values: their professional abilities mattered less, in these depictions, than their sewing and recipes, like other women lauded on women's pages of that time.

In a women's page article entitled "Pretty Rose Wentworth: A Remarkable Woman Who Does Many Things in the Circus," in 1895, the *New York Times* gave some attention to the performer's equestrian routines: "In a trig habit, [she] dashes madly around the course in the Madison Square Garden in a jockey race, drives a chariot, swings in a trapeze from a giddy height, or bends her slender body into impossible postures as she slips easily through a small ring." The rest of the article, however, concerns the "many things" she contributes to life with her husband, clown Harry Wentworth: "They are the most domestic creatures imaginable, and they do fancy work," which here means elaborate sewing, which Rose places in their home in Philadelphia. These details are given more attention than her performance.

Similarly, an article on the *New York Sun*'s women's page, in April of 1932, focuses less on how a woman working as a human projectile flew through the air during a performance and more on the garments and decorations that she created while "always knitting or crocheting" (Dayton). The *Boston Evening Traveler*'s women's page did not discuss equestrian May Wirth's act but instead quoted her at length, proffering the same view of the domestic circus woman about which press agents also expounded: "When a woman can roast a chicken in a chafing dish, serve a square meal upon a dress suit case laid in the middle of her sleeping car berth and keep her temper, I think she can safely be set down as domestic. When she can do a couple of turns every day on the flying trapeze or on a barebacked horse, make all of her circus costumes, darn her husband's socks, and take care of a baby or two, she is entitled to the blue ribbon for housewifeliness" (quoted in Dickinson 23).

In *Hampton's Broadway Magazine,* mostly read by women, Hugh Weir wrote about circus women having chafing dish parties and playing cards, dominoes, and checkers in their railway drawing rooms. And he continues, "The Jordan sisters frequently carry their sewing to the door of the arena, leaving it with reluctance when their 'flying' feat is announced.... Mrs. David, equestrienne, is deep in the mysteries of an embroidered pillow top; one of the Jackson girls, bicycle riders, is knitting a necktie" (800). Julia Lowanda, a bareback rider with Carl Hagenbeck Shows, in an article entitled "How Circus Women Enjoy Life," published in the *Sunday Leader* in Eau Claire, Wisconsin, in June 1906, claims that circus performers sew and gossip like women at church sewing societies. This article discusses Lowanda's loving marriage, her visits on Sundays, and her attendance at church services.

Perhaps creating a more startling effect, articles about circus freaks also stressed their allegiance to the home and to traditional home values. With Barnum & Bailey in 1897, the very popular Ella Ewing, billed as the tallest woman in the world, was constructed in pamphlets and newspapers as a traditional rural girl. An article on the women's page of the *New York Times* that season, which put her height at 8 feet, four inches, discusses her average-size parents, her average size as a baby, and her youth on a farm in Missouri. Though Ella Ewing's size is constructed as abnormal, readers learn that she likes to read, play guitar, make butter, milk cows, play Parcheesi — she is a farm girl who had to be talked into exhibition. Her mother came with her regularly on tour but was sick that season, the article continues, and Ella had used her money, as a good and dutiful daughter, to move her parents and herself into a much bigger Missouri farm house where Ella's mother was recuperating ("Tall Miss Ella Ewing").

With the very few women clowns, fewer even than women tiger trainers, a magazine primarily read by men might again deem their domesticity a newsworthy item. In *Popular Mechanics* in 1927, in an article about circus clowns called "With the 'Merry Joeys' of the Tent World," Earl Chapin May does not consider the act done by Loretta LaPearl, who worked as a clown for Ringling. Instead readers learn that in the off-season she repairs all the props for the clown act while also "you will find her making potato pancakes or turning out roast chicken with oyster dressing, in which she takes due pride" (598).

In an article entitled "With the Ladies of the Circus," from the *New York Times'* women's page in the Sunday magazine in 1906, the readers, addressed in the second person, encounter the surprise of learning just how normal circus women are, even in comparison to those working in the theatre, who don't live their work in the same way. The feature story opens with women in conversation, their talk about sewing a smoking jacket for a husband, making gravy, curing a child with the croup, dealing with dressmakers. Then "you" realize that the scene is not an afternoon tea party or a planning meeting for a charity bazaar but the ladies' dressing tent at the circus, with the audience and the contrast clearly delineated: "You, a woman from the every-day world, find you are merely in a large dressing room in the midst of the ladies of the circus." The writer next provides the surprising specifics of how these circus women can physically transform themselves in the dressing tent to pass as normal women out on the street: "A minute ago she was wearing yellow tights and pumps, flying through the air, turning a somersault, bowing her acknowledgments to the applauding crowd in seats and boxes. Now she is wearing a brown cloth dress, a modest hat to match, a pair of rubbers over her heavy walking shoes, and off she goes saying, 'Now to buy the beefsteak for dinner.'" And thus, on the street, "there is no possible way" that "you" could tell a circus performer from a quiet, home-loving woman, except for her exhibiting the more graceful walk of an athlete, a fact both reassuring and a bit shocking. Indeed, the article continues, a circus performer can pass for normal more readily than a "theatrical person," who can generally be identified by "a certain style of get-up and dressing."

In all of these descriptions on women's pages, circus women seem able to "pass," with their professions shown to be their only abnormality: though they work in tents wearing scanty costumes and heavy makeup, they can leave there and join other women leading "normal" lives: the woman in yellow tights transforms herself through a brown cloth dress; a woman clown cooks pancakes and chicken; and the giant supports her parents and longs for her farm home. Even these women can thus seem appropriate and can thus participate in the circus nostalgia, in the lure of an earlier and simpler time.

In the traditional media of newspapers and magazines, though many articles warned of circus dangers, another sort of rhetoric, molded by press agents, made the circus into the best of all possible places, a site of classic fun and nostalgia, where the women performers were beautiful and skilled and normal, not too scary at all. This rhetoric made the circus into a wholesome site of excitement as well as difference, even for the girl and woman who visited the big top and might dream of remaining there. Even in the same magazine issues or during the same week, the press thus made the circus, and especially the appearance of women there, into extremes of right and wrong, both wholesome and hideous, just what women should and should not do.

CHAPTER 3

# Circus Books for Children: Gendered Romantic Dreams

In 1931, a columnist in the *Nation* commented about the nostalgic and thrilling American circus:

> Like a magic hoop it rolls on forever. And everything within it, animate or inanimate, shares its never-ending glamor, its persistent unreality. The circus is a mass affair, gaudy and spectacular, sentimental without shame as its golden trappings are obviously not gold. Here is no place for fastidiousness or intellectual pride. The first unabashed notes of the calliope send them scuttling. The circus is intemperate, resplendent with false splendor. Take it or leave it. Most of us take it ["In the Driftway" Mar. 1931, 272].

This "it" of the circus that "most of us take" had a more complex presence in American life than just appearing as magical and spectacular or seedy and dangerous. As the *Nation* columnist realized, the circus ultimately offered much more to Americans than either of these visions, something in fact much more elemental: "There is probably no single other medium which caters to a greater variety of human frailties or satisfies a wider range of human desires; which offers such complete relaxation from things as they are" ("In the Driftway" Mar. 1931, 272). This depiction of the circus and its performers, as catering to both human frailties and human desires, certainly occurred in newspaper and magazine articles, but it occurred much more fully in other popular media — especially in a huge number of popular children's books — where the "relaxation" from "things as they are" would influence generations of girls and women as well as boys and men.

Between 1880 and 1940, about four hundred children's novels concerned the child visiting the circus or running away to join it. Circus historian Fred Pfening III referred to these texts as "masses of children's circus fiction," their general theme being escape ("The Circus and Fiction"). Much of this literature was intended for an audience of boys, but fictional girls had circus dreams also, of a getaway that involved physical strength and skill as well as adventure, of circus as a symbolic site beyond the home and small town where a girl could stretch her wings and prove her abilities. In children's literature, the small-town child wants to join this wondrous place and often does so, though this choice appears different for boys than for girls.

## What Boys Dream About

The earliest examples of this genre concerned boys dreaming of adventure. James Otis' *Toby Tyler, or Ten Weeks with a Circus* in 1881 may have begun the circus novel genre, with the trope of a boy's running away to join a circus and working his way up from peanut salesman to star. Toby, with short red hair and a freckled face, is an orphan living with other boys in the care of a man that they call Uncle Daniel. A circus candy seller, aptly named Job Lord, lures the boy away from this solid but dull home, where Toby feels unappreciated, by offering excitement that immediately wears off when the boy encounters the reality:

> How different everything looked now, compared to the time when the cavalcade marched into Guilford, dazzling every one with the gorgeous display! Then the horses pranced gayly under their gaudy decorations, the wagons were bright with glass, gilt, and flags, the lumbering elephants and awkward camels were covered with fancifully embroidered velvets, and even the drivers of the wagons were resplendent in their uniforms of scarlet and gold. Now, in the gray light of the early morning, everything was changed. The horses were tired and muddy, and wore old and dirty harness; the gilded chariots were covered with mud-bespattered canvas, which caused them to look like the most ordinary of market wagons; the elephants and camels looked dingy, dirty, almost repulsive; and the drivers were only a sleepy-looking set of men, who, in their shirt-sleeves, were getting ready for the change which would dazzle the eyes of the inhabitants of the town [42–43].

The worst reality is the daily cruelty of Job Lord, who forces Toby into servitude. But even in this difficult situation, Toby gets to become one of a duo on horseback when an equestrian star needs a quick substitute. As Mademoiselle Jeannette and Monsieur Ajax (the boy having been assured that no star horseman had ever been named Toby), they have the moments of glory of which he had dreamed when he left home:

> The act consisted in their riding side by side, jumping over banners and through hoops covered with paper, and then the most difficult portion began.
> The saddles were taken off the horses, and they were to ride first on one horse and then on the other, until they concluded their performance by riding twice around the ring side by side, standing on their horses, each one with a hand on the other's shoulder.
> All this was successfully accomplished without a single error, and when they rode out of the ring the applause was so great as to leave no doubt but that they would be recalled, and thus earn the promised money [204].

Even after such a triumph, Toby realizes that he has given up his childhood for hard work and that he was better off in the perhaps dull, but safe world of his Uncle Daniel and the other orphan boys. His return is depicted in a scene that casts him as the prodigal son, more precious for having returned home:

> Toby crept softly in, and, going up to the old man, knelt down and said, very humbly, and with his whole soul in the words, "Oh, Uncle Dan'l! if you'll only forgive me for bein' so wicked an' runnin' away, an' let me stay here again — for it's all the home I ever had — I'll do everything you tell me to, an' never whisper in meetin' or do anything bad."
> And then he waited for the words which would seal his fate. They were not long in coming.
> "My poor boy," said Uncle Daniel, softly, as he stroked Toby's refractory red hair, "my love for you was greater than I knew, and when you left me I cried aloud to the Lord as if it had been my own flesh and blood that had gone afar from me. Stay here, Toby, my son, and help to support this poor old body as it goes down into the dark valley of the shadow of death" [262].

*Toby Tyler* was first published as a serial in the children's magazine *Harper's Young People* in 1877, and then as a book in 1881. It was an immediate classic and, even though it scripted the circus as a dangerous, hard place and it moralized on what could happen to a bad boy who ran away, it became a favorite among young boys and girls who dreamed of an exciting and different life.

As an adventure, perhaps regardless of its moral dimension, the story of Toby sparked an interest in the American bad boy, operating outside of the developing schools and towns at the end of the nineteenth century, a story type that included circus scenes and performers as a natural ingredient of rebellion, with these circuses generally presented as much more fun and nostalgic than sordid. George Wilbur Peck, a governor of Wisconsin who founded newspapers in Ripon, La Crosse, and Milwaukee, published his own "Peck's Bad Boy" stories, tales of outlandish pranks and rude behavior, leading to the publication of a number of books about the character, beginning in 1883. One of them was *Peck's Bad Boy with the Circus* (1905), and many others featured dialogue about and visits to the circus, a site of transgressive behavior as in *Toby Tyler*. Following the original story, the film version from 1938 featured the boy Peck, along with Spanky McFarland, at the circus, where they embarrass the lion tamer in a khaki jungle suit and his female assistant in leotards by giving sleeping pills to the lion. Peck also appears in a wig and dress to replace his friend, the young equestrian Miss Fleurette, The Child Wonder, before he goes off to summer camp and further madcap scenes. Here the circus nourishes the best sort of boy as a classic site for high spirits and hijinks.

The success of *Toby Tyler* also influenced Mark Twain as he wrote his own story of an orphan who runs away. In *The Adventures of Huckleberry Finn* (1884), while traveling with the duke and dauphin, Huck sneaks under a circus tent to see all the action of a show and especially the stunning equestrians:

> It was a real bully circus. It was the splendidest sight that ever was when they all come riding in, two and two, and gentleman and lady, side by side, the men just in their drawers and undershirts, and no shoes nor stirrups, and resting their hands on their thighs easy and comfortable — there must 'a' been twenty of them — and every lady with a lovely complexion, and perfectly beautiful, and looking just like a gang of real sure-enough queens, and dressed in clothes that cost millions of dollars, and just littered with diamonds. It was a powerful fine sight; I never see anything so lovely [221].

Huck segues from the beauty of the performers to their thrilling movement: "And then faster and faster they went, all of them dancing, first one foot out in the air and then the other, the horses leaning more and more, and the ringmaster going round and round the center pole, cracking his whip and shouting 'Hi! — hi!'" (222). In this text, the "real bully" circus seems no stranger a reality than so much else that might assail a boy out on the road, another part of the wild nonsense beyond the reach of the Widow Douglas.

At the beginning of the twentieth century, this circus/boy-on-the-road literature continued most notably in a series by Edgar B.P. Darlington, featuring The Circus Boys in five books with long descriptive adventure titles, such as *The Circus Boys on the Flying Rings, or Making the Start in the Sawdust Life* (1910) and *The Circus Boys on the Plains, or the Advance Agents Ahead of the Show* (1920). In this series, Phil Forrest and Teddy Tucker, like Toby Tyler, are orphans, taken in by an uncle who does not want them; they run away to a circus decidedly less sordid than the one depicted in *Toby Tyler*. In the first book, the two boys get their chance when a performer's foot becomes caught in a stirrup and she is dragged across the arena floor as they sit in the front row. When Phil hangs on to save her, the horse "was plunging like a ship in a gale, cracking the whip with Phil Forrest until it seemed as if every bone in the lad's body would be broken. He could hear his own neck snap with every jerk" (30). After Phil saves the star equestrian, the boys get a chance to join up with the show, to take on challenging stunts, and to have great adventures on the road, continued in the other popular books.

This ubiquitous circus-boy genre, with its repeated element of running away to join in something thrilling and virile, was an influential part of growing up after 1880. Carl Sandburg, for example, placed *Toby Tyler* among his favorite adventure stories. In primary school in Galesburg, Illinois, where he was born in 1878, as one of his biographers recently described in a book for children, *Toby Tyler* was the literary work that described adventures in which he could possibly "share":

> Carl daydreamed about stories he read. He pictured Paul Revere galloping through the night to warn the British were coming, and George Washington leading ragged soldiers into battle. He read a popular children's book *Toby Tyler; or, Ten Weeks with a Circus,* and wished he could share Toby's circus adventures [Niven np].

Even if a boy like Carl Sandburg didn't run away to join the circus, it represented an outside world about which to dream.

## What Girls Dream About

This circus literature that piqued a young Carl Sandburg's interest, though most commonly a genre about boys, did not concern boys only. Much of the literature aimed at girls in the late nineteenth and early twentieth century sought to delineate their "proper" role as the "light of the home" ("Beyond Nancy Drew"). Many hugely popular novels written for and about girls, by primarily women writers, depicted the spunky heroine, one who could return family and even towns to better, more essential values. She does not light out for the territory, but instead transforms her relatives and neighborhood, a different form of challenge and adventure. In Johanna Spyri's very popular *Heidi,* for example, translated into English and published in the United States in 1884, the Swiss orphan is heartbroken when she must leave her beloved grandfather and their happy home in the mountains to care for an invalid girl in the city. But ultimately her return home, with the disabled Klara, is healing for everyone. In *Anne of Green Gables* (1908) by Lucy Maud Montgomery, who wrote as "L.M.," Anne, an eleven-year-old orphan, is sent by mistake to live with a lonely, middle-aged brother and sister on a Prince Edward Island farm and proceeds to rejuvenate those around her even as she accidentally dyes her hair green and gets her best friend drunk.

In some books for children, this spunky character, like the boys, longs for the circus. Her desire at least to see the show, if not run away to it, is a sign of her special character, even though she might react in traditionally gendered ways, not at all like a more independent boy. Mary S. Deering's *An Average Boy's Vacation,* first published in 1876 and reissued in a second popular edition in 1878, was one such text in which the spunky girl who longs to see the show interacts with it very differently than the "average boy," a sign of their appropriate characters. In this story, both little Louise and three boys, Phil, Rob, and Louis, ask to go to the circus after they see posters of fat boys and dogs in mid air, posters that have been slathered across fences and stores in their small town where nothing ever happens. After much persuasion, their aunt allows them to go to what they call the "truly Circus," with a ringmaster, clowns, beautiful horses, and laughing crowds, not just a small traveling carnival but the real thing (120).

But though the boys find the visit thrilling, and a chapter's details concern their excited responses to all the animals and performers, Louise worries about the risk involved, especially for the smallest trapeze artist. Like her aunt, she keeps her gaze on his mother, who watches him perform and then escorts him away: "Aunt Marion and Louise were very glad, and the boys very sorry, when the mother, wrapping the Prodigy in her own old shawl, led him behind the curtain" (125). Louise differs from the boys in judging the older trapeze performers also, whose level of risk seems too high and whose actions are not for her something to attempt at home, as they are for her brothers: "Next the trapeze. Louise thought it 'perfectly horrid,' but the boys watched every motion, and Phil and Rob decided between themselves that there was a first-rate chance for two trapeze bars out in Uncle Tim's barn" (123–24). Like her aunt, Louise has a good time, and she loves seeing the opening parade, the beautiful women riders, and all the exotic animals. But she worries too much about families and injury, here clearly constructed as gendered concerns in which she participates along with her aunt, to fully enjoy the show as do the boys.

Other children's books from the late nineteenth century go further in involving girls in enjoyment of the show, in the desire at least to view it if not to join. Louisa May Alcott's much reprinted *Under the Lilacs,* first published in 1877, provides a sentimental story of rural life though, like *An Average Boy's Vacation,* it also highlights the children's desire to escape. On the Fourth of July, the children are not allowed to set off fireworks because they might be too dangerous, with parents giving dire warnings about scaring horses and blowing up arms and barns. Pulling them immediately out of small-town doldrums is sudden news brought by a friend on the run: in a town nearby, Berryville, will be appearing Van Amburg & Co.'s New Great Golden Menagerie, Circus and Colosseum, with shows at one and at seven, for fifty cents and children half price, a chance not to be missed (115).

The boys taunt each other and decide to undertake the four-mile walk without permission, hoping to get a ride home afterwards. But a little cousin, Bab, does not want to take the dog and walk home, as the boys instruct her to do, and in the ensuing dialogue counters every argument against her taking the risk and going along:

> "Circus! Oh, Ben, *do* take me!" cried Bab, falling into a state of great excitement at the mere thought of such delight.
> "You couldn't walk four miles," began Ben.
> "Yes, I could, as easy as not."
> "You haven't got any money."
> "You have; I saw you showing your dollar, and you could pay for me, and Ma would pay you back."
> "Can't wait for you to get ready."
> "I'll go as I am. I don't care if it is my old hat," and Bab jerked it onto her head.
> "Your mother wouldn't like it."
> "She won't like you going, either."

Ben continues by making a judgment not just about Bab but about girls when an adventure is on: "Girls are such a bother when you want to knock round. No, Bab, you *can't* go. Travel right home and don't make a fuss. Come along, boys; it's most eleven, and we don't want to walk fast" (119).

But Bab walks the four miles by herself and then gives the excuse that the dog wouldn't go home. The boys finally let her and the dog go with them, quite a moment for the little girl who walks excitedly with Ben: "Bab held tight to the flap of his jacket, staring about her with round eyes, and listening with little gasps of astonishment or delight to the roaring of lions, the snarling of tigers, the chatter of the monkeys, the groaning of camels, and the music of the very brass band shut up in a red bin" (125).

Unlike Louise in *An Average Boy's Vacation*, Bab enjoys the risk taken by the performers as well as the pageantry of their entrance: she is "kept in a breathless state by the marvelous agility and skill of the gauzy lady who drove four horses at once, leaped through hoops, over banners and bars, sprang off and on at full speed, and seemed to enjoy it all so much it was impossible to believe that there could be any danger or exertion in it." And she feels especially engaged with the tumblers and trapeze artists because her mother calls her "a little monkey." Like the boys in so many books, she dreams of being able to practice the acts at home: she hopes that if she does her chores her mother will let her "wear red-and-gold trousers, and climb around like these girls" (130–31). Though the small town represents security in this nostalgic novel, as in so many written for and about children, these scenes reflect the call of the exotic life, for the small girl as well as the older boys.

In *Rebecca of Sunnybrook Farm,* another favorite family novel, written in 1903 by Kate Douglas Wiggin, an attraction to the circus, to leaving home and social boundaries, is again tied to the high spirits of a young girl, one with an imaginative mind and strong will. At the beginning of the novel, when Rebecca has to leave with the carriage driver, Mr. Cobb, to go to the house of her aunts Miranda and Jane, because her widowed mother is unable to support seven children, her strong spirit is symbolized by her immediate desire to tell Cobb about a circus visit, one of the highlights of her life so far, a vision of life completely apart from her reality of a home with too many children and too little money:

> Last summer the circus came to Temperance, and they had a procession in the morning. Mother let us all walk in and wheel Mira in the baby carriage, because we couldn't afford to go to the circus in the afternoon. And there were lovely horses and animals in cages, and clowns on horseback; and at the very end came a little red and gold chariot drawn by two ponies, and in it, sitting on a velvet cushion, was the snake charmer, all dressed in satin and spangles. She was so beautiful beyond compare, Mr. Cobb, that you had to swallow lumps in your throat when you looked at her, and little cold feelings crept up and down your back. Don't you know how I mean? Didn't you ever see anybody that made you feel like that? [20].

Here her attraction to "satin and spangles," even if glimpsed just momentarily in a passing parade, points to the high spirits that will ultimately alter her aunts and their town.

For the film version of *Rebecca of Sunnybrook Farm* in 1917, screenwriter Frances Marion and star Mary Pickford added a circus scene, not just one recalled during a carriage ride, to emphasize Rebecca's independence and spirit in a more visual manner. After she arrives in her aunts' village, she puts on a circus with the other children on a day when her restrictive and bitter aunts are not home. The spectacle begins with a parade involving girls as clowns, boys padded to be strong men, and a piano with children popping out as the notes. In a barn filled with a huge crowd, Pickford appears as a bareback performer called Rebeccaretta, suspended on a wire in the air above a horse. She is going so quickly, in fact, whipped around by the wire, that she comes off the horse entirely. As in sequences in many films in which Pickford played a child, she appears as an exotic performer, indeed as a slightly dangerous, scantily clad adult, a shock to the aunts when they unexpectedly return home. She spins out into space, clearly beyond control, providing an evocative indicator that the aunts' staid and depressive world will not contain her.

The voluminous children's circus literature had a clear gender line. So many books concerned boys joining the circus, having an adventure and then perhaps going back home, where a moral about family could ensue — after the reader, and the book's hero, had enjoyed circus riders, flyers, and animals. Though of a much lesser number, books also featured girls drawn to the circus but not leaving home for it as boys might. The literature clearly focuses on the girl as attracted to the stimulation, entranced by the beauty and even the risk, her circus exhilaration a sign of unusual character, of the high spirits that could alter her family and town. The girl might be a bit frightened by the circus or completely enthralled, but she is clearly looking into a foreign world, one coming to her town for a day or two, something to hold in memory but not to join. She might only dream about going, but the spunky and independent girl in this period of literature, as portrayed by renowned children's authors such as Alcott and Wiggin, seeks a world beyond the normal and everyday. She envisions circus and thus a grown-up life that does not involve the restrictions of the traditional home and town. In this literature resides the possibility of a site and occupation for girls that would offer something more than normal routines of the past.

# CHAPTER 4

## Romanticized Books for Men and Women

A voluminous children's literature of the late nineteenth and early twentieth century features adventurous boys going to the circus and girls dreaming of this exciting world. The circus also shaped two separate genres of books for adult men and adult women, in which circuses create a thrilling parallel existence, its traits determined by the reader's gender. Jim Tully's *Circus Parade,* published in 1927, was as circus historian Fred Pfening III maintained the first novel that "bothered to show a somewhat derogatory picture of the circus," the rest using it in a highly symbolic, positive manner to showcase what men and women might seek. For women especially, the circus was created and reflected in a voluminous literature, suggesting a place where they would be free to make their own personal choices and pursue their own careers.

### For Men Only

With the circus growing in popularity after 1880, it became a recurring topic of short "dime novels" about adolescent boys and young men, written primarily for an audience of young working-class men. This genre label began as a brand name, Beadle's Dime Novels, published from 1860 to 1874, a series of inexpensive paper-covered booklets, numbered in a series, and soon widely imitated by many publishers. These novellas almost always involved young male heroes, at first in legends of early America but later more commonly in tales of cowboys, detectives, fire fighters, and other adventurers vaguely of the current day (Cox xiii). In this genre, as J. Randolph Cox notes in *The Dime Novel Companion,* "there were few publications designed for and marketed to young female readers" (xxi).

Circus historian Fred Pfening III claims that the quickly written and exaggerated dime novels about the circus "represent an all time low" for circus fiction, but they were certainly a popular item. This genre first featured the circus in Frank S. Finn's *The Boy Clown* from 1878, at the time that circuses were increasing in size and number across the United States (Cox 55). The use of longer titles, such as Richard Montgomery's *Barnum's Hunters, or Trapping Wild Animals for the Greatest Show on Earth* (1887) and Hal Standish's *Fred Fearnot and the Snake-Charmer; or, Out with the Circus Fakirs* (1906), provided a clear rendition of the books' contents (Cox 55–56). Most of the dime novels about the heroes of Wild West shows concern their exploits on the Plains — at least twenty writers penned some five hundred dime novels about the life of Buffalo Bill Cody — but some books, such as Standish's *Fred Fearnot's Wild West Show, or, The Biggest Thing on Earth,* describe the adventure of traveling with these shows (Cox 43). Whether the male hero solves a crime, learns a new aerial or equestrian trick, or hunts down wild animals or freaks, he lives in a circus world of risk, which he conquers through his own gumption and luck. For the young man, then, the circus represents a faraway work world, excitement and challenge on the road, what a young man might dream about and seek.

## For Women Only

For women readers, as well as for men, the circus provided a powerfully symbolic rendering of an exciting outside world, a life of adventure and freedom. The young girl in children's fiction might be represented by her attraction to the circus, a symbol of her imagination. But in novels for adults, women did not just dream of joining — they joined — and their choices provided commentary on the codes that they left behind. In an interview in the *Saturday Evening Post* in 1920, trapeze artist Lucy Lightfoot commented that, in fiction, as an artistic convention, women like herself were often "exploited as the heroines of hectic melodrama," and indeed they were (Yates, "The Circus Girl" 30).

For the adult woman reader, the circus symbolized part of a wild, exotic world out there beyond the dull and normal, but not the hard-scrabble world seen in many dime novels or even in *Toby Tyler.* Instead, the circus provides a freeing, romantic space — where women can shape their own adult lives, finding meaningful work for which they are respected and well compensated. Many of the books feature contrasts between circus and society people, with the circus providing an alternative where the characters, and thus the readers, can evaluate regular life and consider an escape from it. Like news articles fostered by press agents, these books depict fun and adventure, but they also feature critiques of "normal" life and relationships, of established codes. As they concentrate on relationships between circus insiders and outsiders, and thus both the regular and the circus world, these books' alternative world focuses on excitement, purpose, skill — and perhaps most fully on a redefinition of love and marriage.

Some of these books, published beginning in the late nineteenth century, question whether the husband should have the right to control the wife. Equestrian Madame D'Arbonne in Charles Theodore Murray's *A Modern Gypsy: A Romance of Circus Life* (1897), for example, finds the nomadic circus life much more enthralling than a regular marriage: "It was not that she despised or even thought lightly of the marriage-tie. The fact that it was a tie made it impossible. That it was an obligation to live in one place according to rule, subject to the wishes and whims of one man, bound like a slave to the same oar every day, made it intolerable. She had tried it, like many another high-spirited woman, and had found the chains galling." Here Murray emphasizes the unique choice that his heroine makes, which readers can enjoy if only vicariously: "Unlike others, however, she arose and snapped the bonds" (30).

This equestrian leaves her first husband William Arnold, who had sought to enchain her in the "indoor domestic life," and joins the circus (31). But she leaves a second husband, a rich French count, because "he was so dark and fierce and vengeful" (107). Here Murray describes another male extreme, not the drearily domestic but the violent, both of which she must get away from: "The transition had been from the monotony of a calm, gently-rolling, unfathomable sea, to being swallowed up in the roaring breakers, and thumped and bruised, and left quivering upon unknown sands" (143). Even though she has a baby with the second husband, she leaves them both because of what these men have in common: containing her.

When the violent count sends someone to America, where D'Arbonne is performing, to buy or abduct his child, she asks William Arnold for his help. The previously stolid Arnold is willing to venture to Paris and duel the count, after which he telegraphs her: "Have no further fear. Count Frederic dead. Boy acknowledged. Full story mailed" (274). And then D'Arbonne chooses to return to Arnold: this time he does not ask her to leave the circus, but instead he takes a job with the show to be with her. He has transformed himself, in his willingness to accept, help, and join her, into an acceptable husband.

While *A Modern Gypsy* employed the outside space of circus to show a world in which women did not have to submit to their husbands, circus romances also critiqued other social stereotypes. In *Her Elephant Man: A Story of the Sawdust Ring* from 1919, Pearl Doles Bell uses a circus as the site of one of her popular romances, many of which had evocative titles: *Gloria Gray, Love Pirate* (1914), *The Love Link* (1925), *Slaves of Destiny* (1926). In the friendship between Philip and Joan, *Her Elephant Man* contrasts the circus with the outside world, ironically with the circus as the more honest and civilized place, and evaluates the judgments inherent in American marriage codes, especially the belief that performing women or other outsiders might be late-night girlfriends but not wives. The "elephant man" is wealthy Philip Warner, who marries a grasping harpie, a member of his own social group, after she tells him that she is pregnant with his child. To get out of her clutches, he goes to India, where he works with elephants under an assumed name and is then presumed dead. He finally finds out that his wife had not been pregnant, had gone to Reno for a divorce, and had then adopted a child in hopes of inheriting his large fortune since money and position mattered so much to her.

Ultimately, Philip finds kindness and acceptance not in India but at the circus, which he joins as an elephant trainer when he returns to the United States. There he can get away from the greed and cruelty of society life and forget his bad youthful choices. In work with elephants and circus performers, he begins to regain a sense of purpose and community and to develop a close friendship with a young orphan named Joan, looked after by the kindly Jerimy, who had nurtured her from infancy.

In various scenes, the book discusses the divisions between high society and the kinder and purer circus, especially the harsh judgments of the circus woman as the lesser Other. Circus star Tricie Snyder expects that Philip resembles other men dabbling in a circus life: "No *circus girl* is anything to *him*. He's like the rest of his rotten world — ready to be entertained by us, but by no means ready to take us into his home" (28–29). She comments sarcastically about social judgments: a man could abandon his wife and child and take another name but still be viewed as far superior to a circus performer. Philip, however, vehemently disagrees with these standards, though his response does acknowledge them: "Why, Joan, there was a time when the public was prejudiced against circus folk. Against actor folk, too. But that day is past. Now it weighs all artists with the same scales." Joan tells Philip that she will not be surprised if he leaves her because of this prejudice, much more virulent against women who would choose a circus life than men: "'I — I reckon it's a different thing being a woman in a circus and being a man.... I reckon the world don't call the men the names they have for the women" (100).

Even though Philip is the divorced man, who abandoned his wife for India and the circus, she feels that his family would never forgive him if he married her. But Joan chooses Philip, and Philip chooses Joan, turning away from the worst of the restrictive pressures that led him into his first marriage, allowing him to step outside of what had been coded as normal for a man of his class and time and to value a woman for her own superior qualities.

While *Her Elephant Man* posits the circus as the purer locale, from which sojourners can examine social restrictions, it also provides a place in which Joan can have a chance for professional success, one that society women probably would never have. The young orphan Joan becomes a new star equestrian, with her abilities and her stardom, and not a love interest, moving her into adulthood, as Jerimy recognizes immediately: "He had stood with old Kennerly in the pad room near the wide back doors of the Big Top, and had looked in at the center ring where a mere slip of a girl, in swirling pink draperies, was dancing on the sleek back of a running horse. She had come out to them under a storm of applause." As Jerimy tells Joan, referring to the circus owner, "You never again can be my little playmate. Lawson has let you leap through a hoop into womanhood" (15).

In this world of great physical risk, readers indeed find a world less risky than the rough-and-tumble realities of high society. The circus here stands for a world in which women can exist outside of social pressures and restrictive views of normality and can be judged by their character and their skills.

Some writers' tales of the circus as release from normality had ties to their own personal lives. Writer and press agent Nellie Revell was bedridden in a hospital for four years after an automobile accident in 1920 crumpled her spine. She continued to write for newspapers and magazines, "on a pad across her chest while lying rigid on the flat of her back," a plaster cast covering her from neck to heels (Row, Feld). As soon as she left the hospital, she began working on her novel *Spangles,* published in 1926 (with a film version coming out that same year). For Revell her circus story represented not just a release from a normal restrictive life but also from four years in a hospital bed.

Revell had the family history to write this novel. Her mother's family had been in the circus; she had grown up traveling with Barnum & Bailey, though she never performed. She got a job as an advance man for Uncle Dick Sutton's Circus and then as a circus press agent. As she described it, referring to a freak-show performer with an oddly shaped head, his employment occurred during "the days when a girl press agent was as much of a curiosity as Barnum's 'Zip.'" She felt that the circus would make an inspiring subject for a popular novel, as she wrote in a book about plans made during her difficult hospital stay: "It is the universal touch of the circus that makes the world kin. It has no affinity with dialogue for a Chinaman can understand it as well as a bishop. It gives to human nature the spirit of spring. Youngsters chalk up the walls with the glad tidings, 'Ten more days till Circus Day — Hoo-rah.'" A circus story, she maintained, would help connect adults with a possible source of freedom and vitality: "The childlike emotions that 'grown-ups' sometimes conserve should be among their dearest possessions" (*Right off the Chest* 246).

Like Revell's own story, *Spangles* concerns a young woman, living a free and happy life, who becomes entangled in a restrictive reality and then breaks away from it to regain her freedom, the worthwhile existence here being at the circus. Like so many other circus novels, this one critiques established codes of high society. In this story, Spangles' mother was a circus rider who married a "man of very excellent family," a man of adventure, who soon left the mother for the gold rush in the Yukon (40). The mother died in childbirth, and the father never came back; circus people raised the child on the road in a loving community: "The show, she felt forcibly, was not only a part of her. It was her home, her life, her little world, which she knew and understood and loved so dearly" (11).

When Spangles is in her teens, appearing as a bareback rider as did her mother, her father's brother claims her and takes her to Paris where she becomes a debutante. The move to Paris is not a rescue, a chance for a better life, but instead an entanglement in capitalistic greed: living with an uncle bent on controlling her, so that he can gain the deed to land that his brother purchased in the Yukon. Though she is called Spangles in the circus, these relatives insist on using her given name of Helen, and they keep her from ever mentioning the life she left. They don't want any of their high society friends to find out that they are housing a circus performer.

When she meets a nice young man in Paris, she confides in him concerning the ironic comparison she sees between what are for her real and unreal worlds, with security and purpose existing at the circus, not in the drawing room. As she describes it to him: "'I have been here for some time now, but I haven't met any real people yet. There is nobody here I'd call real. All these fancy Counts and Barons with their silly manners and empty flattery don't mean a thing to me. Let me tell you,' her tone became confidential, 'I know trapeze artists back in America that's ten times as real as this whole bunch.... These people don't seem to know or understand anything but dancing and flirting and drinking" (132–33).

When Helen makes her aunt mad at a party by mentioning the circus, the aunt says that she has tried to make her niece into a lady but that Helen prefers "the thieves and the snakes of the circus." In reply, again comparing the two worlds in which she has lived, Helen claims that although thieves come to circuses, the circus people themselves are "good and hard-working." And then she argues that upper-class dwellers of the drawing room do not make the positive impact of circus stars: "Have they ever carried men back to the days of their childhood, when they gave water to elephants or applauded a clown?" She claims in conclusion that "the drawing-room has more artificiality than the circus, but none of its kindness" (232–33).

When Helen finally gets away from these selfish relatives, she returns to the circus and tries to remake her life as Spangles. Since she has lived in regular society for five years, she fears that she will no longer fit in or be welcome: "But even as she was nearing the flag-bedecked entrance to the lot, a subtle, insidious fear stole into her heart. All this was familiar to her, she told herself, and yet, somehow, she didn't quite recognize it; did not feel completely at home. She wondered whether she really belonged to the circus or not" (267). But Spangles reorients herself to the circus life as the better of the two worlds. Ironically, the drawing room is the place where truly hardened grafters play destructive and selfish games, caring nothing about improving the lives of others.

In depicting the circus world, some books go beyond the romantic moment of marriage. They provide a romance, but they also comment on the expectations women may have that are rarely met in the life beyond "I do": these books give a sense that a charmed life may not go on, that we are discussing an escape with which adult responsibilities, given the current social realities, ultimately may not mix. John D. Barry, who wrote many popular romances such as *The Intriguers* (1896) and *The Congressman's Wife* (1903), published *Mademoiselle Blanche* in 1896, a book reprinted eight times in the next ten years. This novel fully considers the romantic potential of being a circus performer and having a dashing man fall in love with first your image, and then you.

Jules Le Baron goes to a circus performance at a Paris theatre, where before buying the ticket he looks carefully at the posters in the entrance. First he reads the advertisement that makes Mademoiselle Blanche seem enticing, since it is "announcing the most marvelous acrobat in the world, and proclaiming that, in addition to giving her act on the trapeze, she would plunge backward from the top of the theatre, a height of more than seventy-five feet, into a net below." Upon reading this description, the man first returns to the boy: "Jules smiles, and felt a thrill of his old boyish excitement at the prospect of seeing that feat performed" (12).

Then as he is buying the ticket, he sees her photograph on an easel near the box office, moving him to adult male attraction to the female body: "The acrobat, her long sinuous limbs encased in white tights, was suspended in mid-air, one arm bent at the elbow, clinging to a trapeze. The tense muscles of the arm made a curious contrast with the expression of the face, which was marked by unusual simplicity and gentleness. The profile was clear, the curving eyelashes were delicately outlined, and the eyes were large and dark" (12).

This description posits that the man can enjoy the sensuous body while also gaining entrance to her private life through her facial expressions. He worries, though, because he knows that the appearance of youth in her limbs could be a result of trickery, stemming from a star's knowledge of make-up: "He wondered if the appearance of youth that she presented were also due to her cleverness. She might easily pass for twenty. Her figure looked marvelously supple; she had probably been trained for the circus from infancy, and she might be fifty years old" (13). Intrigued though skeptical, he waits through clowns, performing dogs, knife-throwing, and trick riding to examine Mademoiselle Blanche for himself.

At the end of the show, as the finale act, Blanche finally comes out to applause, and Jules gets the chance to determine her actual age, a subject of much importance to him. "Jules Le Baron drew a long breath. The long supple limbs, the firm white arms and throat, the pale oval face, framed in dark hair that curled around the forehead, created a kind of beauty that seemed almost ethereal. The glamour of youth was over her, too; she could not be, at most, more than twenty." As she swings on a trapeze "with a bewildering swiftness," her actions lead to wild applause and to a completely enthralled Jules, who feels a grown-up version of a child's sense of enchantment with the circus: "He felt as if his heart had stopped beating. He had never seen such a thrilling exhibition before. All his old delight in the circus had come back to him" (17).

Blanche's magnetism leads to Jules' desire to possess her, but to do so happily he must overcome the stereotypes of circus people that his society endorses, stereotypes like those discussed in *Her Elephant Man*, that circus performers are less moral, less religious, less normal-looking on the street: "Then he wondered what she was like out of the circus — ignorant and vulgar, probably, like the rest of them. Yet in her looks she was different from the rest" (19). But soon he finds himself in love — and amazed by his fascination with a woman not of his class and experience: "To be in love with an acrobat, a woman who earned her bread by hurling herself from the top of a building, who risked her life every day, sometimes twice a day, that she might live!" (47). Blanche finally consents to let him accompany her to church, where he marvels at her devotion as well as her ability to transform herself outside of the ring: "A few of the men recognized the girl, and turned to look after her. She seemed not to see them, but Jules did, and he felt very proud to be her escort. She looked very pretty in her tight-fitting black jacket and little hat tipped with fur, her cheeks scarlet with the early frost, She was the last person in the crowd, Jules thought, who would be taken for an acrobat. It seemed to him wonderful that she should appear so unlike the marvel that she was, and this lack of resemblance to herself made her the more attractive to him" (76–77). Blanche, also, falls in love, happy to be the object of this intense gaze and fascination and acceptance. And she sees their love as transformative for Jules.

But the couple's experience beyond their happy-ever-after moment complicates the picture. Jules wants a wife and even a child, but he does not actually want a more mature version of Blanche. To be his circus star, Blanche returns to the ring after giving birth to their daughter, before she is strong enough to do so, a desperate attempt to keep Jules' attention that ends in her death:

> The black mass below seemed to dance before her, then to beckon to her, and in her ears she kept hearing the voice of little Jeanne and the sound of her laughter. Oh, she had known that this moment would come some time; she had known it ever since Jeanne was born. But she could not sit there forever; the crowd below was waiting to see her fall. If she did not make an effort she should lose her self-control and go plunging into the blackness. She must lift her hands and gather herself together, and hurl herself out as she had always done. But she had no strength; she could only lift her arms weakly. Then she tried to give her body the necessary impetus, and she plunged wildly into the air.
>
> There was a cry of horror from the crowd, and a moment later the white figure lay motionless in the net [328].

Blanche is changed by the marriage and child birth, in ways that Jules does not want her to change. She cannot inhabit both the worlds of ethereal star and of mother. The romantic heroine is not supposed to age: her value is to remain in her youthful achievements and body. The circus dream about challenging work combined with marriage and motherhood here seems difficult to sustain.

## Picking the Circus Man

Circus novels present not just the society man with the circus woman; they also concern the regular small-town woman who runs away to the circus because of love of a performer — though again the decision becomes more complex if the text continues after marriage. Published in 1920, D.H. Lawrence's *The Lost Girl* concerns not just this thrilling choice of life but the complications occurring afterwards, as it relates the story of Alvina Houghton, a girl from a middle-class English family, who chooses a mate from a traveling show.

In 1920, Lawrence's *Women in Love* was published in New York City only in a limited edition available to 1250 subscribers because of the controversy caused by his previous work, *The Rainbow* (1915), the two written as parts of a single novel. Great Britain banned *The Rainbow* for eleven years following an obscenity trial; British publishers would not release *Women in Love*. Coming out in 1920 in the midst of this controversy, *The Lost Girl* gained extra attention with reviewers and the public. The *Brooklyn Eagle* requested serial rights; the *New York Times* commented intriguingly that the book, with its "occasionally profound and startling variations from the stereotyped," might be judged as salacious, but the story was actually "set forth with skill and complete freedom from vulgarity" (Field 22).

In *The Lost Girl*, readers encountered a dutiful young woman, Alvina, caring for older family members, caught in the desperation of the unchosen:

> She was withering towards old-maiddom. Already in her twenty-eighth year, she spent her days grubbing in the house, whilst her father became an elderly, frail man still too lively in mind and spirit, Miss Pinnegar began to grow grey and elderly too, money became scarcer and scarcer, there was a black day ahead when her father would die and the home be broken up and she would have to tackle life as a worker [95].

Alvina perceives only a few work options within her restrictive small town. These jobs, taken only to eke out subsistence, do not seem likely to make life meaningful:

> There lay the only alternative: in work. She might slave her days away teaching the piano, as Miss Frost had done: she might find a subordinate post as nurse: she might sit in the cash-desk of some shop. Some work of some sort would be found for her. And she would sink into the routine of her job, as did so many women, and grow old and die, chattering and fluttering. She would have what is called her independence. But, seriously faced with that treasure, and without the right of refusing it, strange how hideous she found it [81].

Although Alvina is approached by a staid, older doctor who offers an "Honorable Engagement," as a chapter title indicates, and thus a way out of stifling work, Alvina judges this loveless and polite alternative to be another sort of bondage. But when a troupe of Italian performers arrives, she enjoys these "odd eccentric people" who drink and have a "streak of imagination — the eccentric manager, the foreign acrobats, the musicians, the tattoo artist" (119). But most of her attention goes to the Italian Cicio, whose looks and dark color symbolize for her the completely foreign and even pre-civilized man: "His beautiful lashes seemed to screen his eyes. He was fairly tall, but loosely built for an Italian, with slightly sloping shoulders. Alvina noticed the brown, slender Mediterranean hand, as he put his fingers to his lips. It was a hand such as she did not know, prehensile and tender and dusky" (127). When Cicio appears in a show bare-chested, costumed as an Indian brave, his exotic darkness leads Alvina to marry him and leave for Italy.

Though Cicio changes her name from Alvina to Allaye, she is not totally remade as she struggles to cope with a foreign culture and a theatrical life that her upperclass English upbringing causes her to judge as inferior. The roaming that had seemed adventurous begins to seem wrong: "She was beginning to realize something about him: how he had no sense of home and domestic life, as an Englishman had. Cicio's home would never be his castle" (341). And in his unsettled world, she "was a lost girl. She was cut off from everything she belonged to" (324). She also must cope with his impending departure to the world war. But still she recognizes that she has entered a more exhilarating world, one that may next lead her to America, and has left the restrictive family and the meaningless drudgery of home — and she does not ultimately regret her choice.

In the huge literature about the circus at the end of the nineteenth century and beginning of the twentieth, boys run away to the circus and encounter adventures. Girls do not run away, but they want to, and a liking for the circus is taken as a sign of independence and spunk. While older boys and men found adventure at the circus in dime novels, women found an electrifying version of love. The circus performer and performance provide a vision of a thrilling and meaningful existence: a dream, certainly, one that might not stretch so easily beyond a woman's youth, the subject of most romances. In this literature, the circus represents a chance to get away from the withering realities of a woman's usual existence: staying in a small town, caring for older people, moving into a marriage with whoever might deign to ask her, raising children without much help, and keeping house. At the circus, in this vision of it, women have the freedom to move and make choices; they learn exciting skills for which their peers and audiences admire them; older social distinctions, about what a woman must do and be, do not matter; purposeful performers within a tent are superior to pompous drones within a drawing room. Right outside of town, or at least within the covers of so many books, the circus seemed iconically always the same for women: a site of purpose, excitement, freedom, and equality in love.

CHAPTER 5

# The Complexities of Filmic Representation

Books for children and adults involved readers in a world beyond their own, as a place to go to (or at least think about going to) outside the reach of restrictive, conventional life. This literature of excitement and escape certainly extended to the motion picture. From the beginning, the circus appeared in both documentaries and features, at least 180 between 1900 and 1939. The circus' emphasis on movement and quick transition, as well as its lack of dialogue, made it a perfect subject matter for silent film. As films became longer and added sound, the circus hullabaloo, portrayed in fuller narratives, continued to secure attention. In this array of silents and talkies, this visual genre quite effectively reiterated themes found in other media: films presented the circus as both a frightening place to avoid and as a highly romanticized place to run away to as soon as possible.

Many of the first short silent films relied on the drama and movement of actual circus visits to present the startling adventure of these shows. *Panorama of Circus Train Unloading Horses* (1903) shows circus employees unloading high-strung horses from train cars. *Bostock's Circus Fording a Stream* (1903) portrays an entire circus crossing a shallow river where a bridge is out, the elephants and camels drawing heavy circus wagons. The wonders of a circus parade appear in *Buffalo Bill's Parade* (1903), led by Buffalo Bill himself on his famous white steed and followed by mounted Native Americans, Arabs, English troopers, Boer cavalry, Rough Riders, and a cowboy band. *Circus Street Parade* (1903) features a lion perched on top of a bespangled wagon, camels walking side by side with elephants, beautiful women driving gold chariots, clowns performing tricks, and women in cages facing fierce Bengal tigers and poisonous snakes. Other films provide snapshots from throughout a circus day. *Day at the Circus* (1901), for example, concerning the Great Forepaugh and Sells Bros. Circus, shows the parade through town, the grand entry into the tent, and a horse race.

Documentary style films throughout the period also focused positively and dramatically on specific acts by well-known circus families. *Equestrian Acrobats* (1937), for example, showcases the famed Cristiani Family as they mount and dismount moving horses and perform acrobatic feats on horseback. *Circus Co-Ed* (1940) features stunts by the equally well-known Clarke family in a story concerning the training of a young girl for a career on the trapeze.

# Comedies

In many film series created for children, circus scenes provided an exotic locale for ongoing hijinks, just as they did in children's books such as the Peck's Bad Boy series. The circus in all its glory could be expanded and exaggerated in cartoons. In Walt Disney's *Alice's Circus Daze* (1927), part of a cartoon series in which a child actress, Lois Hardwick, appears along with cartoon characters, the circus acts appear at frantic speed with animals and men switching heads, a rubber man bouncing like a ball, elephants skating and leopards jumping rope, and animals filling the audience. On a tightrope, Alice balances on the top of six chairs held up by her partner Julius. When he lights a cigar, he accidentally throws the match onto the rope, burning it and sending both of them clattering to the ground, an exciting moment with no harm done. Live-action series featuring favorite child stars also brought them to the circus for wild fun. In *Clown Princes* (1939), the landlord has given final notice to poor Porky and his family — pay the rent or get out. The Little Rascals put on a show — a circus, with Alfalfa on the trapeze — to raise the needed money. In film versions of *Rebecca of Sunnybrook Farm* and *Peck's Bad Boy with the Circus,* the children's hijinks, a sign of high spirits and independence, lead straight to the circus tent.

In comedies for adults, the circus also provided a site for fun. Charlie Chaplin helped maintain interest in his Tramp character by taking him to the big top. In *The Circus* (1928), the Tramp gets chased around by the police through a mirror maze and the sideshows because they think he is a pickpocket. Running into the big top, he creates an accidental sensation as he collides with clowns, the magician and his assistant, and the crew. The owner immediately hires him, but discovers the Tramp cannot be funny on purpose. The owner solves this problem by making the Tramp a janitor who just happens to always be in the big top at showtime.

The Marx Brothers also found themselves drawn to the circus story as a means of presenting outlandish comedy. *At the Circus* (1939) concerns the Wilson Wonder Circus, where moviegoers could watch a singing equestrian along with a trapeze artist who used suction cups to walk upside down from the top of the tent. Groucho interacts with his classic partner Margaret Dumont, the high-class mother of the show's owner, and sings "Lydia, the Tattooed Lady," which mentions her inkings of the Battle of Waterloo (on her back), the cities of Kankakee and "Paree," Leutze's *Washington Crossing the Delaware*, Andrew Jackson, Niagara Falls, Alcatraz, Buffalo Bill, Lady Godiva (with her pajamas on), a fleet of ships (on Lydia's hips), and her own Social Security number.

# Romances

In both cartoons and live-action, films represented the circus as a place of thrilling action. This image of excitement reiterated the positive iconic imagery of many front-page feature articles and children's books. In these films, the circus scene can only mean American fun. Instead of simply supplying antics and action, some films presented the vision of the circus that appeared in women's romantic novels, as a place to find love, meaningful work, and a purer existence, outside of the restrictions of society. Several films, for example, featured the key words "circus" and "romance" together in their titles. In fact, Muriel Ostriche, silent film star, appeared in two films with that title. In *A Circus Romance* (1914), she stars as Papita, a bareback rider, whom a fortune teller talks into dating a local doctor even though his father will disapprove. In *A Circus Romance* (1916), written by Frances Marion, she also stars as Babette, a dancer with a traveling carnival whose mother, fortune teller Zaidee, had been secretly married to a wealthy man. Babette enjoys meeting her father but doesn't seek to leave the circus or her circus boyfriend Pete.

## Or a Pit...

But films also soon embraced a more negative vision of the circus, as was also found in the injury headlines and weird body articles featured in newspapers. In the imagery of film, the circus repeatedly appeared as a seedy reality, not a place to run away to and fall in love, but an intimidating and violent place, without moral fiber, filled with pickpockets and other grafters — as well as improper women. The visual power of films, many of them silent, admirably created the stereotypical extreme of circus life as not a utopia but a pit. These films not only emphasized the possible injury in the acts but also the treachery of performers, thus not the romance of novels but something much more corrupt.

The emphasis on the circus as sordid may be easiest to document in films adapted from women's novels. The book version of *Susan Lenox: Her Fall and Rise*, by David Graham Phillips, featured a woman dancing in a showboat theatre, vaudeville halls, and then on Broadway, but in the film version, with Greta Garbo and Clark Gable, from 1931, her much more extreme path downwards begins at the circus. Helga, living with her aunt and uncle on their farm, is an orphan made to feel ashamed and act as a servant because her mother, who died in childbirth, had not been married. She escapes on a stormy night when the fiancé that the uncle chose for her tries to rape her. That night she meets up with Rodney, a kind architect, but the wicked uncle catches up with her, and she must flee again. Her next rescuer is a tattooed lady in the Burlington Circus, but she can't save Helga, now called Susie and appearing as a hootchie cootchie dancer named Belle Fatima, from the clutches of the circus manager. Rodney shows up, sees the manager treat "Susie" as sexual property, and dismisses her as a fallen woman, saying, "I am a sap who didn't realize how cheap you are." Susie leaves the circus and, as Susan, moves into the penthouse of a politician who can offer a construction contract to Rodney. He says no and flees to the jungle, where Susan pursues him. Here though the tattooed lady tries to help her, the circus is a seedy place of displayed and exploited women, their names and identities altered, and there are no kind circus managers — details that did not appear at all in the book. In the film, though the fiancé had tried to rape her, the circus turns her into a whore.

Another film adaptation of a popular novel further emphasizes the film's preference for the seediness of circus. In Nellie Revell's novel *Spangles* (1926), the child grows up in a kind and wholesome circus and finds high society the site of brutality and greed. But a film version starring Marian Nixon, made in the same year that the novel appeared, features instead a plot full of horrifics about the show: a possible murderer on a circus train; a jealous older lion tamer, Mademoiselle Dazie, whom the management fires and abandons; an owner that bribes Spangles to get her to marry him; an elephant that kills the owner. Though here Spangles and her young man ultimately find love, it provides a contrast to a depraved circus world, not an indication of the circus' inherent kindness.

In this filmed circus world, the good people do not find respite there, but intrigue, sordidness, and evil. In *The Circus Queen Murder* (1933), starring Adolphe Menjou, suave, lip-reading police commissioner Thatcher Colt plans to get away from the big city for a few days. So he and his secretary, Miss Kelly, hop on a train for an upstate New York town called Gideon. They expect a calm oasis, but the small time Rainey Traveling Circus involves them in crime: out of jealousy, one aerial artist, Flandrin, tries to kill another by unraveling the rope on which his rival performs. Flandrin then kills his own wife with a poisoned dart while hiding out among the cannibals in the sideshow tent. To end the film, Flandrin kills himself by letting go of the high wire and plunging into the crowd. Like Gideon in the Book of Judges, who destroys false idols and returns disobedient Israelites to God, Thatcher Colt conquers a circus morass of adultery, murder, suicide, and cannibalism.

In these films, love triangles can become violent and destructive. In *Circus Girl* (1937), trapeze apprentice Kay Rogers marries aerial performer Charles Jerome, who at the same time is involved with Miss Carlotta, the lion tamer. This "two-timing egotistical heel," as Carlotta calls him, immediately becomes jealous of fellow trapeze artist Bob McAvoy and sets out to kill him by punching him in the eye right before their performance and then cutting the rope to a trapeze on which McAvoy is performing; McAvoy is performing right above vicious, untrained lions that Jerome has placed there so that he can advertise a Suicide Act. In *Dangerous Curves* (1929), trapeze star Larry Lee is so enthralled with fellow trapeze artist and vamp Zara Flynn that he cannot see that she is just using him to get better performance opportunities and that she is having a secret affair with his partner. Lee is driven to drunkenness and near death by her betrayal.

In *Charlie Chan at the Circus* (1936), the big top again appears as a malevolent and bewildering environment, an antithesis to the famous detective's calm authority. Charlie receives fourteen free passes to the Kinney & Gaines Combined Circus for his entire family, but once they arrive, the co-owner asks him to investigate threatening letters that he has received. Even though the circus may look like the site of a fun family activity in the first well-lit scene, it soon appears as an untrustworthy world — dark, with a labyrinth of tents and cages, with performers lurking in the shadows. When the owner, Kinney, is murdered, the culprit could be his partner, the snake charmer, or the menagerie's gorilla, all equally suspect. Chan also mistrusts an older trapeze star, Nellie, working as a wardrobe mistress, angry and rejected because Kinney prefers the younger star, Marie. In this world, where so many people and animals seem dangerous, one performer tells her boyfriend, "Let's get away from here and live like regular people."

Some of these films that create the seedy environment make harsh points about the necessary separation between normal men and performing women: these films present no romantic picture of marriage and equality. In *Pink Tights* (1920), Mazie Darton, a high-wire performer with a traveling circus, longs for a peaceful country life. Forced to stay in a small town while laid up with an injury, Darton is spurned by the conservative towns-people. When the Rev. Jonathon Meek, the local parson, befriends Darton, he opens himself to criticism from his flock, who protest his closeness with show people: it is inappropriate for him or for any other regular small-town man to even be her friend.

In the film version of circus life, for the normal woman to fall for the circus man is just as offensive as for the normal man to get involved with the circus floozy. Choosing the circus man, in fact, can lead the good, normal girl to degradation and crime. In *The Woman Always Pays* (1910), after small-town girl and preacher's daughter, Magda, goes with her fiancé to the circus, she leaves him to run away with a performer named Rudolf. But soon he shows interest an exotic singer named Lilly. Magda becomes jealous and starts a fight in which she accidentally kills Rudolf, the film ending in the police arresting her for murder.

In films, the circus performer could be just as bad, as visually exotic and immoral, as male viewers might want her to be. She could be a darkly ruined figure like Magda, a dangerous vixen like Lilly, or a more fun version of the bad girl, like Tira in *I'm No Angel* (1933), starring Mae West and Cary Grant. The bold Tira, no last name given, works as dancing beauty and lion tamer at a fair. Tira is an exotic sexual woman, her exploits handled as comedy but still presented as exploits. The film begins with the barker at Bill Barton's Wonder Show trying to attract men to her tent. When Tira comes out to lure them, they all go inside to see her do the shimmy-shake in a semi-revealing gown and sing "Sister Honky Tonk." She has a hotel room in town to which she takes men and plays them songs recorded for each hometown, like "No One Can Love Me Like a Dallas Man," to get them to hand over gifts and money. When a boyfriend, easily labeled and condemned as "one of those circus people," seemingly kills her latest admirer, she tells the circus owner that she will do anything for money to hire an attorney, even put her head in a lion's mouth. These managers think that this act can get them all to "the big show," as indeed it does, in New York. There posters featuring the roaring lion and her legs hail her as "feminine beauty triumphant and unafraid." While appearing as a lion tamer at the big show, Tira continues to pursue her other occupation: flirting with rich men and accepting expensive presents, for which she is labeled as "crude and ill bred." When Jack Clayton (Cary Grant) abandons her and she sues him for breach of promise, the court scene is humorous and she prevails. But several men argue that her immoral past acts invalidate her claim, a funny scene but still a judgmental one. This scene is classic Mae West, all saucy, with great innuendo, but here a circus woman has a seedy past and present and no recourse in society except her own wits.

While stories about lion tamers or dancers might warn of a dangerous circus existence, films involving freaks could do so at another level entirely. The best known of such a horror movie type is *Freaks* (1932), directed by Tod Browning, who had worked as a promoter for the Wild Man of Borneo and as "The Living Corpse" in a live-burial act at various carnivals and as a clown with Ringling Bros. This film opens with a promoter who tells the sideshow crowd that they will see "living, breathing monstrosities" whose appearance separates them from normal viewers: "But for the accident of birth, you might be as they are." As he engages the crowd, the film flashes back to tell the story of the most hideous attraction. At a sideshow circus, where the greatest attractions are little people and people with microcephaly, trapeze artist Cleopatra, a "big woman" advertised as Queen of the Air, sleeps with the strongman Hercules but pretends to care for the little person Hans, a wealthy man. With Hercules as accomplice, Cleo decides to marry Hans and then poison him to inherit his fortune. At the wedding feast, where the freaks chant "one of us, we accept her," she openly flirts with Hercules and mocks the sideshow performers. With Hans very ill from poison, the freaks snoop around and find out what Cleopatra has been doing. During a stormy night, they transform Cleopatra into a monstrous half woman, The Feathered Hen, available for viewing in the sideshow pit at the end. This dark film reveals a hatred between big and little people, no community at the circus but layers of cruel judgment, a relentless drive for money, and a terrifying potential for the worst forms of violence. This film is another that makes the original much more horrific. In the short story from 1926, "Spurs" by Tod Robbins, the plot concerns the little person ultimately getting control over a cruel bareback rider who had married him for his money and killing the "circus Romeo" who had been her lover (279). Though the story includes a group of sideshow freaks at a wedding party, there is no group action, no group vengeance.

Across an array of film types, this genre took advantage of the drama of circus. In short

**Poster for *I'm No Angel*, with Mae West as sideshow dancer (courtesy Universal Studios Licensing LLC).**

silents, circus scenes gave directors a chance to show audiences what these artistic sites, both the circus and the new film, could achieve. In films for children, live and cartoon, the circus became a thrilling site to visit, filled with action and surprise. Similarly, it created an excellent backdrop for slapstick comedy aimed at children and adults as well as for idyllic "circus romances" aimed at women. But in most filmic depictions, the circus provided not just a vague romantic place to run away to but a sexual and seedy reality, where women were gazed upon as bodies, attractive and dangerous, as outsiders that might fascinate but that should be avoided, a warning that audience members might or might not seek to heed.

Across the genres of popular media, both children and adults embraced contrasting myths of circus. As Timothy Morton has noted, in this depiction of an art form "everything is seen from the outside," thus with only a tangential relationship to what an insider might see and experience. All of these extremes presented an "exoticized" vision, involving only sparse attention to the details of an actual work life. Circus stood for the desire for independence shared by both the girl and woman, for a new and exotic world that they could inhabit, well beyond the normal. As these genres took on the ekphrastic task of "embedding us in a deep, dark inside," they showed not a mirror version of any circus's actual operations, but an "inside" that could describe richly iconic and nostalgic family fun as well as the modern girl and woman's desire to seek adventure and love beyond the confines of home (145). The woman's entrance into a traveling world of artistic work, or even just into the tent as spectator, could be glorious and freeing, as some texts argued, but it could also appear as dangerous and even deadly. The American media thus created a dichotomy — of unreal extremes — concerning this life and work beyond the confines of home.

# PART TWO

---

# Circus Depictions:
# The Stories Circus People Told

In so many media depictions, women in the circus provided extremes of danger and freedom. The mass media warned of ruination, but also offered the circus as an exciting alternative life, two opposite — and alluring — commentaries on the more regular existence of Americans.

But though the circus could be constructed in articles, books, and films so that it would dramatically both warn and lure, it also involved real performers doing a real job. They participated, of course, in extreme constructions that intrigued readers: they used fake names and repeated fake biographies. But they also created their own descriptions — in autobiographies, interviews, letters, speeches, visitations with dignitaries, and even amended contracts — that contrasted with and complicated the public versions of themselves.

## Suffrage

As outsiders and as workers, circus performers saw the need for change in the position of women. Many of them advocated for legislation that could engage all women more fully in American life. In 1912, women performers in the Barnum & Bailey Circus started their own Women's Equal Rights Society, with Josie DeMott Robinson as president and Kate Sandwina, strongwoman, as vice-president. May Wirth was an active member who helped the group communicate with women at other circuses. This association shared many members with The Suffragette Ladies of the Barnum & Bailey Circus, an association with eight hundred members that held meetings with activist organizations across the country ("Enlist Suffragists"). At one meeting in New York, Emily Pierson, a member of the Women's Political Union (WPU), said in a speech that "I saw Mrs. Sandine [sic] throwing those men around, and I thought that men, seeing their own sex done up in that way, could never say that women hadn't physical force." The WPU's Elizabeth Cook addressed circus women at another meeting and declared that, "We are all part of a great sisterhood, and that is what suffrage is." Along with New Yorker Eunice Dana Brannan, influential member of the National Woman's Party whose father founded and edited the *New York Sun*, this group planned a benefit circus performance in San Francisco for the suffrage cause, the performers organized and led by Zella Florence, acrobat; Victoria Davenport, bareback rider; Victoria Codona, aerialist; and May Wirth and her sister Stella ("Enlist Suffragists"; "Suffragists at Tea").

Besides planning special benefit performances for the suffrage campaign, circus women brought the cause to big-top shows. On the Fourth of July in 1912, members of the Wisconsin's Woman's Suffrage Association drove automobiles to the Ringling Bros. circus grounds in Racine, where circus employees distributed literature to the crowd ("Ringling Bros. Help"). Some performers, both women and men, wore suffrage sashes as they performed. At Madison Square Garden that same year, suffragists in the Barnum & Bailey Circus held a press conference before the show began at which they made speeches, posed for photographers, and crowned a giraffe as "Miss Suffrage" ("Enlist Suffragists").

Circus performers also participated in suffrage parades and rallies, their appearances well publicized. At many events in New York, equestrian Josie DeMott Robinson posed atop her rearing horse for publicity photographs. She wrote in her autobiography about joining in suffrage parades that at first had looked to her like "excited mobs of women":

> Before long I was in the midst of it too. I suppose I was rather a valuable acquisition, for I had horses and could make them do anything the leader of our district wanted. I could ride Comet and make him stand up straight in the air, while I waved a suffrage banner with a firm hand and a high arm. I could lead a parade [*The Circus Lady* 276–77].

The *Brooklyn Eagle* featured a large picture of her and her horse Nauty jumping off of a set of steps at the Mineola Fairgrounds on Long Island, a widely reprinted photograph that built excitement for the suffrage campaign. She also gave platform lectures in New York on women's need to keep fit to aid the suffrage cause and prepare for full citizenry (*The Circus Lady* 280).

Circus personnel extended their participation by lending animals to the cause. In a terrible rainstorm, women by the thousands gathered in Chicago in 1915 to march four abreast from Michigan Avenue to the Coliseum where the Republican National Convention was being held. All in white, led by Carrie Chapman Catt, they followed a baby elephant, borrowed from a local circus menagerie, and a large marching band, classic elements of an exciting circus parade ("Suffrage Movement").

## Other Activism

While many circus performers advocated for women's suffrage and equal rights, they also argued for women's fuller participation during wartime. Annie Oakley believed that women should learn to be proficient with firearms to have an additional career option and to defend themselves and their country (G. Riley 142). Just before the Spanish American War, she wrote to President William McKinley and volunteered for an unusual service.

> Hon Wm. McKinley, President
> Dear Sir
>   I for one feel confident that your good judgment will carry America safely through without war. But in case of such an event I am ready to place a company of fifty lady sharpshooters at your disposal. Every one of them will be an American and as they will furnish their own arms and ammunition will be little if any expense to the government.
>   Very truly,
>   Annie Oakley

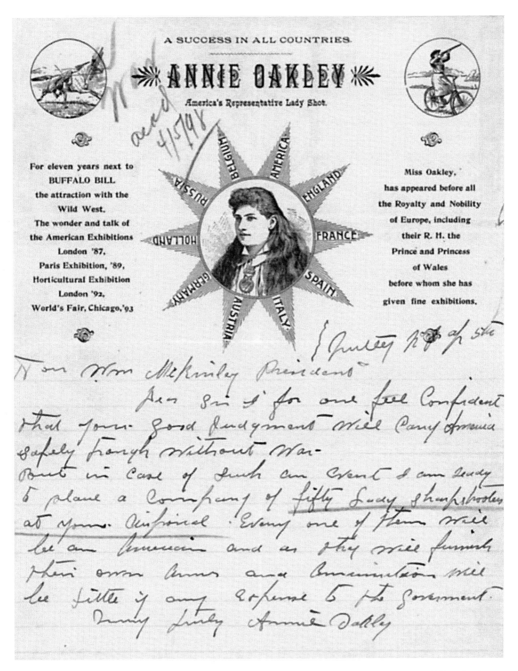

Letter from Annie Oakley to William McKinley, April 5, 1898, regarding a company of female sharp-shooters (U.S. National Archives and Records Administration).

When the United States entered World War I, Oakley again offered to raise a regiment of woman volunteers. At neither time was her proposal accepted. During World War I, she also offered to teach marksmanship to the troops. Though the army did not choose to employ her, she traveled across the country for the National War Council of the Young Men's Christian Association and for the War Camp Community Service, giving shooting demonstrations and lessons (G. Riley 187). Similarly, in talks given throughout World War I, often titled "How to Keep Fit and Not Become a Misfit in Government Service,"

Josie DeMott Robinson argued for thorough fitness training so that all American women could make a significant contribution during wartime ("Women Hear How to Train").

Though just some circus women thus embraced activist causes, they all reiterated what Earl Chapin May called "pronounced feminism" in their long careers as working women in a difficult, competitive industry ("Why Women Dominate" 3). Cultural historian Susan Glenn made a point about late nineteenth century theatre that certainly also applies to women who engaged in circus performance: "The feminism of women on stage was a form of cultural and professional practice" (4). Regardless of whether they entered in direct discussion of equal rights, women circus performers forged new paths for women as they reflected on their status as Other, their reasons for entering this profession, their contract negotiations, their daily practice, their physical and mental risks, and their constant travel. As women performers made and remade the story of the circus, they departed from the extreme though exciting versions of their lives in journalism, fiction, and film. They created their own compelling depictions of circus women. Over the decades the thousands of women working within the circus industry brought before the public their presence as, and their stories of, American women workers. Certainly, like other writers, they had their own rhetorical purposes, often to explain or defend or remember, and their own varied audiences. But these versions, coming from women performers themselves, greatly complicated the picture of this life, making it not just a matter of romance or sordidness, but a fully engaging profession.

# CHAPTER 6

# Separation and the Status of Other

Once in the circus always in it is a rule of the business. No circus rider was ever known to forsake the fascinations of the sawdust ring to go to housekeeping. — "The Latest New Woman" 1896

Occupying a central place in the performer's discourse about an American working life was discussion of their own status. In the circus life of practice and performance, both on the road and in winter quarters, circus members perceived themselves as living a life separate from "regular" Americans: they recognized the gap between the circus performer and the town dweller as clearly as anyone else. Tiger and lion tamer Mabel Stark spoke of this split in her own account of her life: "We all live in private worlds of our own making, absorbed in our own hopes and dreams. But circus people especially live to themselves. A circus is a traveling city complete in itself" (Stark and Orr 248). Similarly, in an interview in the *Saturday Evening Post,* trapeze artist Lucy Lightfoot said of troupers and towners that "their lives are as wide apart as the poles" (Yates, "The Circus Girl" 30). In evaluating this separation and status as Other, however, circus women presented another reading of themselves than the extremes found in journalism, fiction, and film: they were not simplistic romantic heroines and certainly not the evil lesser. Instead of embracing either popular choice, they viewed themselves as complex women, living lives in many ways superior to what was commonly judged as normal.

In recognizing a separation between town dweller and performer, many circus women wrote about the possible unhappiness of trying to fit in or be accepted in the towns where they lived during the off-season. When as an adult equestrian Dorothy Herbert and her mother spent winters in Scottsburg, Indiana, they did not mention that Dorothy was in the circus: they wanted to be accepted in their neighborhood and town ("Herbert's Horses" I. 22).

Equestrian Josie DeMott Robinson suffered when her family was well known as not being among the normal locals. As a child, as she wrote in her 1925 autobiography, what she labeled with capital letters as the Outside World had possessed "great mystery and fairy charm" (*The Circus Lady* 54). But living during the off-season in Frankfort, Pennsylvania, she recognized that outsiders thought of her family as perhaps fascinating but also as inappropriate and lesser. Indeed, her father's sister did not want to be seen with him. Her friends' parents wouldn't let their children go to see her at a performance in their own town, but would let them go to the circus in another nearby town where no one they knew would see them. At a child's birthday party, where parents asked children to sing or recite or display some other talent, DeMott Robinson did gymnastics: her body movements seemed immoral to the parents, and she was never asked to a party again. As she declared about these neighbors, "They made us feel aliens in every word they spoke.... They were the folk who lived as they should, we the gypsies of the road" (*The Circus Lady* 51, 80). Trapeze artist Fritzi Huber, a member of a multigenerational circus family, similarly described the separation and judgment in an interview book about his circus family: "If you grow up in the circus, you know that you will be treated as an oddity. It's inevitable" (Frega 272).

Performers were aware that separation and judgment occurred on the circus lot as well as in the town. DeMott Robinson remarked that when she was a child, visitors to the lot assumed that she was being forced to work and abused. When she was caught crying because she wanted to perform a dangerous trick and her father would not allow her to do so, outsiders did not believe what such a "hardened little thing" might say: "They were always sure that my tears were because of fear of my coming performance, and they talked of taking it up with the society, such cruelty to a little girl — hardened little thing, but it was too bad" (49). It took her "long, bitter years" to understand that trying to explain her life to such an appraiser was "a useless, hopeless thing to try to do" (43). This negative judgment that she experienced was a common one about children and training, as the *New York Times* noted in 1872: "There is, however, a popular belief that these children are cruelly treated to make them learn these various tricks, which some suppose to be hurtful to the infant frame" ("Children of the Sawdust").

For the circus freak, certainly, the separation from the realm of the normal was even more pronounced. Krao, for example, appeared as a bearded lady but also as a missing link and ape woman for Ringling Bros. and Barnum & Bailey. She was "said to come" from the jungles of Siam, small and dark, with a beard to her waist and, as often described in pamphlets and newspapers, a "thick growth of hair something like a horse's mane" between her shoulder blades. "When called upon to travel through city streets she always wore a veil," one of her friends told a *New York Times* reporter. "She was in terror of curiosity when away from the 'big top.'" Such curiosity might be controlled at the circus, but could reach to violence outside of that space ("Circus Folk Mourn").

As sideshow visitors stopped to stare at and comment upon that which was not themselves, the stares on the circus lot itself could also be painful to bear. Christine, the alligator lady, found it painful to be watched even as part of her job, as a friend recalled: "She suffered terribly and yet withstood, with exceptional tolerance, unkind and cruel remarks thrown at her by the more indiscriminate individuals who paid to investigate the 'human grotesqueries' of the freak show" (Rossi 64). In 1913, Baronness de Barcy, a bearded lady, was asked, "How does it feel to have hundreds of people go by daily staring at you?" Her reply alluded to the painfulness of being stared upon as well as her own professionalism: "'Sometimes I mind it — sometimes the blood rushes to my head, but usually ... I feel that I am a matter of interest. I am something unusual, and if people look at me I feel that they are justified'" ("The Circus Freak").

Like many other performers, Josie DeMott Robinson felt that these negative judgments, of the circus person's immorality or cruelty or strangeness, were especially pronounced in the United States, her comparison being to Mexico, where she had performed: "The feeling of the Mexican towards anyone who was an artist in his profession was so very different from our own, where I felt the outsider, the gypsy. Here [in Mexico] there was only one attitude; if you could do something well, you were admired for it" (*The Circus Lady* 118). In other countries from which large circus families came to the United States, performers claimed, tradition ceded respect to generations of hard work and success. This common praise for distant lands made the negative judgments about the United States seem even more pronounced.

Circus performers certainly knew about the extreme judgments of the larger society and felt the weight of the worst of those judgments. But though they agreed that a separation existed, they often described it in terms that contradicted media assumptions. Ironically, given the common fictional view of the circus as a separate site of freedom and wildness, as a break from discipline, Josie DeMott Robinson argued in her autobiography that other children had many more choices: town girls "always seemed to live in a delightful state of uncertainty" since they could choose where to go and what to do and did not have to practice and travel constantly as circus performers did (54). For her, this "Outside World" was a "dreamy place, where people moved as they pleased" (61). And she felt as a child that all the great pleasures lay in this easier and exciting, undisciplined space: "This outside life, where things seemed to go on without apparent necessity, held me in thrall" (55).

Many other circus people looked at their lives as different, but without drawing the lines where popular media did: their distinctions involved not just discipline and freedom but morality. They argued, very differently from what appeared in most headlines and in film, that the highly structured life within the circus and the presence of extended families made circus performers more ethical and proper than townspeople and other entertainers. Clown Eveta Mathews, known as Miss Williams in her act for Barnum & Bailey, had planned to quit when she married, she told an interviewer in 1895, but then she saw female equestrian and trapeze artists working within families and staying in the business, a career taking these women from apprentice, to star, and then later to ringmaster and trainer. With that stability of "place" and family, Mathews argued, circus performers could remain throughout their lives in a highly honorable situation: "That is why the standard of morality in the circus is far better" ("Why Miss Williams"). Josie DeMott Robinson argued further that circus life was superior in its emphasis — not just on discipline but on community and responsibility within an entire cast: "There is a fraternity there, that we of the circus who have ventured into the Outside World do not find in that strange place — a fellow feeling that transcends money and position, that applies the Golden Rule and practices it" (*The Circus Lady* 2).

Bobby Huber, son of acrobat and dancer Betty Huber, spoke to an interviewer of missing this superior circus community once his parents got older and his family stopped touring: "It was a different life once we had gotten off the road.... Fritzi [his sister] and I missed it very much. We had had security in that life.... We had so many friends, constant company and joking. It was a very civilized way of life" (Frega 226). In her memoir, aerialist Tiny Kline argued, as she frequently did in interviews, that this community made the circus superior to the theatre: "To a performer of the theatre, once having gotten a taste of the circus, in spite of all its hardships, rain, cold, and heat in extreme, it is still the most fascinating and advantageous branch of show business. There is a feeling of security and brotherly love among these folks who live and work in such close association, together twenty-four hours a day" (189).

Circus performers evaluated freedom, discipline, and morality in more complex ways than did many extreme newspaper articles and novels; they also differed from those articles and novels in their judgments of women's physicality and thus of physical freedom. Because circus performers were not simple romantic idols, or evil wanderers, but working professionals, they often argued that they were not inappropriately on view in the circus or inappropriately fit and aggressive. Instead, it was city dwellers that used their bodies unnaturally, their movements limited and thus unhealthy. When as a famous equestrian Josie DeMott Robinson married the owner of the Robinson Circus, left the business, and went with him to Cincinnati, she began turning into a "timid, fearful gillie," as she wrote in her autobiography: "I tried so hard to wear the clothes and manners of this Outside World, this strange world which I had wondered about when I was little" (174). After years of exercise and performance, she had to adjust to the stolid life of a middle-aged matron, which required slow motion: "I used to practice doing things slowly. No one will ever know how hard I tried to be a proper gillie. I came down the stairs slowly as if to Chopin's Funeral March, and folded my hands elegantly. I smiled gently at the butler. I ate as if I were listening to a dirge and keeping time to it. I rose again as slowly and went sweepingly out to the cook to order for the day" (175).

Along with suffering from an unhealthy lack of movement, DeMott Robinson wrote, city women lived in unhealthy clothes: "Tighter in the waist line, with tight long sleeves that scarcely showed a wrist, and had high puffs at the shoulder. The body was held in a vise, and we vied with one another in seeing how small a waist we could succeed in squeezing into" (175). When she met women in Cincinnati, she wanted to say, "You poor thing, how can you stand it? How can you breathe? Why, you can't even raise your arm" (176). And then she reacted strongly when she realized that she was becoming a member of this unhealthy society: "I who used to swing upside down on a living horse, who always danced when mere walking would do, so glad was I of life, so full of health. It was the most gruesome thought I had ever had in my life" (178). Her body "was actually beginning to get frail and it needed rest after any social event. I would come home and drop on my chaise lounge, and rest" (187). When, after fifteen years, in 1905, DeMott Robinson sought to enter the circus again, as she wrote, " I cried to find what a weak, worthless body I owned" (*The Circus Lady* 208).

Many other stars found the outside world physically restrictive, especially for women. As Mary Enos, a perch pole performer, told interviewers about the off-seasons with her husband Gene: "When we are not with the circus sometimes it seems we simply cannot stay in a house. It is stuffy and uncomfortable after being out in the open as we are at work on the road. Life is so much more pleasant if lived out of doors and the circus people know and love it…. I started as a child to be an acrobat and I like it. I like all kinds of sports, too. Swimming and golf are perhaps my favorites, but I also like basketball and baseball" (Gossard, "Gene and Mary Enos" 20).

In many types of texts, the circus woman depicted herself as Other, but generally not as the extreme of romantic hero or dangerous, sleazy risk-taker, as the popular media often judged her. Instead of simply reiterating those stereotypes, she might tell another more complex story of being the Other in American society — as she spoke for women's discipline, sense of purpose, physical development, and involvement in a working community.

CHAPTER 7

# Entering a Circus Career

While circus performers altered the view of the separation between the circus and the non-circus, creating their own picture of superior worth, they also complicated the discussion of why girls and women embarked on circus careers. In the popular media, women became performers because of their unnatural attraction to risk and scandal, the cruel requirements of circus parents, or their own romantic dreams of excitement and love. The depictions created by circus women themselves told a more complex, and compelling, story about why women chose this challenging career and future.

## Choosing This Life from the Inside

An article entitled "With the Ladies of the Circus," from the *New York Times'* women's page in the Sunday magazine in 1906, states that "everybody" at the circus was working within circus families: grandfathers in clown makeup, husbands and wives on trapeze, children working as apprentices. Women performers born into circus families, the author continues, often married and started their own families within this world.

Although the reality was not so extreme, perhaps seventy percent of women working in the circus were born into the life. Some like Josie DeMott Robinson came from American circus families, but most were born outside of the United States into families that immigrated for career opportunities (Yates, "The Circus Girl"). "Last season," ringmaster Fred Bradna claimed in 1914, "although 250 girls had their headquarters there, the English language was almost never heard in our dressing room at Madison Square Garden." As Ella Bradna, his famous equestrian wife, asserted, "Almost all circus riders are French, Italian, or English" ("Circus Girls to War"). Circus writer Diana Starr Cooper described this diversity throughout the program: "A great many people of different sizes and shapes turn up in the course of this show, in various stages of brilliant dress and brilliant undress. This beautiful woman is black. As the show proceeds, you become aware that people come in a variety of colors. There are performers from China, a troupe of Moroccan tumblers, three dancing gauchos from Argentina. In the ring, everyone is exposed, heightened, illuminated, and you realize anew that our kind comes in a myriad of shades" (28). In her 1931 book about growing up in a circus that her father managed, Betty Boyd Bell similarly described the cast: "You know when Mr. Kipling wrote that 'East is East, and West is West, and never the twain shall meet,' I don't believe he had ever been to a circus. I was thinking about that one day when I was on the Lot and right near by me I counted more than a dozen nationalities" (68).

Many foreign-born performers immigrated to the United States within large circus families. Lizzie Hanneford Clarke, second child of the Hanneford circus family, was born in a van when the E. H. Bostock Circus exhibited in Shaftesbury, Dorsetshire. In 1903, her parents, after years of saving, started their own circus in Ireland, while their children continued working in other shows for the additional income. In 1903, Lizzie made her debut in the pantomime *Cinderella* for the traveling Algy's Circus and then performed in Poole and Bosco's Circus, housed in Belfast. In 1908, when Lizzie was fifteen, her father started a second family circus, which she managed. "I can still vividly remember," she recalled to an interviewer, "coming to a cross roads and going on by myself with my little show while Mother and Father and the rest of the family kept on with the No. 1 show. The pride of having my own living wagon and an illustrious title was nearly lost in my tears and the lump in my throat" (Smith, "Elizabeth Hanneford Clarke," I. 26). Lizzie was quite a performer in all of these shows, including the one that she managed. She did a Roman ladder act, in which four or more people performed acrobatics on specially made ladders. She also rode an elephant, appeared in the family horse riding act, walked a tight wire, juggled, and performed tricks aboard a large, rolling globe. In addition, she helped make the wardrobe. The Hannefords came to the United States and opened with Ringling in 1919 when Lizzie was twenty-two. She performed with her brothers Poodles and George, dancing on horseback, very athletic and beautiful, playing off between them in moments serious and comedic.

Within many of these families that came to the United States, it was the woman's success that led to the move to a better circus job, a part of family immigration little discussed in the press. Victoria Codona, for example, a member of a well-established circus family, performed as a dancer on the slack wire, a loose wire that moves with the performer. She told an interviewer that she was "raised in a trunk" as the family traveled, joining her brothers in their aerial act at age twelve, in Mexico, in 1904. When Otto Ringling saw her there in 1909, he hired her and thus her brothers; they opened in the Ringling center ring that year for $125 a week. It was a move to the big time, and the crowds were wowed by her talents, as a Chicago review commented: Victoria appeared as a "marvel on the slack wire, swinging, revolving, dancing, gliding," and she finished the marvelous exhibition "by swinging to and fro in a tremendous arc, as the wire was slowly lowered to the ground," with nothing in her hands with which to balance (Parkinson 11–12).

As the popular media discussed, circus performers often married and raised children within the circus, who learned from their mothers as well as their fathers. In the United States, Lizzie Hanneford met Ernie Clarke, a great trapeze artist in his own family act, and they married in 1920. She stayed with her family's act afterwards and had a daughter Elizabeth, called Ernie or Ernestine, who began traveling with her circus parents and learned to be both a high-wire performer and a bareback rider. As Ernestine described it, her own childhood resembled her mother's: "When I was just three months old, I began to travel with my parents, and typical of many circus children, my parents took me into the ring as soon as I was old enough to be put on a horse and ride around. I honestly cannot remember learning to ride. I can remember learning individual tricks, but not learning to ride a horse. It was just something I always did. It was part of our family life" (McConnell 114–15).

Contrary to popular depictions, though many performers engaged their children in family acts, others vehemently opposed this choice. In fact, some young people that faced stern parental opposition about this career choice were circus children. Rose Holland's parents were circus people who left her to be raised by a grandmother in the 1870s and tried to keep her away from their itinerant life. Her mother was Elise Dockrill, a well-known equestrian, a star with Barnum & Bailey, who had hoped for her daughter "to be spared the hardships of circus life." But as an adult, as Holland told an interviewer, she became an equestrian, the thrilling realization of a "childhood ambition." She had been drawn to the circus: "How many of us would have given all we possessed to abandon our school books and our humdrum existence to become part of that thrilling circus world? If we had been summoned from the curbside where we danced up and down in excited anticipation as we waited for the parade to pass, we would have joined the clowns, the acrobats, and the bareback riders without a moment's hesitation, a childhood ambition suddenly and completely realized" (Palmer 7).

Other circus parents who sent their child away to school or to relatives described themselves as extremely disappointed when the child chose the life from which they had kept her away. Against the wishes of her parents, who did not want her entering the business, Agnes Robinson, daughter of Gilbert Robinson, a circus manager, married a performer, France Reed, and went west with him. She had met Reed in Cincinnati, while she was visiting her uncle John Robinson, another circus manager, and her parents had made her leave when they heard about this budding relationship. Her mother and grandmother had been riders, but her parents did not want this future for her. An article concerning her story quotes her father speaking his disappointment through sarcasm: "I can see that girl, brought up amid refining influences, educated as carefully as we knew how, sitting on the top of a — show wagon" ("Circus Life Attracts Her").

In all of these facts of growing up, marrying, and raising children within the circus world, performers did not especially differ from other Americans of the time period. That circus performers came from foreign families, facts of their lives often used to emphasize their exotic and separate reality, actually proved that they were very much like other Americans. Many cities in the United States contained a percentage of foreigners similar to a circus crew: in New York City in 1910, 40 percent of residents were foreign-born and 38 percent were in the first generation of their family to be born in the United States (Jackson 582–85). In cities, as within the circus, Americans tended to marry people within their own neighborhood and social group. And while the circus involved child labor, 1.7 million children worked in industry in 1900 and 2 million in 1910 (Brinkley 473–74). Like circus performers in this time of more limited occupational mobility, other young people participated in a trade that had involved their parents and grandparents, on farms and in mines, factories, and stores, deciding to remain within the family work world as adults. About this situation some parents were very pleased; others hoped for their children to rise above the family situation and seek a different, better future. These facts of circus life, then, were not particularly extreme or unique, but given the separation between the circus and normal, they could easily be made to look tawdry, immoral, romantic, or exotic.

In the basics of their stories, circus women were very American. They came into the country as immigrants, joining in a family business and marrying within the group. Children of several generations stayed in the same occupation, trained by those that went before (though some parents sought different opportunities for their children). The truly exotic feature, in fact, was not one of these circumstances but another one not so frequently remarked upon: that daughters, and not just sons, were trained professionals within the family business—who could earn the highest of incomes and whose success could insure the future of the group.

## Choosing This Life from the Outside

Other young women, almost a third of performers, followed an American archetype by running away to join the circus. With constantly changing large staffs, performance locations outside of town several times a year, and winter sites across the country, this art form offered something that American women indeed might join, much more easily than running away to Hollywood and becoming movie stars. In children's fiction, this possibility existed for boys and was for girls to dream about. In romances, women took this step, but only for romantic love. Real accounts, however, extend and alter the fictional tropes: these performing women's narratives often involved freedom and love, but with many renditions and complications of these themes (as well as other ones entirely).

Just as in fiction, many women began dreaming of joining, as their interviews and autobiographies testify, when they first saw a parade and show in their own small towns. Lucia Zora, who became an elephant trainer, wrote in her autobiography that "The wandering instinct was upon me early, taking the form quite naturally of a desire 'to go with the circus.' An investigative child, and by my predilection to stray from home, more than a usual source of annoyance to watchful parents, I wandered, one day when I was about five, down the shady street upon which stood our home, in the sleepy little upstate town of Cazenovia, New York. The sound of brass-throated music came from a distant street and I hurried there to stand with other children, watching the meager parade of a small wagon show. The clown fascinated me, the horses were beautiful, the performers held for me the same magic lure that they possess for any child, but the one thing that stood out above all others was the elephant" (4). Zora, like so many children, viewed the circus as the ultimate "personification of dreams which are natural to childhood: far-away places, strange, mysterious happenings, adventures, and fields of golden fulfillment, just beyond the horizon" (5). On an extended holiday with her family when she was a young woman, Zora got her chance: "We were in New Orleans. A circus was there also. They could use another woman in a position known in the circus world as 'generally useful.' That meant dancing in the ballet, riding in the grand entrée, appearing as the background for other acts" (7).

Some women who sought a circus job viewed it as a youthful lark, for which they might even have parental permission. One of them in 1940 was Gloria Haight, a debutante from Long Island. "Half the year she rides with the circus, guiding a great white steed about the sawdust ring at the opening spectacle, taking part in the trick riding acts and trotting sedately around the ring again in the grand finale," the *Chicago Sun Parade* reported, yet she also still participated in the upperclass life at home: "During the late summer and autumn, Gloria leads the life of a sports loving sub debutante at her parents' home on Long Island's South Shore. There she rides, runs a speed boat, flies an airplane and—during her spare hours—paints." She had joined the circus, she claimed to the reporter, "just for fun," and because of her great love for horses. As the article claims about this pairing, "Gloria's has been a life of sharp contrasts. She knows the haunting cry of a circus train at night, the glare of the spot on a high trapeze, the strange little world under canvas. And she knows the rich, plush comforts of home, the sweet smell of a Long Island glade" ("Circus Deb").

Few women, however, who did not come from circus families had approval for entering this outsider life. In the face of stern disapproval, some daughters rebelled and joined, especially if they saw the circus as their way out of an unfulfilling grind. Toward the end of her career, circus performer Marjorie Hackett declared of her youthful motives in an after-dinner speech: "I got my start in the Circus Ballet that was produced by Portis Rowley for the Moslem Shrine in Detroit. I fell in love with the whole concept. I was 'hooked' but knew nothing about how to join a show.... I say I wouldn't have passed it up for any amount of money. It was never my end-all ambition to be a star. I just thought that it [would be] sort of fun and it was a way out of Detroit and I enjoyed it" (3). When Hackett told her parents about this goal, she immediately faced opposition, especially from her father who felt that he needed to control his wayward daughter: "In his mind, circuses were all evil and no daughter of his was ever going to be in such a show! ... My father said, 'I'll disown you if you go in the circus,' and I said, 'So! What.'" She left for California, where an uncle lived, and got a job with an ice show. But she wanted to join a real circus, something she did not know how to do, as she recalled her own questioning and delays: "How do you get in the Circus? Who is who? I don't know anybody to ask. I came back and hung around our apartment on east Grand Boulevard. I gave myself a bathrobe with prancing horses on the back" (1). Then Hackett answered an ad in the *Detroit News* for Lewis Brothers Circus of Jackson, Michigan, and received an invitation to come to the winter quarters, an opportunity creating further conflict at home: "Again when I broached this to my father, he said, 'We're not goin' to drive you up there because we don't want you to go on that show'" (2). She talked a neighbor into driving her. Speaking toward the end of her career, Hackett recognized that her father had perhaps known better than she thought: "As I look back on the conditions we lived under at winter quarters out at Grass Lake, I think I can understand and I don't think I would let my daughter go" (2).

Hackett joined up with a strong desire but no discernible talent and had to go from 115 to 92 pounds that winter to even get a chance to try out for an acrobatic act. She did some tumbling, then became part of a Wild West act with the Lewis Brothers, part of a bull whip trick in which a male partner used the whip to "cut papers and a cigarette out of my mouth" (3). She then went on to various roles with Hunt Bros. Circus and Cole Bros. Circus, with the dream of running away, of choosing a path outside of her hometown and her father's control, propelling her forward like many boys and men.

Many other women were willing to learn this trade to get away from home and take control of their own lives. Betty Broadbent, for example, at seventeen quit a babysitting job in Atlantic City, nothing else being available to her locally, to join the circus in 1927. "She wanted to be her own woman," said Charles Roark, a ventriloquist who was one of her husbands. She started out as an illusionist whose head was projected, through mirrors, onto a stuffed spider's body to create the effect of a human-headed spider. After a carnival performer told her that tattoos would enable her to earn a much better living, she got the inkings that enabled her to be billed in a Ringling Bros. and Barnum & Bailey act as the youngest tattooed woman in the world, and she enjoyed a forty-year career as a tattoo artist with several major circuses. Her act began as she entered a sideshow tent in a satin or velvet robe; then, as she turned slowly, she lowered the robe to reveal a short bath skirt and her tattoos: Pancho Villa on her left leg; Charles Lindbergh on her right; a Madonna and child on her back. At the 1939 world's fair in New York, she competed in a televised beauty contest; she knew that she didn't have a chance of winning, but she sought the free publicity that might improve her circus billings (Cheong).

For other women, as in romance novels, the circus was worth joining not just for freedom but for love. In Josie DeMott Robinson's autobiography, she describes her own mother as a woman not particularly desirous of a career in the ring but willing to take on such a life and become an equestrian to remain with her husband after she married in 1861: "Mother herself went into the ring for only one reason: the match between herself and my father had been a genuine love match, and they hated to be away from each other" (*The Circus Lady* 17). They had eight children who went along, traveling by wagons, the father going ahead to find lodging for his family in each town in which they would perform. "Life was an exciting thing in those early wagon days," DeMott Robinson wrote of those years in which the whole family was on the road (*The Circus Lady* 18).

For many women the circus did not just symbolize a chance for the freedom or love of romances; instead it represented the chance to reach toward professional success doing something that they loved. Olga Celeste, the Leopard Woman, trained many types of animals for over fifty years. When she was a child in Sweden, as she told an interviewer, her father sold her horse to the Circus Madigan; right then, she wanted "to run away from home, join the circus and be with her horse" (Taber 33). In 1904, when Celeste came to the United States to visit a sister in Chicago, she got her opportunity to work with animals: "When she learned there was an animal show in Riverview park she couldn't get there quick enough." At the local Big Otto Show, which trained animals for circuses, she met Essie Fay, a famous equestrian who worked with sixty-three horses in an act for the Walter L. Main Circus. Celeste worked with Fay at Big Otto and then with traveling circuses, where she presented a mixed group of lions, leopards, and pumas (Taber).

For other women, a desire to work with animals or on the high wire fulfilled another very real need — to support their families — and thus provided another type of freedom and fulfillment difficult for women to find, the space in which to both realize ambitions and secure a good living. Mabel Garrard Chipman dreamed of a circus life from childhood but got permission only when her work became necessary to help support her family. Born in 1878 in Monmouth, Illinois, Chipman read about the circus in picture magazines and children's books from the time she started school and spent most of her free time practicing acts. When she was nine, she became acquainted with the neighboring Davis family, which operated a medicine show, selling "miracle elixirs," and in their home she learned to play the saxophone. Chipman became so proficient that the Davises asked to take her on the road with them as a member of their family band, but her parents declined.

When Chipman was eleven, her father fell from a bridge that he was building at Quincy, Illinois, and drowned in the Mississippi River. Mabel's mother then needed financial help and gave permission for Mabel to tour with the Davis family, which had by that time joined forces with showman Murray Childs in operating the Davis and Childs Medicine Show. From this beginning in the business, Chipman went on to the Joe Bennett Tent Show as a horn player and acrobat and, at the age of nineteen, moved on to the high trapeze. She then moved to the bigger Frank C. Bostock Show, later known as the Bostock-Ferrari Shows. In 1898, with this circus, she met Bert J. Chipman, and following their marriage, in 1899, they took their own show on the road, played a number of fairs and street celebrations, and then joined the Lemen Brothers World's Best Shows, a twenty-car railroad show, with Bert selling tickets and serving as a ringmaster and Mabel, who had acquired the professional name of the Original Ma Belle, performing on the trapeze. In these shows, she could fulfill her own ambitions while supporting herself as well as her mother and her younger siblings (Smith, "Ma Belle Chipman").

In some families left without male providers, the circus provided employment for both mother and daughter, a meaningful means of securing their own support. Dorothy Herbert, born in 1910, grew up in Kentucky, where she learned to ride horses. She moved to Detroit with her mother when her parents separated. There she took a dancing class and attended school while her mother clerked at a department store. When the members of the dancing class, including Herbert, served as extras on horseback for a pageant production, *Rome under Nero,* Herbert's mother appeared in a mob scene. After the show ended, the master of the horses asked if Herbert would like to join his performing group, and she also secured a place for her mother, a way out of a dull existence for both of them: "Mother thought this might be more interesting than going back to the department store, so we went with this outfit to Ann Arbor, Michigan, where we went into training" ("Herbert's Horses" I.6). They began performing in fairs and circuses, her mother on horseback in parades and Dorothy in a horse comedy act for which she dressed as a clown and rode a mule.

Other women embarked on circus careers not just to support themselves or their parents and siblings, but to support their own children. Balinda Merriam Spencer needed to work to support her sons at a time when factories or domestic work were her other choices. She performed as an equestrian with John Robinson Big Ten Shows Combined (Dickinson 26). She had married John L. Spencer, a Civil War veteran in 1866, had two sons, and divorced him in 1872, the children remaining with her (Dickinson 39). She did standard riding tricks, such as standing, dancing, and juggling on the back of a galloping horse, to earn their living and later incorporated her sons into the act.

As women performers described it, the dream of circus was a dream of freedom and love, but of a much more complex nature than in romance novels. The circus offered so many possibilities beyond what was considered normal for women. Those born into circus families could choose to enter a proud tradition, their future ensured not just by heredity but by daily practice and hard work. By running away to the circus, other women with no family history in the industry might have a chance not just to choose their own spouses and marry for love but to leave restrictive home environments, learn a creative art and practice it, support themselves and their families, and reach to ever higher levels of professional success. The performers' own stories, appearing in various venues for various purposes, create a much fuller rendering of what was sought by the women in the circus.

# CHAPTER 8

## Behavior Rules for Women and Their Contracts

We should want the "town folks" to feel that the "show folks" are real men and women and ladies and gentlemen as well. — Rule Sheet, 1912, Ringling Bros.

Women joined the circus not just for a simply constructed sort of freedom and love: they also joined to support themselves and others and to achieve professional success. When they joined the circus, whatever their motivation, they entered a contractual status, participating in an American business, one of the very few in which women had a chance at advancement. Part of the circus experience — these women's work experience — involved facing, and sometimes overcoming through confidence and persistence, the harsh realities of American capitalism, including the many restrictions that it placed on women.

### The Rules

When performers signed contracts for a year on the road, these documents spelled out much more than just salaries and dates. Women worked under detailed agreements, not required of men, that dictated their behavior on the road. When female performers signed "Rules Concerning Ballet Girls Supplementary in Contract," for the season of October 1912 to March 1913 for Ringling Bros., for example, they agreed to the luggage they could bring on the road ("No trunks carried larger than 15 × 18 × 24") as well as to detailed regulations concerning their social life:

> No intoxicants of any kind permitted in sleeping cars, dressing rooms, or show grounds.
> Ladies should be in sleeping cars at a reasonable hour after the night performance, as per instruction from Ballet Master.
> Male companions during hours when not on duty, strictly prohibited.
> Flirting and boisterous conduct at all times and places, prohibited.

A further rule sheet states that the "girls" could not stop at hotels along the way, could not visit relatives in towns where the circus went, could not visit with any male members of the show except for the management. A third code sheet goes further in enumerating inappropriate behaviors:

> No pet animals, revolvers, intoxicants or inflammables allowed in the sleeping cars.
> Do not chew gum while taking part in spectacle.
> Male performers are not to visit with the ballet girls. The excuse of "accidental" meetings on Sunday, in parks, at picture shows, etc., will not be accepted.
> Do not change position of trunks as placed in the dressing room.

This document claims that the rules are necessary, as experience had shown, to "protect the girls." Appropriate personal appearance and behavior matter, the rule sheet continues, because they help control what happens among employees and because they help shape the impression made on the public. In fact, the rules state that ballet girls need to comport themselves well in the circus tent, around the lot, and in town so that locals will judge them to be "real" women and "ladies" and not some lesser or morally suspect other: "We should want the 'town folks' to feel that the 'show folks' are real men and women and ladies and gentlemen as well" (Rule Sheet, 1912).

Though contracts for young and single ballet girls had the most morality clauses, married women also signed contracts that concerned their personal lives. They guaranteed that they would remain married for the season and that they would room with their husbands if the men traveled with the show. They could stay in hotel rooms only if accompanied by their husbands, and they would not be seen socially in contact with other men. These rules for women thus controlled the personal decisions that women performers, and especially the well-publicized stars, might make. Cat trainer Mabel Stark lived unhappily with her husband, Al Drivin, a bookkeeper and administrator with the Al G. Barnes show, but she was afraid to divorce him after she first went to Ringling because she might have been dismissed under the morality clauses in her contract. She wrote in a letter to a biographer about her fear of even voicing her unhappiness: "I knew no one there, was afraid to speak for fear there would be some scandal" (Letter to May, 28 May 1933).

## The Risk

While contracts tightly controlled what a woman performer could do, they also highlighted her vulnerability in practice and performance. Shows carried no insurance, and the physical risk was entirely the artist's. Indeed, the 1912–13 contract for Ringling Bros., signed by the ballet girls and other performers, "exempts and releases" the circus from any liability for "death, injuries, accidents, sickness, claims and damage of whatever nature" and for any resulting medical care or loss of work. Further, the contract states that the performer understands "that the character of the services to be performed involves hazard" and that results of hazard are to be born not by the circus but the artist. Any missed performance, for injury or any other reason, could result in a week of lost wages. Upholding their long-standing relationships with the railroads, circuses also made provisions for indemnifying them: a performer could not hold a railway liable for damaged property or for injuries incurred in any train accident. Many other contract provisions ceded power to the circus management: circus performers could not join up with other shows during the term of the contract even if they were let go; after a season ended, the circus had the option to renew the contract — the performer was then legally obligated though management did not have to renew; posters belonged to the circus management even if the image was of the performer (Rule Sheet, 1912).

While the contract stated so many things that the circus would not do for performers, it also gave some sense of what the circus would do for them. On a train and in circus lots, the job included room and board and perhaps costumes, especially if a group all wore the same outfit, as in an opening parade. Some circuses, however, provided just room and board and none of the salary until almost the end of the season so that performers would not go home early or jump to another show. Even with controls on the pay schedule with some organizations, a woman who joined the circus to support herself and her family would generally be able to do so. In the contract for 1912–13 signed by new and unskilled ballet girl Kathryn Edwards, the amount paid is $8.00 a week, to cover parades and rehearsals as well as twelve performances, two a day for Monday through Saturday. At that time, in several Midwestern states, for example, unskilled women laborers made between $5.28 and $9.58 a week at factory jobs, so the pay was similar, and the circus job did provide room and board ("Wages, Hours and Speed" 96–97).

## Bargaining

As performers reached higher skill levels, they often gained more power to maneuver, and thus they entered into lengthy bargaining for increases in salary and applied with different circuses to obtain the best possible offer. In a competitive marketplace, contract negotiations could be protracted and highly rhetorical, the argument necessary to the future of the performer, as it was for Gene and Mary Enos, perch-pole performers, her balancing role called "the understander." A newspaper article thus described their act: "On the top of a pole 30 feet high Gene Enos balances and does lay-outs and plunges while Mary balances. Onto this Gene climbs to the top. The most dangerous stunt of the turn is a freestand done on the top of the pole" ("Gene and Mary Enos"). This pair worked for various American Circus Corporation circuses in the 1920s though they continuously sought a post with Ringling, the top of the line (Gossard, "Gene and Mary Enos"). In November 1913, Gene wrote to Al Ringling from Cartegena, Colombia, where he and his wife were touring with the Barlow and Dunham Circus, describing the great feats of "understanding" done by "the little lady" along with their other skills, in an attempt to change jobs:

> We do a combination act, consisting of acrobats, rolling globe and high carrying perch. All the understanding in this act is done by the little lady. She throws me somersaults, I do juggling while standing on her head, also a head to head. She goes up and down a six foot high incline on a globe, forward and backwards. We finish with our 20 ft. high carrying perch. I weigh only 130 lbs., and the little understander only 117. I do about a three minute routine while on the perch, consisting of different layouts, planges and etc. I also fill in clowning and have a little Boston bull dog I use as a pad dog. My apparatus is all nickel plated and my wardrobe is all first class.... My price is $85.00 a week. We are real circus people, good and useful.

Al Ringling replied that "We find that we cannot place you to advantage for the coming season as we are now well filled in your line." With Ringling Bros. not interested, the couple went with Hagenbeck-Wallace, trying to stay with this circus as long as possible for they saw it as a home base for being with their friends, a show that was not quite Ringling but was doing well and remaining in the United States. When they began working for Hagenbeck-Wallace, they received a weekly salary of $85.00 for the two of them, the amount that they had asked of Al Ringling, with their salary increasing over the years. In a contract signed in November 1927 with Downie Bros. World's Best Shows, for which they did a perch-pole act as well as his serving as equestrian director and her as wardrobe mistress, they worked for a combined salary of $101 a week. In November of 1928, with Mary also contracted for a trained goat act, their salary increased to $113 per week (Gossard, "Gene and Mary Enos").

While good performers like Mary and Gene Enos could increase their wages, the highest amounts certainly went to the best known of stars, who could easily be lost to other outfits. Aerialist Lillian Leitzel had to sign the morals clauses required of other performers, but nothing else about her contracts followed the standard form. For the 1915 season, with Ringling Bros., as her contract for that year noted, Leitzel made $200 a week while the show stayed in Chicago and $150 a week on the road. In her 1931 contract, she was guaranteed $350 per week. With an increased income, such a star might be expected to provide many of her own amenities, each item subject to negotiation. Leitzel's contract for the 1931 season, for example, signed in November 1930, contained the following stipulations, agreed to after extended negotiations:

> Aerial Ring Act of at least what was previously presented by the Artist in the circus of the Employers.
> Employers to supply stateroom in sleeping car.
> Artist to carry her own property man to properly install the apparatus and also carry a maid, the Artist to pay for their services but not for their meals. Miss Leitzel to supply her own private dressing tent (size four breadths by four breadths canvas) and all rope, blocks and falls used in connection with her apparatus.
> Miss Leitzel to be excused from Tournament and parade.

The biggest stars, like Leitzel, generally weren't required to participate in parades through town or the opening spec, or spectacle, a privilege, but one that added to the suspense and excitement since circus goers eagerly awaited their appearance.

Circus owners bargained carefully to avoid providing more pay and benefits than necessary to stars like Leitzel. With some stars, when possible, they also used low pay amounts, and the continuous promise of more, to achieve the desired level of risk, but experienced performers learned to bargain for better terms and more respect. Equestrian Dorothy Herbert, taking out loans to support her mother and teaching riding in the winter for extra money, realized in 1937, twelve years into her career, that Ringling Bros. and Barnum & Bailey had been underpaying her quite purposefully, as the manager, Sam Gumpertz finally told her: "'I must admit,' he confessed, 'our motive was a purely selfish one. Our intention was to keep you ever striving to reach greater heights'" ("Herbert's Horses" III. 21). Once Herbert became aware of this underpaying technique, she asked for, and received, regular increases in pay though she kept taking risks to further advance her career and her salary.

Whether women worked at the circus for freedom of various sorts or for love, they were entering not just an extremely seedy, nostalgic, or romantic space but a profession. They there encountered a gendered sort of employment, where the terms of their private lives were often dictated to them, the superiority of their skills their best protection. Like other American employees, they bargained for fair pay and better benefits, especially as they attained the skill level, confidence, and knowledge required for making such demands. Though in almost all industries in the United States at that time, only men held such labor power, women also did so in the circus.

CHAPTER 9

# The Rigors of Practice

As performers of all types sought contracts, as they prepared for the season, and as they traveled with the troupe, there was always practice, the means to keeping their jobs and achieving higher levels of success. The circus career required hard work every day, the few moments of glory in the center ring reflecting regular devotion to the craft. What might look easy or natural in the ring actually resulted from each day's challenging work. Circus articles, books, and films, when they were not focusing on a performer's love life, centered attention on the act in the big top as either glorious or deadly: they missed the daily discipline that so many performers described as the majority of the job and as essential to success.

Many circus children toured with their families, rehearsing as they traveled. Ernestine Clarke, for example, indicated that "I enjoyed the profession I was learning, and practice was the most fun of the day for me. The worse punishment I ever received was to be told I couldn't practice." Like so many girls and young women in the business, she worked under the tutelage of a parent, the aerialist Ernie Clarke, each day: "My father didn't care what you did as long as you tried and kept trying. If you fell, and of course we had the safety mechanic on, you would pick yourself up, everyone would laugh and then you tried again. Practice was just a big fun time. I remember in practice the first time I missed grabbing the fly bar. My mother was watching. As I fell into the net, she fainted, and they had to carry her out." Since this mother was Lizzie Hanneford Clarke, Ernestine also worked on an equestrian act: "I became part of the bareback act when I was nine years old. At eleven years old I did my first flying trick, but it was sometime before I actually went into the act." Working with both parents, who also taught school subjects to circus children, took up her day: "My total childhood was spent with my family" (McConnell 115).

Other performers growing up in circus families practiced with their parents during the off-season and with trainers during the season, staying off the road until they were ready to perform. Celia Fortuna came from a high-wire circus family in Europe, one of eight children, "each a star" who spoke "five or six different languages." She came to the United States at fifteen and went into serious training, as the fan magazine *White Tops* reported: "She practiced assiduously in the family attic, and persevered in spite of many bumps and bruises until she had achieved the muscle grind, the double planche and all the other intricacies of a real bar act." When the family left to go out on tour, her parents secured a retired performer to instruct her until she was ready to join them on the road (Anawalt "Snapshots").

**Aerialists practice in Sarasota. Photograph by Allen Lester (John and Mable Ringling Museum of Art).**

Many circus performers and managers offered long-term training in the winter for both stars and young adult apprentices. John Davenport, Sr., circus manager, never rode professionally, was too big to do so, but ran a facility, beginning in the 1890s, in Chicago, where equestrians trained for long hours daily: "In 1910 the Davenport ring barn was the only one in Chicago. It was known to virtually every circus rider in America. Here there were no gay trappings or radiant costumes. It was a place for hard, tiresome work which

**Dress rehearsal for The Riding Davenports in an outdoor ring beside the Hagenbeck-Wallace big top, 1937. Photograph by H.A. Atwell (Circus World Museum, Baraboo, Wisconsin).**

called for iron nerves, conditioned muscles, and clear brains." At this barn as well as others, individual moves and complete acts evolved slowly throughout the winter: "Feats which were to seem so matter of fact when executed in the big top were rehearsed for months on end before the critical eyes of the masters whose axiom was that perfection was always sought but was never completely attained" (Draper, "The Davenport Family" 25).

Parents and trainers could certainly insist on disciplined work. Tosca Canestrelli, born into a circus family of five generations in Venice, Italy, in 1923, came to Ringling Bros. and Barnum & Bailey in 1932, with her mother and brother as well as two uncles and their wives. The family intended for Tosca, at age nine, to learn to catapult from a bounding rope, like a "giant rubber band," stretched between two supports forty feet apart, from which the performer bounced to get to a huge height, as from a trampoline; the trick ended as the performer landed on a "relatively small one-inch rope." Her sister Celeste, who herself perfected an unsupported ladder act while also riding horses and elephants, wrote that Tosca had been coached from age nine, at Ringling Bros., by their father:

> Not only did he train her in the pure mechanics, but he also worked to coordinate her mental and muscular skills so as to impart the vital element of timing into her performance. And, he directed her every move, not only in practice, but later on when she was performing.
> It was a grueling regimen, repeating the same maneuvers, day after day after day, for six

years, while all the time maintaining the high degree of concentration that is necessary to avoid a serious accident ["Suggested Comments by Celeste Atayde" 3–4].

Each day, their mother taught Tosca ballet skills, the instruction of both parents ultimately enabling her to reach the high wire via the bounding rope, something few women did; to balance on the wire without fan, parasol, or balance pole; and from there to do splits, a somersault through a hoop, and a backward double somersault, what no other woman had done. Of their parents and Tosca, Celeste wrote, "it was their love for her that made all of her successes possible," a key element also of her own training ("Suggested Comments by Celeste Atayde" 6).

Many other women practiced with parents who were stern taskmasters. Equestrian Josephine DeMott Robinson, in fact, wrote similarly of the training discipline: "I was trained by my father, John DeMott, from whose vocabulary three words were omitted. I never heard him say 'can't,' 'tired,' or 'afraid.' It never occurred to him that I would get tired, knowing that my body was being so conditioned that it automatically threw up barriers against fatigue. In short, I worked without tiring" ("Exercise as Rest"). This disciplined approach could seem cruel, and certainly grueling, but it also indicated that the young artist was being taken seriously and being prepared for a career.

This training was not just part of youth or of winter stops, but also of every day and week on the road, not just for equestrians but for all types of performers, to get to the top and stay there. During an off-day or an early morning, as aerialist Tiny Kline wrote, "Bears were practicing their skating and cycling on one stage, an acrobatic troupe was just breaking the four-high pyramid in the ring next to it, liberty horses were going through their drills in another ring, and yes, the boss trainer, Mooney, was putting through a herd of his charges in the new act: baseball, played by elephants in the third ring" (105).

Even the greatest stars — or perhaps especially those stars — continued to improve their acts, on the road as well as in the winter. Working in the mornings before her shows was the best known of equestrians, May Wirth, with an entirely different appearance than in the show, as described in the autobiography *Circus*, written by Betty Boyd Bell, who grew up traveling with the circus that her father managed: "Mornings I used to watch May practicing with her horses, perhaps breaking in a new one for the act; you never would have thought she was the May Wirth of the afternoon and evening shows. Her spangles and chiffon skirts, and her silk tights and ballet slippers were all put away in her dressing tent; she wore dark blue bloomers and a white silk blouse with an open collar; and her sleeves were rolled up, and the dark hair that made a cloud around her pretty face in the ring under the lights during the show was braided into a little tight pigtail" (105). In this practice garb, Wirth painstakingly reviewed everything from the show of the previous day and honed new routines.

Performers needed regular practice to maintain their skills — and to accomplish the new, dangerous tricks that kept crowds coming back and salaries increasing. What managers always sought was something new to advertise, something new that would continue to bring patrons to the seats, and performers wanted to be the best, certainly, but they also responded to the pressure of creating the ever new. Aerialist Fritzi Huber maintained, Frega wrote, "Ideally, you want to be the first or even the only person performing a certain stunt, but this is part of the reason why you push the edge" (Frega 270).

On the road and in the off-season, practice was a permanent part of the job, necessary to be able to perform the old acts and to develop the new that would further secure a manager's and an audience's attention. Women worked with the best trainers they could find, with family members and others. To learn, they dealt with prejudice, impatience, and risk. Like women in other professions, they relied on hard work, which at the circus could lead to the highest levels of stardom and salary. To succeed at this career, often faced with the hardest of circumstances, women performers renewed their education and commitment every day.

# CHAPTER 10

# Life on the Road and Rails

Though the career combined hard practice and physical risk, it also involved the daily realities of being out on the road. In newspapers and in films, this itinerant life might be all about wicked choices. In novels for boys and dime novels for young men, it meant great days of adventure. In romances for women, it provided a time for love to bloom. But March to November for circus performers actually involved day after day of risk, hard work, and dullness in changing spaces and places, the road a real and complex requirement for earning their living. During the season of 1889, Balinda Merriam Spencer, then forty years old, a divorced mother with two sons, worked as an equestrian with John Robinson Big Ten Shows Combined. Her daily journal provides a detailed picture of this nomadic yet structured life, the specifics of which apprentices learned about when they took their first jobs and that many performers, like Spencer, discussed with family, other visitors, and interviewers, both during the season and off-season, a reality that in many ways diverged from stories common in the press and in fiction.

As many newspapers reported on their women's pages, circus travel could involve the same types of domestic moments that occurred at home. Spencer was from Ohio and tried to let her family know when she might be coming near so that she could visit with them. She took in sewing while traveling, for other performers and the management, to make extra money, and she also made her own costumes and those of her older son, Henry. As her journal attests about the circus' trip into Virginia, she tried to take in sites that they passed on the way while also enjoying nice, and perhaps attractive, people that she met: "July 7, (Sun): We made a run of 285 miles. On the way, we passed the Natural Bridge and a newly discovered cave and thousand other objects of interest. We skirted the Blue Peak Range for a long distance. I find the conductor a very pleasant and instructive young man. His name is William Conners" (13).

Throughout the season, though, her concerns as a working woman must reach beyond the sewing of costumes that might interest a newspaper's women's page. Her employment depending on it, she comments on variations in attendance, along with reasons for them. Bad business might come from revival meetings, competition between circuses, poor crops, or bad weather. Good business was a nicer thing to report: "July 8, (Mon) Roanoke (Roanoke Co) Va: We did the banner business of the season. Had a lovely day — only very warm and a long parade and long walk to hotel and cars. Stopped at the City Hotel and met some very nice southern ladies there" (13).

In her entries, she covers small moments, like visits with nice ladies, but she also keeps her attention on many variables that could produce problems for the show. She frequently remarks on the squabbles that people traveling for long (or short) periods together could enter into: "May 27, (Mon) Bremen (Marshall Co) Ind: Nice little town. Rained nearly all day. One-ring show. Zigzag entry and Tournament. Henry had his picture taken. Paid party three dollars. Got Miss Lizzie Garvins picture. Miss Josie Marks is very sick. Lulu and Sally had some battle. Too many mischief makers around." She also notes the injuries of various sorts that seem to befall human and animal performers at almost every show. Most often the accidents were slight: "July 8, (Mon) Roanoke (Roanoke Co) Va: Mr. LouLou and Will Marks had a quarrel in the dressing room. Will Marks got drunk at supper time and Henry helped Josie get him to the lot. Will fell in the Two-Horse Act with Josie. Not much hurt" (13).

Sometimes accidents, including more serious ones, came in groups, humans and horses, like one named Messenger, seemingly spooked and thus mistake prone: "May 28, (Tues) Albion (Noble Co) Ind: This day has been a chapter of accidents. During entry, Miss Nellie Aiken fell from her horse and was dragged around the ring and her clothes entirely torn off. 'Messenger' fell in the races with Charlie and hurt him quite badly, but he rode the next race. At night, Messenger fell up on him and knocked him senseless. He was carried out for dead. Henry and Arthur Spencer and Johnnie Robinson took him to the cars. Two colored men fell in fits after the obstacle races. Lulu and Sally had trouble in which Mr. Hughes was somewhat interested" (5). Lulu and Sally, it seemed, were perennial trouble-makers, and perhaps both were involved with Hughes.

The bad luck of accidents, as Spencer continued to describe them, could involve more of the animals as well as children in the circus and people in the stands: "August 13, (Tues) Canton (Stark co) Ohio: Stopped at the Barnett House. This was a rainy cold raw day and a day of accidents—enough to confirm any superstitious persons in their belief that the 13th is unlucky. First, the elephant boy fell from the elephant in parade, breaking his leg. Next Bruce DeMott Robinson fell in the Pony Races, being badly hurt. Horse hurt in Man and Horse Race. Nellie Aikin's horse fell in entry. The lady we met at Coshocton on Sunday fell on the seats—badly hurt" (21).

Frequently on the road, as she wrote, accidents and delays could also be caused by the weather: "August 24, (Sat) Toledo (Lucas Co) Ohio: The day opened beautiful. A long parade. Mattie went on the pony chariot and carried the snake. When the show was half over the rain came on and in 15 minutes everything around us in wind, hail and confusion. The big top collapsed, the center pole broke and hundreds of persons were buried beneath a sea of wet canvas. However, no one was much hurt. One girl it is reported, had her arm broken. However, that finished us for the show in Toledo. We packed up and pulled out for Decatur, Ind." (23).

Travel with the circus involved visiting among friends, raising children, seeing new sites, living as a member of a community. But it also entailed much vulnerability—to a whole host of troubles that ultimately might cause a decrease in the show's revenues or the loss of a job. This career offered adventure, true, but not just like in *Toby Tyler*. Instead it was an adult adventure, of trying to market one's skills and continue on in safety while still participating in family life and seeking to achieve higher levels of success. The circus life could be exciting and dangerous as well as dull and tiring. It was a road job.

# CHAPTER 11

## Scanty Dress

The transforming ability of a costume or mask is spiritual. Putting on a costume is almost a ritual; you are performing to transform yourself. — Donalee Frega, *Women of Illusion* 269

As circus women dealt with contracts, constant travel, and daily practice, they also faced the challenge of their employers' changing views of costuming. The pressure was to wear less and less, yet another way to emphasize the new and daring and keep the crowds coming back. Circus historian Earl Chapin May wrote in 1933 that many changes had occurred in the circus in the previous fifty years, one being "the disappearance of what one of my friends once referred to as 'its damnable morality,'" meaning the traditional modesty which compelled all women to wear full-length tights and all men to appear in the ring with full-length sleeves." By 1933, he noted, the standard had become "bare legs for the women and bare arms for the men," changes that might shock and challenge the performers themselves even as they created the new and risky to add to the circus draw and thus their own security and salary ("Bigger and Better" 15).

Though the circus demanded skill, it also increasingly sold sexuality, with the requirements of the acts sometimes providing a reason for ever decreasing cloth, but the desire of the crowd to see the highly sexualized woman also creating the alteration. Women throughout the decades, in a changing environment concerning female propriety, chose costumes to sell their acts, reacting to the pressure of employers and audiences while also attempting to please themselves. Like women employed in other American businesses, including offices and stores, they repeatedly encountered the complications of reconciling beauty and skill as they sold a product to the public.

Not all the costumes chosen by owners to shock and entrance viewers consisted of a smaller circumference. Indeed, in 1895 and 1896, when Barnum & Bailey featured the gimmick of a separate ring devoted to women performers, the cast included eight women attendants in topcoats, scarlet cravats and vests, tan silk hats, and the controversial divided skirt called bloomers, named for Amelia Bloomer, women's rights and temperance advocate who died in 1894. The circus advertised these costumes and their import as well as the performers' "aristocratic" looks while adopting an ironic tone about New Women and circus women: "Mr. Bailey declares it was hard to find eight young women to properly embody the idea

Aerialists started the trend toward more revealing costumes, seen here in a Barnum & Bailey poster from 1909 by the Strobridge Lithograph Co. (John and Mable Ringling Museum of Art).

of the bloomer attendants. They had to be girls of height and style and dash, and swell girls of aristocratic bearing are scarce in the circus set." These New Women attendants held ribbons and loops for the bareback riders and also faced the antics of a specially hired clown, Evetta Mathews ("The Latest New Woman").

Though the bloomers could shock as a marker of the New Woman, it was generally a lack of clothes that riveted attention. Like burlesque and other theatre shows, circuses included tableaux: women posed topless and nearly bottomless as nymphs, Venuses, or maidens, generally covered in thick white greasepaint to create a marble look. In the parades that might begin and end a show, young women often wore elaborate eastern harem costumes, diaphanous Greek tunics, or little more than paint.

Trapeze artists, like tableau standers and paraders, especially secured attention for their decided lack of clothes. Costumes were very short. When women started appearing on the tightrope in the 1870s, they did so in costumes tightly fitted in the bodice, with a flared or contoured skirt. Soon though they were wearing the shorter and tighter costume that got its name from the act's inventor, Frenchman François Léotard, who debuted in Paris in 1859, leaping from one swinging trapeze forward to another. Acceptance of women in the modern leotard and thin tights began with the argument that any extra cloth could be dangerous on the high wire and trapeze bar.

It was not just trapeze artists who appeared in ever shortening costumes. In the earlier days, when women rode in carts or rode sidesaddle, equestrians appeared in long skirts that lay down over the flank of the horse. A. Morton Smith thus described what he saw in several opening specs in the 1870s and 1880s: "The lady riders wore conventional costumes of that day, with long skirts and small derby hats decorated with ostrich feathers, and they used old-fashioned side-saddles" ("Spec-ology" 51). But, as Earl Chapin May noted in 1933, by that time women had discarded "the long tarlatan skirt" years before ("Bigger and Better" 15). As the emphasis shifted from the abilities of the horse to the abilities of the rider and as women left a seated position and more commonly performed tricks on the horse's bare back, short outfits became part of what would sell the rider and the act.

## Bargaining

Just as women negotiated the terms of their contracts with managers and owners, they also bargained with them concerning what they would wear. Many equestrians, trained as riders in long skirts or in western slacks, found the scanty dress inappropriate. In the early 1930s, Dorothy Herbert reacted strongly when circus management asked her to appear in a gold leotard, along with a red cap, red shoes, and drapes of yellow, orange, and red coming from her shoulders, an outfit in which she had already been portrayed, without her permission, in a poster. In an autobiographical article, she described her response, spoken loudly to her manager: "'I will not wear such a thing on a horse,' I cried. 'Why, I would as soon go out naked.'" Though she felt that a leotard was appropriate for aerialists since it helped them to work without injury, she saw no purpose for such a costume elsewhere: "I can just hear people saying, 'Where is the net? She thinks she's in a flying act'" ("Herbert's Horses" I.18).

When a manager told Herbert that she needed to switch to the scantier costume, she decided on a prank that did not achieve what she hoped. She wanted to emphasize that a leotard, instead of a fuller skirt, was too sexual, and so one night, without prior notice, she shifted to a flesh-colored leotard with gold leaves sewed on at key points, and a long, blonde wig, as she described her entrance with her horse Satan: "The flames were lit, I dropped my cape, and Satan and I dashed out. I heard quite a few gasps from the audience, and immediately after the act, without waiting to take a bow, I ran to my dressing room.... I was scared." She then had to let the bosses in and prove to them that she had on clothes, but they did not get mad or insist on full skirts: shocked spectators, they believed, would bring in a bigger crowd. Though she had intended to repulse circus goers on one night, alienate that town's audience, and thus change the managers' minds, she next had to get their attention away from flesh-colored costume and Lady Godiva scenarios.

Herbert next decided to compromise with her managers by having a sexual and exciting outfit made, but one that would incorporate the fuller and longer skirt that she preferred. "It was a deep pink top covered in rhinestones; a long circular skirt of ostrich feathers, ranging from light pink to deepest rose and a headdress of variegated feathers to match. It was out of this world — and so was the price: several weeks' salary for one costume" ("Herbert's Horses" I.18–20). This choice placated her managers for a time, but she soon thereafter began shifting to the leotard style that they preferred, her contract bargaining involving salary increases as well as alterations to her costumes.

Herbert's choice of more sexual costumes led to larger profits, especially necessary as she began to purchase her own animals and pay for their care. However, she found that the smaller costumes that had shocked her but pleased managers and audiences did not play well to all houses. At an off-season job at the Royal Horse Show, a prestigious, traditional event within the Royal Agricultural Winter Fair in Toronto, she first appeared in an evening gown, stepped back to take off her headdress and the skirt, and then went back onto the horse in the type of leotard that American circus managers were insisting upon. But the Canadian management reacted quite differently: "When I dropped my skirt, you could hear gasps all over the house. (You must remember that this was back in the 1930s.)" She was fired that night. "Mother and I went back to the hotel and I cried all night. Here was my first date with my own horse, and I had been fired" ("Herbert's Horses" II.20).

Other riders tried to strike a balance between the racier costumes requested by managers and their own sense of decorum. The four women in The Davenports riding group provided drama by their simultaneous maneuvers. But circus owners also wanted the drama of the short skirt. In 1930, both on the road and in their winter appearances at New York's Jolson Theatre, they kept their "distended" skirts even as they went to "long backless bodices with gold spangles, elaborately dressed yellow mohair wigs and gold bands and Roman sandals covered with pink iridescent spangles" (Draper, "The Davenport Family" 25). But this compromise would not suffice for long: managers wanted women in leotards.

As more and more women entered circus work from 1880 to 1940, with ever more competition for the spotlight, part of what enabled a woman to keep her job and raise her salary was definitely sexuality. The circus would always require skill, especially for women doing more than standing and marching, but an enticing appearance mattered too, and it could be enhanced by costume. Part of a woman's work involved not just training but dealing with her employers concerning what she would wear as she performed. Like women in many American industries, circus performers exploited, accepted, and rebelled against the complex duality of beauty and skill in their working life.

# CHAPTER 12

# The (Difficult) Road to Success

The stories told by women circus performers stressed the realities that the circus involved, their reasons for going, their contractual status, the constant practice, the life on the road, and the ongoing debate about the costumes they wore. Many women who told these stories performed in the circus for just a few years, working as ballet girls. Those who continued for a full career, like Balinda Merriam Spencer, did so by developing a marketable skill that could carry them beyond youth. This group included the few, like equestrian Dorothy Herbert, who worked their way to the top of this industry — ambitious, hard-working, well-trained, charismatic, and risk-taking performers in a profession in which many of the best rewarded stars were women.

Women who sought to be stars secured as much training as possible, regardless of the difficulty involved. After Dorothy Herbert appeared in a Detroit pageant with her dancing class, she got the chance to appear in a comedy act involving mules, but she wanted to work toward a star equestrian act. She trained in 1925 at Gollmar Bros. Circus with Ray Thompson, a well-known rider and trainer, to get the best of instruction, even though he was extremely cruel: "He would work a horse and rider until both were ready to drop. If a mistake were made, the lash whip would often miss the horse and hit the rider instead." Because he cracked her knuckles if she moved her hands incorrectly, her hands and arms "quickly learned to stay in place" ("Herbert's Horses" I. 6). On ponies, she learned to ride sidesaddle — guiding the horse "to get on a pedestal, waltz, change the ring, lie down, and sit up and rear" — after which she no longer had to ride comedy mules ("Herbert's Horses" I. 7). She also began to do bareback tricks, to jump hurdles, and to race horses. Her skill level enabled her to join Colonel Zack Miller's 101 Ranch Wild West Show in 1927.

As Herbert sought to move from Miller's wild west show into larger circuses, like many other performers seeking to reach to higher career levels, she felt the need to take whatever work was offered, as she noted: "One evening while I was reading *Billboard,* the showman's magazine, I saw an advertisement for people for several shows in Peru, Indiana. Not knowing what to expect when I arrived there, I, nevertheless, packed my bags, put them in the car, said good-bye for now, and started out." In her early days, with Sells-Floto Circus, as she recalled, "I decided I would ride whatever they put me on, no matter what, and that was my attitude for many years to come. I would show them, even if I broke my neck trying" ("Herbert's Horses" I.10). With a high level of skill and even higher level of risk, she climbed the circus ladder, from Sells-Floto, to the Eldridge & Bentum Circus, to the John Robinson Circus, and then to Ringling Bros. and Barnum & Bailey.

All through her career, Herbert attested, she continued to take on new challenges, as did other circus stars who wanted extended time in the center ring and thus higher salaries. In the early 1930s, riding without reins while blindfolded, she began jumping her horse Satan over a hurdle of fire. In 1933 she jumped on Satan over two other horses. In 1934, she appeared in another new act, called The Big Hitch, which consisted of her standing on two horses and controlling eight others as they went around the ring at top speed, after which she immediately went into a blindfold fire jump. In 1936, she and Satan began jumping high hurdles; she also swung from a saddle horn as her rearing horse spun on his hind feet. (See C-7.)

In 1936, Herbert also took on the role that heightened the sexual tension of the woman on horseback: she did the Mazeppa. In developing this act, she was responding to the owners' desire for more dramatic and sexual performances, a pressure placed on all types of performers. In the initial story, from Voltaire's *History of Charles XII, King of Sweden* (1731) as well as a Byron poem, "Mazeppa," from 1819, the court page Mazeppa was punished for his indiscretions with the wife of a Polish nobleman by being bound to a wild horse for a wild ride through eastern Europe. The horse finally died from exhaustion, with Mazeppa still tied to it, having fainted from pain and exposure. In a dramatic version presented at Paris' Cirque Olympique in January 1825, Mazeppa proved his love for the Polish Olinska through the bravery of the wild ride and received her as trophy after galloping on the stage tied to the horse's back. In 1862 in New York and then across the country, Adah Isaacs Menken, from New Orleans, caused a sensation in the role, as a woman playing a man.

In the circus as well as burlesque, the label of Mazeppa came to indicate little more than a wild horse ride, with a woman laid out against the side or back of the horse, in scanty dress, vaguely oriental in appearance, certainly not appearing as a man. The arena space and trained animals of the circus made it the perfect place for the wild Mazeppa ride, especially with an equestrian of Dorothy Herbert's skill level and beauty dressed in a bodystocking or in a bra top, short skirt, and flowing cape. With the ringmaster touting a vague tie to literature and theatre, Herbert appeared on the seemingly out-of-control galloping Satan, lying across the horse's back sideways with her hands dragging the floor, one leg caught in the reins and another in the air, as if she were about to fall, the tension heightened as she went over a hurdle in this pose. Such an act, risky and sexual and yet vaguely literary, kept crowds coming in. As Herbert testified, this laid-out pose in the frenetic ride exacted quite a toll: "On the straightaway it was all right, but going over the hurdle in this position was quite another matter. My arms and legs were black and blue, and my midsection, back, and stomach were taped up like an Egyptian mummy" ("Herbert's Horses" II. 27).

With so many well-known tricks and so much touring, and with hard working circus press agents promoting her, Herbert attained American stardom. In 1935, she appeared on a Wheaties cereal box (the practice of using athletes to coincide with the slogan of "The Breakfast of Champions" having begun the year before). Wheaties ads and boxes in the 1930s also included trapeze star Antoinette Concello and equestrian Jennie Rooney, who starred as Cinderella in a popular parade. A 1936 ad for Camel cigarettes, which maintained that a Camel "stimulates the natural flow of digestive fluids," presented Herbert along with a chef and journalist endorsing the slogan of "for Digestion's sake ... smoke Camel's." The ad quotes Herbert, who appears in a leotard on top of two rearing horses, as saying, "I'm

**A crowd watches Dorothy Herbert on a rearing horse, 1933 (Circus World Museum, Baraboo, Wisconsin).**

a devoted Camel smoker. I smoke all I want — eat anything I care for. Camels make food taste better and digest easier."

In 1939, as Herbert's stardom continued to build, she appeared with Ringling Bros. and Barnum & Bailey, jumping through high hurdles and hoops of flame, doing a madcap act in which her horse appeared to be out of control; she lay down on the flank of rearing horses; and she led a horse through waltzing, rearing, and leaping maneuvers, her movements synchronized with those of as many as seventy other women riders. That year she won a *Billboard* poll as the nation's favorite outdoor performer. In 1940, she played a secretary in the feature film, *Mysterious Doctor Satan,* part of a popular serial from Republic Studios, in which Satan is an evil scientist seeking world domination, possessed of an army of robots, and not a horse. For this film, Herbert worked to make the stunts look as dangerous as possible, insisting on the use of her own horse, Rex. Marshalling her skills from the Mazeppa, to the delight and surprise of the directors and for the continuance of her career in this industry, when faced suddenly with a high fence, "I galloped Rex toward it, and just as he was about to jump, a shot rang out and I fell into my layback, with one leg in the air, hands dragging, as though I had been hit." When she finished, the crew applauded and "the director was delighted" ("Herbert's Horses" III. 32). Like Dorothy Herbert, many other women sought year after year to reach the highest levels of success: by securing the best training, bargaining for fair terms, taking risks, and perfecting their acts. Not all were as famous as Herbert, but circuses employed generations of women well known for their skill and dedication, for their rise to the top of their profession.

Women circus performers may have come into the business led by one of many possible motives, including family loyalty, freedom, love, a chance for steady pay, or a driving ambition. Like other professionals, they took pride in their work, in their separation as a successful group: they, in fact, often viewed themselves as superior to those that issued extreme judgments about circus life. As independent American workers, these women bargained for the best possible contracts; they practiced regularly to improve their skills; they adjusted to life on the road; they negotiated with owners concerning the size of their costumes; and they succeeded with well-wrought acts. Circus women acquainted others with a complex version of women at work, beyond the positive and negative stereotypes appearing in the popular media. They considered themselves to be hard-working, disciplined women devoted to a dangerous and challenging art form, thriving within a difficult world of commerce.

Mary Singleton, "The Circus Parade," a rendition of circus excitement in small-town America (courtesy Mary Singleton).

A very different look, both for Mabel Stark and for the tiger (Circus World Museum, Baraboo, Wisconsin).

Ringling Bros. and Barnum & Bailey became a combined show in 1919, with great stars like Poodles Hanneford, Tiny Kline, Bird Millman (shown here), May Wirth, and Lillian Leitzel appearing throughout the 1920s (Collection of the John and Mable Ringling Museum of Art Tibbals Collection).

The face and body shown here have no resemblance to "the real" Ella Ewing (Collection of the John and Mable Ringling Museum of Art Tibbals Collection).

The image's "freak" status conflicts with the beautiful gowns and faces of the Giraffe Neck Women (Circus World Museum, Baraboo, Wisconsin).

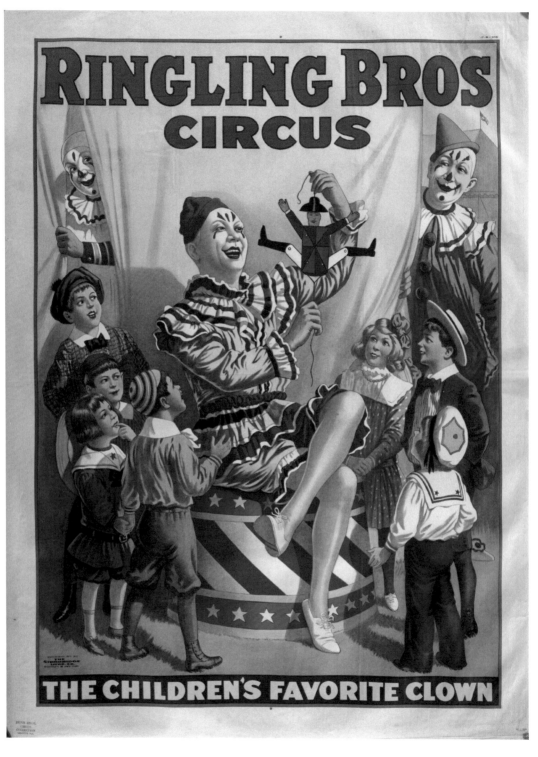

The clown certainly attracted children at the more wholesome circus, as seen in this Ringling Bros. poster from 1917 by the Strobridge Lithograph Co. (The John and Mable Ringling Museum of Art).

A poster featuring Dorothy Herbert, Ringling Bros. and Barnum & Bailey Circus, Erie Lithograph (The John and Mabel Ringling Museum of Art).

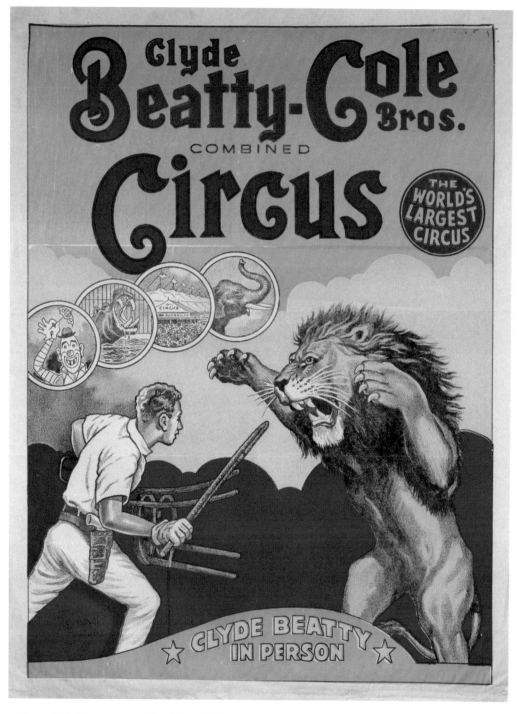

Beatty-Cole Circus poster advertising Clyde Beatty in person, relying on his fierceness of presentation. "People with a fondness for statistics ask me how many chairs I use in fending off attacks in the arena in the course of a season. My records show that I used—'consumed' would be a better word for most of them were utterly demolished by my playful pets—sixty-three chairs last year" (The John and Mable Ringling Museum of Art).

# PART THREE

## The Circus Comes to Town

In the popular media, the circus often appeared bigger than life, as seedy, dangerous, and scandalous as well as romantic and adventurous. But in fact the circus was also a real site of work that performers discussed in their own writing and speech making. They were much more likely than any outsider to write about an array of motives, their freedom and lack thereof, the community of performers, contractual obligations, hard work, calculated risks, and life on the road. Their stories expanded, contradicted, and complicated the stories that others told about them.

Mabel Stark. Are they dancing or fighting? (Circus World Museum, Baraboo, Wisconsin).

93

Though the perspectives of insiders and outsiders certainly differed, leading to contrasting stories of women at work, ultimately for both performers and spectators the circus appeared "live," resembling nothing else seen — in rural areas, small towns, and cities — by an audience of all ages and classes. A special power of space and place occurred in posters on local stores and fences; at the unloading; at the parade; during the circus goer's visits to the menagerie and perhaps the dressing tents; and at the games of skill and chance, sideshows, and tent show, all of which created an intense involvement between performer and spectator.

The impact of circus depended on the repeated presentation of highly decorated and skillful women in close relationship with the audience in all of these sites. Women might be half of the total cast, and the shock of their beauty, their skill, and ugliness, their various forms of difference, were a key to selling circus. As they examined the posters that came to town before the show and participated in the long day itself, women as well as men in audiences across the United States thus interacted with the exotic: fully engaged with a most foreign sort of career.

# CHAPTER 13

## The Power of the Poster

While circuses employed press agents to place an article or two in each town's news-papers, they also had another much more powerful form of publicity, one over which they had complete control. The circus first arrived through the creation of a whole town or county's worth of visuals for the big show. By the time that the performers actually stepped out of circus wagons or trains and the circus parade began, every available space presented a special version of that which was coming to town.

Circus posters were not just abundant: in the weeks before the circus came to town, they were literally everywhere. A typical number of posters or sheets for any one locale might be 5000 to 8000, though that number of course varied with the size of the venue

Posters covering a building near Lynchburg, Virginia, to advertise the Downie Bros. Circus, 1936. Photograph by Walker Evans (Library of Congress Prints and Photographs Division).

and the length of the stop: in 1893 Barnum & Bailey "plastered 227,110 sheets in New York City, including 9,525 on the railways, and an additional 8,186 in surrounding cities" to advertise a one-month stand (J. Davis 44). At a time when American print culture was dominated by the pages of the Bible, *Godey's Lady's Book*, and maybe a seed-store catalog or almanac, circus posters created a much larger presence. According to P.T. Barnum, the secret to success in the circus business was "Advertising — Advertising — nothing else" (Walk 17). And for the most part, that advertising meant posters. As circus historian Neil Cockerline has written, "The key to success for every circus was advertising, and the key to advertising for the first 175 years of the circus in America was the circus poster."

These images appeared literally overnight; they were huge; they stayed up a long time; they were in vivid colors; and they showed worlds otherwise perhaps unimaginable to most viewers. To twenty-first century eyes, so many posters in one small town might seem like overkill. Advertising today typically sells a product or products that may be purchased from among many others and can be used over a long time period. In the heyday of one or two night stands, the circus had to sell itself as a one-shot extravaganza — only *tonight,* only *right here* in *your* town! Unless the circus's title, its date, a graphic representation, and perhaps a "feature" — "See Buffalo Bill on His Farewell Tour!" — came across forcefully night after night, locale after locale, all of the rest of the circus enterprise would be for naught.

As posters developed after 1880 from the much smaller handbills of earlier generations, their increasingly bright and large visuals and decreasing amount of text sought to draw a variety of audiences to the show. By the 1880s, as the circus increasingly marketed itself as a place for children, posters began to have much less text than small handbills of earlier eras. And the circus' purported educational functions therein described — see how it looked when Columbus discovered America, see how "Burmese" women stretched their lips or their necks — made the show more acceptable for the family. These images could also attract the enlarging audience of immigrants in the United States, for whom the show's lack of dialogue made the circus an attractive entertainment form, as well as automobile occupants with less time to scan an advertisement than walkers or horse-cart drivers. Horatio Alger, Jr., in *The Young Acrobat of the Great North American Circus* (1888), described the effect that such large drawings of beautiful women and handsome men seen on every street could generate in any town, like this book's Smyrna: "There was a great excitement in Smyrna, especially among the boys. Arlow's Great American Circus in its triumphal progress from State to State was close at hand, and immense yellow posters announcing its arrival were liberally displayed on fences and barns, while smaller bills were put up in the post office, the hotel, and the principal stores, and distributed from house to house" (1).

Examining circus posters of this period, we can find writ large many of the key qualities that made the American circus such a popular, compelling spectacle. In particular, in the posters' presentations of women, we see many of the contradictions also presented by the larger phenomenon of the circus. Because of the overpowering quantity of these posters as brought to town by advance men, their compelling uses of color and design, and their continuing appearance before the whole populace, the images of women presented on these posters possessed great power. These posters drew potential audiences into a highly rhetorical world of what women could look like and who they could be once their public lives and careers left the realm of normality. They reintroduced many of the extremes represented in books and films while engaging townspeople first hand in the exciting extremes of these women at work.

# The Advance Men

Circus posters seemed to appear overnight, put up by people called advance men. Barnum and Bailey had it down to a science (J. Davis 43–44). Three or four waves of advance men, and they were practically always men, came in railroad cars through each town where the circus would stop. The first car contained the general contractor, who worked out deals for everything the circus would need at each stop, from renting exhibition grounds to procuring permits to contracting for billboard space. The second car contained the advance agent, or press agent, and the actual "billposters," the men who put up the "bills." A good billposter could put up 700 posters in one day; 1000 in a day was considered outstanding.

The third car brought the show's publicity to all other towns within a fifty-mile radius of the stop, advertising special "excursion rates" on wagon or rail to the show site. Then the last car re-ratified everything. And it was nobody's business to take the posters down, so they could last for seasons and seasons, eventually overlaid by other posters for other circuses.

According to circus scholar Fred D. Pfening III, here is how this process worked in one small town:

> The billing for the July 5, 1913 Ringling engagement in Ashtabula, Ohio gives an idea of the extent of advertising in a town of approximately 20,000 people. On June 2 the first advance car arrived. Its billposters put up 2,771 sheets of Strobridge paper ranging from thirty-six sheets to half-sheets. The second advertising car arrived ten days later. Its crew posted only wall work along the rail lines and in the countryside. A week after that the last car hit town, billing locations the other two cars had been unable to contract or had missed.
>
> Overall, Ashtabula took 5,127 lithographed sheets. While the wall work covered over ten times the square footage of the window work, more one sheet and half sheet bills were posted than multi-sheet images, 429 to 295 ["The Strobridge" 40].

# How the Posters Were Made

Often produced by the country's best printers, posters were a big business, typically the single biggest expense for a circus. The biggest companies, such as Strobridge & Company in Cincinnati, printed more than five million posters in a year (Cockerline). The sizes of these posters eventually became standardized, and a "sheet" became the basic unit, at 28 by 42 inches (a "one-sheet"). There were also many multiples, all the way up to "24-sheets," plus "panels" for store windows, and "date stamps" for customizing dates (or pasting over competitors' dates). These sheets were generally high-quality paper, of a medium weight bleached white, the low wood-pulp content leading to remarkable durability that allowed the sheets to remain visible on walls and fences for years after they were fastened, with and without the permission of the owners of these spaces, with a flour paste. Their oil-based inks, often six or seven brilliant colors, accounted for their eye-popping vividness that might last long after the circus left town.

# Images of Women

The women portrayed in posters, before the show arrived and perhaps long afterwards, were not like anyone a small child growing up in Ashtabula, Zanesville, or New York had ever seen. These women flaunted dazzling short costumes as they swung from trapezes, put lions and tigers through their paces, rode horses in every way imaginable, blasted out of cannons, did tumbling routines — as well as appearing in scenes from the sideshow or "ethnological congress of nations," where things could get really strange. Whatever else might be said of their costumes or skills, they presented provocative female bodies all around the town and county.

Although there were at least as many men as women in circus acts throughout this entire period, eighty percent of these posters featured women to attract an audience of men, women, and children to the shows. Even though most posters exhibited a woman performer by name, the posters were mostly composed of stock images, perhaps altered to supply the right hair color but otherwise a generic female form that could be infinitely repeated. Performers' contracts indicated they had no right to these images and could not use them with any other circus. Some posters repeated not just the image but the name of a well-known star, whether she was coming to town for that night or not. Audiences might think they were seeing stars like trapeze artist Bird Millman and equestrian Dorothy Herbert, though they might not in fact be there at all. Star Lillian Leitzel even recalled men who thought that they had dated her in towns where she had never been: "My mail is ever likely to contain letters from erstwhile sweethearts, telling me of the plans we have made for the future — neither plans nor sweethearts being previously known to me" ("Random Recollections").

In featuring superstars as well as less well-known performers, the poster was well crafted to sell, especially with images of women that provided visual shock, from the many skills performed as well as the highly unusual dress and situation of the woman performing those skills.

## The Animal Trainer

In posters for the most dangerous of acts, children and adults in each town saw dramatic combinations of sexuality and risk meant to lead them out to the show. Circus posters featured female animal trainers with big cats and skimpy clothes, women communing with a crowd of animals, physically interactive with the beasts, though they did not wear these short skirts but protective clothing in the ring. In posters featuring male trainers, these performers generally appeared in khaki safari wear and high boots, evincing a practiced and distinguished authority.

Posters of lion-tamer Adgie from 1915 showed her reclining among lions in skimpy garb and dancing the tango with one of the lions. Such a sexual presentation continued in the depictions of Mabel Stark, who worked for various circuses from the 1910s to the 1950s. The poster on page 93, from Ringling Bros. and Barnum & Bailey, shows her in the archetypal "animal trainer" costume — high leather boots, white trousers, and an ornamental jacket with tassels on the sleeves and a high collar. The face of the Mabel Stark character in the poster is generic, bearing no particular resemblance to her. But the hairdo is like a signature for her.

In this poster, a viewer might well ask whether Mabel Stark is "wrestling" with the tiger or dancing with him. The bars behind them are the only suggestion of the larger context of the circus: woman and tiger seem to be alone, doing the footwork of a waltz, in some kind of symbiosis, certainly not something seen before in any small town. And in this relationship, as the text on the right of the poster indicates, she is dancing with the "now friendly and willing once terror of the jungle," as though their relationship has changed him into a partner for her.

If the relationship between Stark and the tiger in that poster is suggestive, the one in a second poster, for Al G. Barnes Circus, featuring a woman who actually looks like Mabel Stark, seems beyond doubt. (See C-2.) The tiger appears about as anthropomorphically smitten with her as would be possible before the age of Disney. Stark's clothes here are radically different—some kind of soft blue formal wear—and the pose between the two definitely could not be considered as a struggle. In this poster, describing Stark as "world's foremost trainer of ferocious jungle beasts," she appears exotic because of her relationship with the tiger, a ferocious animal seemingly trained to be lover or husband.

## The Equestrian

Notice the horse's face dominates the foreground, May Wirth centers the mid-ground, and the clown is either entering, or leaving, the view (Circus World Museum, Baraboo, Wisconsin).

Other posters showed beautiful women in close association with their animals—and in close proximity to circus men who perhaps surprisingly seem secondary to both. May Wirth, originally from Australia, who came to the United States in 1912 as "the world's greatest bareback rider," appears here in a poster with the face of the horse dominating the left middle of the picture. The horse appears big and friendly looking, like Stark's tiger fully anthropomorphic, with a face done in detail, while the rest of the body, from the girth on down, is hardly filled in at all. Wirth's costume is elaborate and detailed, with ballet slippers, a golden garter, tights, a short skirt and abbreviated vest. A large bow in purple and gold sets off her long hair, both trademarks for her. And, ever so delicately, she carries a whip like a wand, like a fairy beauty perched magically aboard her own human-like steed.

Two features of the poster further reveal the lesser nature of circus men. A clown looks on affectionately. Additionally, a man in the upper right hand corner appears in formal riding attire — boots, riding pants, a cutaway jacket, gloves, and a top hat. He looks on, like a ringmaster, as Wirth does her trademark somersault. What we see in the here and now of the foreground is Wirth and her affectionate steed sitting still, admired by the clown, while as a footnote we see her further engaged with a circus man who stands at the side during her act, her physical presence overwhelming both these men and even her own tricks as the "somersaulting queen of the arena."

## The Wire Walker

In posters, the magic of these starring performers could seem to overwhelm every other part of the circus, even the male performers, a sighting of them constructed as the best part of going there. In a poster of Bird Millman, famed tightrope walker, this "charming captivating bewitching sensational high wire artiste" appears in fitted bodice, a corsage, frilly party skirt, ballet shoes, and a red parasol open behind her, very attractive and feminine, with china doll skin and graceful hand positions. (See C-3.) Behind her there is no sense of the rest of the big top — rather a night sky full of stars replaces the crowds, the bleachers, and the tent. Here she appears as the apotheosis of the heights that the greatest of stars could reach: she exists in her own space, at one with stars in the heavens, her wire only barely visible as she soars.

## The Snake Handler

While many posters featured stars of the big top, seeming to soar above everything else, sideshow dancers and other performers commonly appeared in posters, reiterating themes of attraction and exoticism and bestiality, and flirting with themes of evil. The snake handler provided a great theme for such posters for she represented several cultural icons of fear and excitement. In the array of pictures of Uno, Queen Supreme of the Serpent Kingdom in the poster on page 101, the viewer can see her in various short skirts and boots, presenting a fine array of legs and snakes, her poses dramatic and alluring. And she is covered by the highly symbolic snake, wrapped around her head in the smaller pictures and creating a great loop around her in the large, center one. She appears oblivious to these animals that writhe around her, their heads sticking out in odd locales, her body encircled at various sites, bringing to the viewer a strong representation of evil, fear, and sexuality.

## The Giantess

While trapeze artists and equestrians might appear in posters as extremely beautiful, bigger than life and floating into the sky, and while exotic sideshow acts might be constructed as seedy and even evil, posters showed freaks as exaggerated in their freakishness, making the tall woman tower over buildings and the little person appear the same size as a thimble or salt shaker. A popular figure in sideshows for years was Ella Ewing, from LaGrange, Missouri, who at somewhere between seven and a half and eight and a half feet in height (the fine print on the poster on C-4 says "nearly 9 feet high") exhibited as "the Missouri Giantess." This poster labels her as "absolutely the tallest lady on earth," "a veritable female colossus," and "a cyclopean young lady weighing over 300 pounds." Here she appears along with "Great Peter the Small," in reality Peter Adamson from England. Striking is the upper-class dress and posing: the formal attire of the "normal" man on the left, Peter's apparent uniform, the "normal" girl's Sunday-outing attire, and all of it backdropped by Ella Ewing, feminine in full-length gloves and floor-length gown, with big poofy shoulders and lace on the top. (The face and body shown here have no resemblance to "the real" Ella Ewing.) Except for the fact that she's eight and a half feet tall, and Peter perhaps 22 inches, everything is proper and polite. Meanwhile the text running down the right side and across the bottom of the poster shrieks every kind of ballyhoo: "Human Prodigies — Midget Man — Giant Giantess — The Littlest and The Biggest — The Antipodes of Humanity."

Here the woman shocks in her contrast to the "midget man" but perhaps more so in her towering over the "normal" man, who is here forced to look up to her. Beneath the normal man is a male midget, also formally dressed, on a fancy table like a flower decoration, with even the young girl in the foreground much bigger than he. The shock here resides in

Uno. The menagerie and the freak show often combined in unusual ways (John and Mable Ringling Museum of Art, Tibbals Collection).

these freaks having some traits of normality, seeming in fact to be members of the upper class, when in fact comparisons of size render them towering monsters or tiny decoration, shocking size and power threats, again outside of normal.

## The Giraffe-Necked Woman

Other posters of sideshow attractions juxtaposed attractive or normal features with extremes, thus jarring the viewer with difference and with similarity. In the 1930s, the Ringling circuses featured one or more of the "giraffe-necked women from Burma." The fundamental opposition in the minds of those viewing these posters must have been between the freak status conveyed by the brass coils and the exaggerated beauty of the women, with their china-doll features, their striking earrings, their carefully coiled and pinned hair that resembled the bobbed hairdo of the flapper. Abnormal necks and neck coils take up the center part of the poster on C-5, decorative strangeness, the harsh looks on the women's faces making them more exotic and a bit frightening. From their bright and vaguely oriental dresses to the neck coils to the coifed hair to the nails situated in their buns, they create contrasts of beauty and frightfulness, freaks in their abnormality but also in their self-possession and eerie beauty.

In these posters and legions of others, suddenly appearing all over town to announce a soon-to-arrive show, viewers got a large and highly colorful introduction to so many astonishing possibilities of the show. Within the tents in these depictions, women might be hugging tigers, showing off their long legs from atop of horses, dancing in the stars, encircled by dangerous snakes, towering over men of various sizes, appearing with the oddest of features like elongated necks. In these posters, in their beauty, size, sexuality, deviant love life, dominance over men, high level of skill, exoticism, and connection to evil, circus women certainly diverge from what might be seen in a regular American town. Here was a presence, though, on so many fences and store windows, that beckoned viewers into the tents to see the wild possibilities, exaggerated and scintillating, of working women across America.

# CHAPTER 14

---

# The Unloading and the Parade

At the very beginning of the circus day, or even the afternoon before, townspeople began to interact with the real, live circus and the women performers in it. On that most exciting day or weekend, the involvement of children and adults in the live performance started as the crew unloaded all the tents, props, and animals, the first event of the show. In *Popular Mechanics* in 1926, an article on a wagon circus in motion used a second-person presentation to describe the unloading of wagons, which many people attended to see the wonder of all that exoticism not just on posters but actually entering their own town:

> You are awakened at peep of day by that unmistakable rumble of steel-hubbed circus wagons. You tumble out of bed and into your clothes. If you are lucky, you reach the railway yards in time to see the last of the hooded cages roll down the inclines "runs" from the gaudily painted circus "flats."
> You trail this last cage, drawn by a team of dappled grays, to the circus grounds [May, "Keeping the Circus" 387].

With larger shows, and much more commonly in later years, the arrival would be at the train yard, perhaps at five in the morning or the night before, with spectators there to watch women, men, and animals.

While spectators went out to the wagon and train sites, they also came into town for a glorious holiday, whether or not they had tickets to the show, as Charles Murray described in 1897:

> It was circus day.
> The early morning sunshine that bathed a smart Jersey town in a genial spring glow fell upon a scene of extraordinary activity and excitement.
> At the first dawn of this beautiful spring day all roads radiating from the town had been enlivened by the appearance of all sorts of vehicles, crowded with all sorts of people; and at this hour a bird's-eye view of the surrounding country would have shown every highway enveloped in unbroken miles of dust.
> The business streets were already alive with the early arrivals, and the long rows of country wagons packed along the curbs boded ill for those to come [5].

People lined up for the grand event that came right through town in front of all the posters: the circus parade. Generations of Americans described the excitement in an array of genres. In 1857, for example, Emily Dickinson wrote to her sister that "Friday, I tasted life. It was

**Unloading of elephants and camels in front of a crowd of spectators, Hagenbeck-Wallace Circus, 1932. Photograph by H.A. Atwell (Circus World Museum, Baraboo, Wisconsin).**

a vast morsel. A Circus passed the house — still I feel the red in my mind though the drums are out" (45). In 1898, James Whitcomb Riley described the town-changing parade in poetry:

> In the Circus parade there is glory clean down
> From the first spangled horse to the mule of the Clown,
> With the gleam and the glint and the glamour and glare.
> Of the days of enchantment all glimmering there [5–8].

And in her autobiography in 1931, Betty Boyd Bell also described this magic scene on small-town streets: "There was a street parade that was a sort of Grand Entry in the daylight; most of the performers put on their costumes and there was a parade of wagons and chariots and people and animals through the principal streets" (25).

The parade, itself the finest of advertising features, involved ever more colorful and intricately carved wagons, often with beautiful women atop or on attached trapezes; elephants that marched along with horses, both ridden by beautiful women; tigers and lions in wheeled cages; brass bands and a calliope; and clowns interacting with the crowd. (See C-1.) Women on floats might pose in stilled tableaux of easily recognizable scenes, from fairy tales like Cinderella or well-known history. In 1892, for example, the Barnum & Bailey parade featured floats depicting Captain Smith with Pocahontas along with scenes from *Sleeping Beauty*, the *Beauty and the Beast*, and *Cinderella* ("The Great Circus Parade").

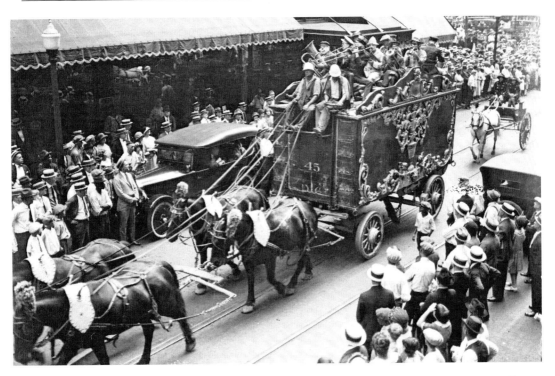

The big circus parade comes through town, Sells-Floto Circus, 1924. Photograph by H.A. Atwell (Circus World Museum, Baraboo, Wisconsin).

With posters in town a week before, with the unloading, and then with the circus parade, the circus transformed the American town. On town streets already filled with colorful poster images, the unloading and then the parade made a big splash, remaking a well-known area into a space of wonderment. Here was the anti-version of American life, an image of everything missing in the everyday. At the parade, spectators rarely saw the biggest stars, whose contracts exempted them from attendance, or the freaks, whose viewing would take away any reason to pay to see them. But an amazing array of what women could wear and could do, of a different vision of life, came off the train cars and right down Main Street. Townspeople saw women well beyond the realm of the normal or regular, a sight to behold, beautiful and exotic, quite an anomaly as they came off the train cars and down the street.

# CHAPTER 15

## To the Menageries, Games
## of Chance and the Sideshows

Certainly by circus day, with the combination of posters, the unloading, and the parade, everyone knew that the circus had come to town. When Ringling Bros. toured in 1890, their daily route report, a diary kept by the management, generally said "Afternoon house big. Night house big," as Americans flocked to the show. The minute that locals came on the grounds, they entered a relationship with the performer and the performance unlike that in any other entertainment. The circus offered a heightened sense of choice and involvement, not one linear story to watch unfold as in at play or movie, one set of acts as at a vaudeville show, or one sporting event as might be encountered at a local baseball diamond.

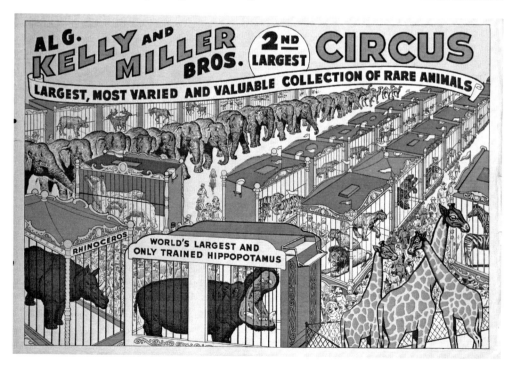

Lead stock and elephants filing into a menagerie tent, Ringling Bros. and Barnum & Bailey Circus, 1928. This destination was especially thought of as appropriate for women and children before the matinee. Photograph by H.A. Atwell (Circus World Museum, Baraboo, Wisconsin).

Here instead entertainment seekers encountered everything at once, with a much higher level of engagement, which began on the show grounds well before the main show began.

An hour before a 2:00 show, doors opened to the menagerie and sideshows, with the main tent opening at 1:15 if customers wanted to go in and get a seat. As townspeople entered the grounds, they found several forms of exotic, interactive entertainment, some at separate prices, all at the customer's own choosing, exhibits geared to please various ages and both genders. The same schedule began again at 7:00 for an 8:00 show, often attended by more adults and especially more men, with the sideshows perhaps opening again afterwards for these mostly men.

When customers entered the circus area, they could choose to go to the menageries that traveled with many circuses, in the early days seen in the wagons in which the animals traveled, generally without an additional fee. This destination was especially thought of as appropriate for women and children before the matinee. In fact, the 1908 program for the Barnum & Bailey Circus indicates that "an hour's time is given to ladies, children, and other visitors, before the regular performances take place, in which to visit the Double Menageries, which the program promised would include giraffes, elephants, a rhinoceros, and the smallest horse in the world" (1). The "other visitors" were presumably the men that accompanied their families.

As customers entered the grounds, they could head instead to what was sometimes labeled with the carnival term of "the Midway," generally a small area in front of the sideshow

*Opposite:* Poster advertising the menagerie at the Al G. Kelly-Miller Circus (John and Mable Ringling Museum of Art).

**A midway scene at the Sells-Floto Circus, 1922. Photograph by H.A. Atwell (Circus World Museum, Baraboo, Wisconsin).**

tents that housed games of chance and skill. Other vendors offered such games right outside of the show grounds. In both positions, these games encouraged both the positive and negative image of circus.

Games of chance frequently drew in the young children so sought as customers by the Ringlings and other circus owners. In the often seen Pingpong Ball and Fish Bowl, for example, children threw pingpong balls at a table filled with rows of small bowls, getting a prize if their ball entered one of them. A game like the Duck Pond, geared for even the youngest children, often accompanied by their mothers or older siblings, could be "won" every time: the player selected a rubber duck floating in water and turned it over to read the name of a prize.

Games of skill more frequently attracted older boys and men who could test their own mettle on the circus lot where strangers, seen in the parade, would be soon be appearing as strong men and tiger trainers, competitors for the admiration of their girlfriends and wives. These games often tested a player's skills at hitting a target with either a ball or a weapon. Games of this type include Cross Bow Shoot, the Milk Bottle Game, and the Balloon and Dart game. Another popular game that tested physical abilities, "Ring the Bell," involved a large mallet with which the player struck a pivot board, causing an indicator to be driven vertically up a scaled board. By hitting the pivot hard enough, the contestant could win a prize. In these games, winning a small prize could lead to more investment for the chance at a larger one.

As primarily older boys and men competed at these skill games, often with their sisters, friends, girlfriends, wives, and children watching, they frequently made accusations that the games were fixed, a seedy possibility of circus. Games, in fact, might be rigged in various ways: with weighted milk bottles, rings that didn't quite fit their target; guns that didn't shoot straight; underinflated balloons that wouldn't pop. With men from town there to impress their companions, and with cheating a possible explanation if they didn't win, these rows of games could be a volatile male space, especially before and after the evening show.

While various members of the circus audience might visit the menageries or games of chance before the circus performance began, others chose their own entertainment by going directly to the sideshows. At a circus, as at a carnival or amusement park, customers walked past a talker or drummer, speaking in dramatic terms and using a bally or a ballyhoo, an exhibitor who would came out front to lure in customers. Next a "shill" rushed forward to excitedly buy tickets, with the aim of encouraging those standing nearby to part with money and follow him inside to see an array of acts.

Inside the sideshow tents, as at city museums, exhibits appeared on the periphery on raised platforms to which a lecturer would lead the crowd one by one while telling fabricated tales, his presence giving a pseudo-scientific tone to the proceedings and often luring in women customers with children as well as men. Spectators thus did not just choose the sideshow but which tent to enter, where to linger, and where to ask questions, thus determining the success of the sideshow performers.

The traditional ten-in-one found within many sideshow tents included people whose deviations from normal made them "born freaks," such as little people or giants, as well as "made freaks" like tattooed people, appearing along with those presenting "working acts" like magic tricks or daredevil stunts. Customers might also be lured into a tent offering a "Single-O," or single attraction, such as a "What Is It?," a woman or man proclaimed to be the missing link or a monstrosity of a human being. The ten-in-one or Single-O would often end in a "blowoff" or "ding," an extra act not advertised on the outside, which could be viewed for an additional fee. The blowoff act would be described provocatively, often as something deemed too bizarre for viewing by women and children. These additional attractions, especially in the evening for male visitors, might include a "Girlie Show," with fully-clothed dancers or racier "cootch" dancers, shaking all over and doing striptease numbers, the act predating the term "striptease," which was coined at Minsky's in New York City in 1931 and entered common usage in *Variety* in the 1930s (Stencell 7).

Sideshow talker or drummer, Klamath Falls, Oregon, 1942. At a circus, as at a carnival or amusement park, customers walked past a talker or drummer, speaking in dramatic terms and using a bally or a ballyhoo, an exhibitor who would came out front to lure in customers. Photograph by Russell Lee (Library of Congress Prints and Photographs Division).

Lithograph of crowds at a circus sideshow, 1900. Inside the sideshow tents, as at city museums, exhibits appeared on the periphery on raised platforms to which a lecturer would lead the crowd one by one while telling fabricated tales, his presence giving a pseudo-scientific tone to the proceedings and often luring in women customers with children as well as men. Courier Litho. Co., Buffalo (Library of Congress Prints and Photographs Division).

When customers entered the show grounds, they could also go into the main tent, where the circus orchestra would begin playing well-known tunes an hour before the show. At the Barnum & Bailey Circus of 1908, for example, the orchestra's pre-show music included pieces by Wagner, Rossini, Schubert, Verdi, and Dvorak. Thus with a menagerie, games of chance, sideshows, and the orchestra, circus goers found much available for them. They had entered a domain where they could pick their own entertainments, each vendor dependent on those choices. Women as well as men could choose where to go and what to see, a chance to engage in an exotic un-reality generally missing from the regular hometown.

## CHAPTER 16

<hr>

# Into the Dressing Tents

Before the show began, many circus goers came even closer to especially the women performers by visiting the dressing tents located on the circus lot, generally attached to the big top by a covered runway so that performers could quickly change and reenter the ring throughout the show. To get an inside view, customers tried to pull back tent flaps, enter the dressing tents, look into the performers' trunks, and speak to them. Most had no invitation; they snuck in and then began snooping around while asking questions and stating judgments. Beyond the romances and newspapers, beyond the posters and the parades, here was the opportunity to interact with the stars themselves.

## Men Visitors

Many of the unwanted visitors were men hoping to attain a salacious view by slipping through an entrance, a tent bottom, or a canvas seam. Circus historian Charles Murray described the rude behavior, and the sense of difference, operating especially as men thus encroached on women performers in their private sphere: "It is a curious and disgusting fact that people who would think it disgraceful to be peeping and listening at the keyhole of a private chamber, and who would consider a horsewhip light punishment for a 'Peeping Tom,' where their wives and daughters are concerned, will stand unblushingly looking in upon the circus dressing-rooms." With men trying to thus invade the women's dressing tents, circuses hired watchmen to keep them away—and these employees had to remain vigilant. Indeed, Murray said, men would "raise the canvas whenever the watchman's back is turned without compunction" (37–38).

Sometimes violence erupted from this desire to spy. According to Murray, in fact, "If there is anything that will rouse the anger of a circus performer, it is this despicable trait of thoughtless human nature" (37–38). In April 1910, in Evansville, Indiana, Jennie Mallar, a wardrobe mistress, killed 36-year-old James Simpson, as a reporter described Mallar's motivation and the action: "She said that peepers had been warned away from her dressing tent many times. Finally, when annoyed again, she seized a pistol and fired, thinking she was shooting too high to hit anyone outside. Simpson, who was less than twenty feet from the tent, was shot in the head. Her charge was murder" ("Killed by Circus Woman").

## Women Visitors

But not only men sought to enter women's dressing tents without invitation. Indeed, local women seemed enthralled with getting a look at this exotic space: these uninvited inspectors came with preconceptions of how circus women would comport themselves in private, what they might be wearing under their costumes, and how the women would (not) organize these private spaces. Female intruders, according to a *New York Times* article in 1906, especially sought to gaze into the performers' trunks because of what they might reveal about a circus woman's lack of feminine standards: "Your idea of the artistic nature will be, doubtless, that of a trunk which is stirred with a broom handle when anything is wanted in the hope that the desired article will finally come to the top" ("With the Ladies").

What they encountered, however, was another sort of structure, perhaps superior to that in their own homes. In the dressing tents for women, at each stop along the way, the performers' trunks were numbered and arranged by a code respecting differences in status. The first aisle, as aerialist Tiny Kline described the scene and the ranks, held the trunks of "the aristocrats, those top-notch ladies of the circus," with bareback riders on the left and aerial performers on the right. With the trunks in small circles, their lids placed up, each group could simulate private dressing rooms, shut off from others. As Kline noted also, about moving through this large tent, "the farther from this queens' row, the lower the rank of the performers, in a second and third row" (118). Within a busy and constantly moving world, female performers thus had an etiquette that enabled them to be dignified and private when visitors stayed away.

In the *Saturday Evening Post* in 1920, Lucy Lightfoot described the organization of her own trunk that amazed those women who snuck in for a look. In the same tent row in each town, her trunk neatly housed all her costumes and make-up, with a top tray that divided in the middle, and with halves that could be raised and swung out on either side. There she could reach what she needed to mend something for the parade and show and to don the costumes for her busy circus day: a costume for the pre-circus parade through town; street clothes for lunch; another dress for the spec that opened the show; then maybe five changes of costume during the show as she did acrobatics, horse riding, and Roman chariot races (Yates, "The Circus Girl" 32). Much to their surprise, those women who sought to see the trunks generally found a well-organized work world, reiterating the structure of the rows of trunks, certainly not a chaos of crazed women away from the mandates of a home.

While some women simply invaded this space to see the performers as they changed clothes and stare into their trunks, others had invitations from managers who viewed the dressing tents as an additional source of profit and public goodwill. Before and after the shows, managers set up appointments for their best known stars. In her unpublished autobiography, Lillian Leitzel wrote positively about these scheduled appointments, often with local dignitaries: "Being, in a way, the hostess of the show entails a lot of peculiar responsibilities. Those people, who for reasons which seem sufficiently important to the management, are given a trip through the back yard are generally entertained in my dressing tent. I have found them charming guests and have tried to be an equally attractive hostess."

Though Lietzel enjoyed talking about her travels and her act and disregarded the more personal questions, she realized that many other performers, especially those who did not speak English well and did not understand the intrusion, found such visitors hard to tolerate: "One of my really important functions is to keep tactless people from associating too intimately with the performers, many of whom are foreigners and consequently unable to accurately estimate the American idiom. They are, incidentally, educated and intelligent people, but with a peculiar acute sensitiveness which is difficult to understand without long association with them." Leitzel realized that many visitors were polite and respectful to the star but much less so with other women in the cast, as she recorded considering one "very prominent" visitor in Boston who had been perfectly nice with her, but then became much more judgmental about the other cast members, expressing criticisms that Leitzel hastened to refute in her autobiography:

> "Oh Miss Leitzel, how glad I am that I had my twins several months ago, before I saw all these perfectly terrible people."
>
> Some of those "perfectly terrible people" she would have met — she didn't incidentally — are the debutante daughter of a millionaire who left society for the life of the circus; the wife of a man who was at one time his country's diplomatic representative in Washington; a Russian princess who is riding in an act on the show because her knowledge of horses was the only thing she had to sell after the Russian debacle; the charming, cosmopolitan wife of a senior officer in the French Army; several college women, one of whom has made a real estate business on the West Coast yield her a fortune of several hundred thousand dollars during the winter months; and a woman whose ability to write has already made her prominent and will, sooner or later, make her famous.

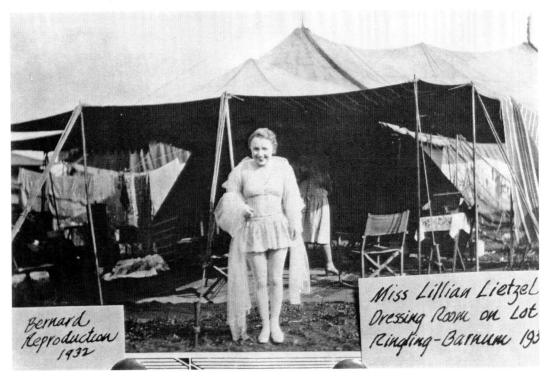

Lillian Leitzel at her dressing tent, 1930. Before and after the shows, managers set up appointments for their best known stars. Leitzel wrote positively about these scheduled appointments: "Being, in a way, the hostess of the show entails a lot of peculiar responsibilities. Those people, who for reasons which seem sufficiently important to the management, are given a trip through the back yard are generally entertained in my dressing tent. I have found them charming guests and have tried to be an equally attractive hostess." Photograph by Robert D. Good (John and Mable Ringling Museum of Art).

Leitzel concludes this section of her autobiography with strongly stated praise of the performers who might be seen in the dressing tent and in the arena and thus with disparagement of the woman who had branded them as "perfectly terrible."

## Social Interchanges

Trapeze artist Lucy Lightfoot commented in the *Saturday Evening Post* about the types of questions that might be rudely aimed at an adult performer, stemming from prejudices concerning the performer as a sleazy and uneducated outsider: "I abhor a certain brand of alleged society women who come here in an endeavor to patronize me. They seem to think they are privileged to ask any rude or personal question that may strike their fancy. Some of them seem surprised beyond words because I read good, wholesome, standard literature and am not a slangy, hard-featured slattern." Lightfoot found these visitors rude and judgmental not just in their speech but in their emotional responses: "I resent having people come to my tent, stare at me ... and then turn away laughing, as if they'd seen some wild animal." She realized that this talk and these actions stemmed from the performers' lesser status that rendered them cavemen, or a zoo exhibit, to the ill informed: "I detest people who haven't brains enough to understand and who don't seem to know anything beyond the bounds of their own little limited world. They seem to assume that circus people have not got beyond the primitive stage of the cave man and are an aggregation of unlettered louts wholly devoid of the commonest sense of social amenities" (Yates 34).

But in these encounters some circus stars met with local women who were open to seeing another life style, who might find it more attractive than their own or who would at least be impressed at the professionalism with which other women worked. Leitzel, in fact, commented on what some women coming to visit ultimately learned, that "the circus is truly a cross section of life. The performers who entertain you so enthrallingly in the big top with their thrilling and often dangerous acts are as charming as they are interesting and are just about as far from being terrible people as they can possibly be" (18–19).

The dressing tent was intended as a place where performers could prepare, dress, and undress, an essential, controlled professional space, like a private office, washroom, or apartment. In attempting to enter there, male and female circus goers demonstrated their desire to see underneath the clothes, as though they had a right to do so, as though the performers that they saw on stage somehow belonged to them and were theirs to view and judge. A fascination stretched from the show to the performer, especially the woman performer, a desire to peer behind the curtain at a private world and question its inhabitants, remarking on their deviations from normal. Americans also sought this intrusion with film stars — but they were much further away, mostly just available to read about in movie magazines. The amazing phenomenon of woman circus performer could be regularly visible right outside of town, and on the show grounds local women often sought interactions with her beyond what was available in the parade and show.

## CHAPTER 17

---

# The Big Show/The Circus Gaze

After circus goers made their own pre-show choices, going to the unloading and parade and then perhaps to the games of chance, sideshows, menagerie, or even the dressing tents, they entered the big top, where at a price manageable by many Americans who would never go to a play or see any other live art form, they witnessed the main event. The program of the circus, its speed and multiplicity, made it unique, with women in well over half of the twenty to forty acts that came before the audience, and with women throughout the stands (J. Davis 5). In this unique entertainment form, circus goers had many ways of continuing the interaction that occurred at the parade and on the show grounds.

A quick review of a circus program demonstrates the array of costumed and performing women that appeared before the audience at a frenetic pace. The Barnum & Bailey 1908 show, for example, began with a spec, or opening spectacle, called "The Grand Tournament": as the program described it, "the finest, richest, and costliest display ever seen." This spec included "four hundred historical characters correctly costumed," primarily garbed as Egyptians and Arabians, walking and riding on floats, among them quite an array of characters and costumes: "mounted guards, trumpeters, heralds, charioteers, knights, nobles, high priests, foot soldiers, archers, warriors, idol men, banner bearers, dancing girls, fan girls, houris" (*Barnum & Bailey's* 3). Circus goers of various ages thus immediately encountered an educational theme along with small and highly decorous costumes, swelling music, grand gestures, and a sense of so much more to come.

Then the main part of the show began, an ever changing array of action. In the 1908 Barnum & Bailey show, to the sound of trumpets and drums, elephants and beautiful riders entered all three rings to perform tricks. Next ten aerial acts entered the arena, performing above all three rings, on single and double trapeze. Additionally an aerialist completed the "slide for life," attached by her jaw to a cable on which she swept down to the floor. Of these ten acts, four involved all-women troupes, including the Silbon Sisters, star Eugenie Silbon advertised separately as creating "dainty and dexterous single trapeze display" (*Barnum & Bailey's* 4). The rest featured combinations of men and women.

Filling the three rings next and quickly were "three royal riding acts by four famous queens of the arena." Of the Sisters Meers, the program advertised "youth, beauty, daring and amazing cleverness in combination. The world's greatest lady riders." Another of these acts featured Julia Shipp and Victoria Davenport, discussed in the program as providing

115

FOREPAUGH'S GREAT AGGREGATION MUSEUM, MENAGERIE AND TRIPLE CIRCUS.

GAMES OF THE ROMAN EMPIRE REVIVED THRILLING CHARIOT RACES

THE LARGEST SHOW IN THE WORLD.

Poster advertising thrilling chariot races at the Adam Forepaugh Circus. In the first of three final chariot races, both drivers were women; then both were men. The next event pitted the female and male winners against each other. Strobridge Lithograph Co. (John and Mable Ringling Museum of Art).

"dainty and dexterous displays of principal bareback equitation, by the charming exemplars of grace and ingenuity" (*Barnum & Bailey's* 5).

Next appeared female tableau artists or silent standers, demonstrating "athletic grace and heroic beauty," standing in formations like Greek statuary, along with five groups of acrobats doing elaborate floor routines. The four groups all included women; they appeared along with three single acts, including Millie Azora, costumed as a Japanese contortionist.

Then came seven groups doing "high-school riding," an equestrian act that featured the expert moves of well-trained horses waltzing and rearing, the women riders generally sidesaddle. Four of the seven groups featured women, appearing with male partners or in all-women teams, seen along with Mary and Petroff's Musical Canines, which wore silver-toned bells and performed to popular songs. This entire array was followed quickly by six comedic acrobatic teams, five of them including women, with acts that would "alternately tickle the visibilities and amaze the sense of sight" (*Barnum & Bailey's* 6).

The action continued without intermission at the same frenetic pace. Comedy continued in many more sets of acts, stretching across all three rings. Within this second segment Miss Emma Stickney exhibited a "delightful display of equine and canine intelligence, in which the prettiest of ponies is ridden by the cutest of dogs." Then came more equestrians;

acrobatic and aerial acts, including the Four Sisters Yellorome on the rolling globe and Nettie Carroll; great equestrian stars in all three rings, including Ella Bradna in the center ring, Victoria Davenport with her husband on one side, and the Sisters Meers on the other. Next appeared clown acts, three aerialist troupes, and horses jumping hurdles (*Barnum & Bailey's* 8–9).

The show ended with twelve horse racing events and an exciting finale. The races began with a "spirited and exciting ladies' jockey race"; they also included rough riders competing in a "riding of the plains" contest, as in a wild west show, and two-horse Roman races, for which the rider had one leg planted on each horse's back. In the first of three final chariot races, both drivers were women; then both were men. The next event pitted the female and male winners against each other (*Barnum & Bailey's* 13).

The climax of the show, another race, involved two women, the French Sisters LaRague as they were advertised, coming down two runways in automobiles, and turning somersaults in the air, a very popular act at the beginning of the century — "the last word in aerial auto sensations" — performed by "nervy French girls who risk their lives in this furor-creating thriller" (*Barnum & Bailey's* 15).

The show presented by Barnum & Bailey and other circuses changed over the years, with some acts losing popularity and other new ones introduced. Contortionists and other

Poster of the Sisters LaRague in the air, Barnum & Bailey Circus, 1908. With women advertised as French, and dressed in a leotard or gown, these acts involved driving as a transgressive act. Strobridge Lithograph Co. (John and Mable Ringling Museum of Art).

floor acrobats, for example, performing bending and tumbling routines, amazed audiences in the 1890s but became less popular in subsequent decades. The "dip of death" somersault act that ended the show in 1908 had been first performed on a bicycle and later would no longer look so thrilling even when executed with a car. New costume types also came and went: the Ringling Bros. show for 1917 featured women aerialists wearing huge butterfly wings, floating on wires, a beautiful sight but an effect soon deemed dangerous since the wings created balance problems (*1917 Courier*). In the 1920s, the combined Ringling Bros. and Barnum & Bailey show featured more stars in center ring, with well-known names like Lillian Leitzel and May Wirth. Wild animal acts became more common in the 1920s and 1930s, headlined by Clyde Beatty and Mabel Stark, as did big-top magic acts, but the shows still featured a familiar array of equestrians, aerialists, acrobats, and clowns. Smaller shows might have fewer acts, though the same basic types, and perhaps just one or two rings in which the action could occur.

In all of this action, circus goers could feel immediately involved, just as they had earlier at the parade and on the show grounds: inside the tent, they could focus on one of the rings; boo or yell (often at the insistence of the ringmaster); interact with clowns who might enter the stands; sit or move around; eat the concessions; and talk with friends and strangers as performers competed to entertain them.

In this varied, interactive site, with much to engage their attention, viewers generally found themselves engrossed, as circus writer Diana Starr Cooper described the scene: "People in the circus audience sit near the edges of their seats. They lean forward. The arrangement of their spaces in the tent awakens all the senses, summoning you to attend to each and every moment and to go with them all as they parade by one another. Then you can return the gaze of the camel's eye and hear, above or below the music, the horses' snorting and the insistent hollow drumming of their hoofbeats. Elephants smell, deliciously, of elephants. Beautiful ladies sweat" (6). In such an exciting and volatile space, with choices always before the audience, spectators might even imagine themselves as transformed from gazers to performers: they could feel that involved in the action. As a *Nation* article commented in March 1931 on the connection between "the[m]" and "every last one of us": "On their trapezes and their tight ropes high above a solid earth they act out a dream of perfectibility. Defying space and gravity and human weakness they weave a fantasy of human infallibility. And the spectators? There are no spectators. Every last one of us, svelte and lithe and sheathed in silk, is swinging in space, walking on air, leaping to the backs of plunging white horses. There is not a flabby muscle, not an awkward limb, not a sagging knee in the whole tent" ("In the Driftway," Mar. 1931, 272).

This power in the crowd, the association between cast and audience members, was very real to the performers, to some extent even determining their skill level and safety. Lillian Leitzel, for example, commented in her autobiographical notes about the need for a sympathetic audience. While she worked, she focused her vision on the crowd and even on one face within it: "It is frequent that one person — often a child — who seems tremendously appreciative of what I am doing, will be the only person in a tent filled with twenty thousand people who really has my attention. Manifestly, it is impossible to play to them all and the logical person to work for is one who palpably appreciates what I am doing" (10). To the contrary, she also noted the power of the negative, often male, gaze. "The contrary of the situation is also unfortunately true. If, as sometimes happens, a baleful, sour-looking person — of course, it's always a man — happens to fix my attention I feel that I cannot do nearly as well. I seem unable to rid myself of the impression that that one man is the embodiment of the entire throng, just daring me, 'Go ahead, but you gotta be good!' I always accept the challenge and do the best I can but I think that it would be a much better performance if I could get rid of the obsession that the crowd is hostile, despite the paradoxical fact that I know it isn't, at all" (10–11). Cat trainer Mabel Stark also wrote about the relationship of performers to the outsiders who exercised control on circus day: "The outside world becomes just so many staring eyes, so many hands to clap us to the ladder of success or pull us down to defeat by withholding the coveted applause" (Stark and Orr 154).

In all these decades and in all sorts of shows, the circus featured three or four things happening at once, nothing in front of the spectator for very long, aerialists followed by equestrians followed by clowns. The performance always involved the ongoing interaction of performers and audience members, with power in the audience beginning with the basic matter of where they looked, which acts they watched for what amount of time, when they chose to clap and boo, when they left for snacks. The small-town and big-city resident was accosted by circus, often amazed by so much, so quickly, an alternate universe in which women moved with grace and skill, by themselves as well as with other women and with men, seemingly outside of external or traditional controls except those exercised by the people with whom and the circus goers for whom they worked.

# CHAPTER 18

# Late-Night Girlie Shows

Part of the sideshow area commonly re-opened at the end of the evening to attract male patrons before they left the show grounds: "after the crowd had come out from seeing the circus performance, not on the way in" (Stencell 37). This attraction, the girlie show, did not appear with Ringling Bros. after it began seeking to be what other circus managers called "the Sunday School Circus." But it was a key selling feature of many smaller shows, such as Cole Bros., Hagenbeck-Wallace, Robinson's United Shows, and the Clyde Beatty Circus, as well as carnivals. At a cheaper price than a burlesque show seen at a theatre or nightclub, and in small-town locales to which such shows never came, spectators could attain a fuller viewing of beautiful women, like those appearing in the specs, and also of some who were a bit terrifying, like those appearing in the other sideshows. While women were less common visitors to this part of the circus grounds at this time of night, they certainly knew about this traveling world, outside of the small-town normal and enthralling to small-town men.

Early banners and false fronts put up for the girlie show made the entrance look like a burlesque theatre to associate the circus sideshow with that exciting entertainment. The lavish carvings, mirrors, and painted scenes of the entrance might in fact be appearing on the sides of wagons, one placed on top of the other. Crowds might especially be drawn by vivid drawings of oriental dancing girls, "hot and blue" as one banner for the Austin Bros. Circus proclaimed. Such banners generally inflated the numbers of women to be seen within: a sign advertising twenty-five models, for example, actually referred to twenty-five poses done by six women (Stencell 57). Outside the sideshow area for Austin Bros., colorful portrayals of almost naked women appeared along with banners for the other sideshow acts like the girl with x-ray eyes and the human pretzel. Performers in robes or partially revealing dress stood outside with the barkers to help draw an audience.

Beyond the banners, customers saw glimpses of a stage, perhaps created from additional stacked-up wagons, which might be big enough for one or two women or twenty women and an orchestra. By the 1920s tents in darker colors replaced the regular canvas to allow for better inside lighting and effects (Stencell 32). Once they paid the fee and entered, patrons saw a variety of acts. The down-in-the-well act had patrons looking down into a circular wooden well, where a scantily clad woman posed wet. A 1911 banner for such an act proclaimed that the customer should mount the ladder to see the beautiful woman "way

Girlie show, Brownsville, Texas, 1942. The main acts involved dramatic posing and dancing. Photograph by Arthur Rothstein (Library of Congress Prints and Photographs Division).

down deep in all her glory" (Stencell 47). Other shows featured tanks in which women did erotic swim movements in small suits. Within the girlie tents, more frequently at carnivals but also at small circuses, also appeared '49 Camp Shows, in which men could enter a saloon area and dance with a woman in western garb for a fixed rate per dance plus tip.

At the girlie show, although patrons might sometimes see women in tanks and dance with women in small saloon areas, the main acts involved dramatic posing and dancing. With the Hagenbeck-Wallace Circus in 1913, for example, women posed in bronze-colored body stockings accompanied by a strong man in gold paint (Stencell 58). Carnivals went further. At the Hennies Bros. Shows in 1937, for example, women posed nude with a gauze curtain separating them from the audience and with back lighting contributing to a dim effect. In circuses and carnivals, women also danced the shimmy and the hootchie-cootchie, with more than three or four together being advertised as a revue. By the 1930s, with fame coming to burlesque dancer Sally Rand, her fan dance also became a girlie show staple. As the night wore on and customers paid an additional fee for the extra or blow-off entertainment, these dances might feature fewer and fewer clothes: Cole Bros. Circus featured cooch dancers down to g-strings in their blow-off in 1937 (Stencell 40). Not all of the performers seen at late-night girlie shows sold traditional sexuality: men paid for disrobing by little women, by women with disabilities of various sorts worthy of observing from beneath their clothing, and by fat ladies who had appeared in girlish clothes earlier in the day.

Such evocative entertainments, along with the possibly rigged games of chance that might also be open at night, contributed to a charged atmosphere and to circus fights. For male customers, here was a possibility that did not occur with film or theatre. With the circus often not leaving until the morning, men often insisted on not leaving the site, attempting to remain there to accost women performers or fight against the circus strong men. Given this volubility, circus owners often hired canvasmen as much for their ability to fight as to work. As a circus veteran testified in 1882:

> A canvasman watching a tent is just like a man watching his home. He will fight in a minute if the outsider cuts the canvas and if a crowd comes to quarrel. He will yell "Hey, Rube!" which is the circus rallying cry and look out for war when you hear it. Almost every man about the show, no matter what he is doing, will start and rush to the place that cry comes from; and he will take any weapon he can lay his hands on, too. Sometimes the parties that cause the trouble are knocked down and the matter ends; sometimes others take their part and the fight lasts a long time. I have heard them yell "Hey, Rube!" many a time, and seen as bad fighting as I did in the war.

Even the most refined male circus performers learned to switch to fighting mode to protect their families and themselves. Though the Cristianis, famed equestrians, were comfortable with royalty and Hollywood celebrities, they could fight when called upon "in the down-and-dirty style of a ruthless gang of Sicilian street fighters" (Rossi 67).

With girlie shows and possible fisticuffs, the circus day often ended with a bit of a seamy underside, with women seen in various modes of exotic dance and undress, as though men could get one more view of women outside the moral standards of their families and towns. The experience could be a bit too much, a bit too alluring, and the men in circus audiences often could not handle the situation.

Circus performers first appeared in full color in posters all over town, and then there they were: up close in the town parade. Then on the lot everything appeared right there at the customer's own choice—to go to the games of chance and choose one; to enter the sideshows and look at particular exhibitors; to attempt to invade a dressing tent; to visit the menageries; to enter the arena. And choice continued through the show as spectators decided what to watch when presented with multiple rings and stages; what to boo and clap for; how to react to clowns who might come into the stands; when to take a break and get something to eat; and whether to stay late for the enticements of the girlie show. All through the day, the circus was right there, the acts controlled to some extent by the crowd.

From the posters' appearance in town to the unloading and parade, the dressing tents, the show, and the sideshows of the day and night, circus goers found themselves engaged with a foreign sort of experience and cast. When the circus came to town, women and men interacted with large groups of strangers as Americans rarely did. The unique envelopment of circus gave Americans a day with the exotic, a day that was a clear contrast to their own hometown. It was too much for some men to process, but it was also a place for women and girls to experience realities beyond the lives they led. Here was close interaction with women in an exciting industry, a connection generally not available with any other type of entertainer or any other group of workers. The circus offered a unique chance to interact with beauty, skill, exoticism, oddity—and the diversity of women at work.

# PART FOUR

# The Women Ranked and Seen

On any circus day, in any American town, locals saw a distinctive art form that engaged their participation and their own decision making much more than any other art form. On that day, in which perhaps fifty percent of the performers might be women, circus goers did not just see acts in general but particular performers with particular skills, each act type communicating to its audience in a unique way. As circus goers watched the array of performers, they witnessed various powerful renditions of female beauty, strength, vulnerability, humor, sexuality, and ugliness; each type of performance conveyed its own meaning and offered its own vision of what women were capable of achieving. Women appeared there renowned for their beauty (and other women for their lack thereof); women provided a beginning and end of the show; women were adornments to a man's tricks; and women were exotic extras in the sideshow tent.

The circus also featured women known not just for their bodies but for their high levels of training and accomplishment. In acts that engaged particular strengths and meanings, the circus presented an array of female talent, women demonstrating the highest levels of achievement as they dominated animals, soared above the crowd, satirized their own nation, shot rifles, and even ran the show. Across the country, there may have been only "circus," but within it there was a considerable a range of talented women.

# CHAPTER 19

# Ballet Girls

For the young and attractive woman, without any definite skill, the first circus job might be the one called "ballet girl." This label actually identified large numbers of women within the circus troupe, women who sang and danced in the circus spectacles, or specs, with which most shows began. Their label stemmed from the inclusion in this troupe of actual ballet dancers, especially from 1880 to 1910, the heyday of this circus fixture. In those years this group often numbered a hundred, especially when a large circus like Barnum & Bailey appeared in Madison Square Garden. In 1903, ninety-five women appeared in Ringling Bros.' "world famous ballet." A similar number appeared with Barnum & Bailey in 1910, presented with "trappings and gilt and ermine, crowns and geegaws and tinsel ... visions of royal splendor and Oriental glamour." Though the numbers decreased after 1910, entry parades continued as a cherished part of the show, featuring many more women than men regardless of the theme ("Horseback at the Circus"). Within this spectacle, as in the parade through town, spectators encountered a mass viewing of beauty and sexuality, beyond anything in their neighborhood, a dazzling presence, not of individual attributes or skills, but of an array of interchangeable arms, legs, and smiles, made mythic through story lines vaguely developed.

As circus historian Fred D. Pfening, Jr., wrote, "The grand entry presented at the beginning of or during a circus performance is the most glamorous, eye-filling and impressive feature of the program." This spec generally had a theme announced in the program and by the ringmaster. A spec might feature well-known stories from ancient history, from the bible, from famous battles, or from fairy tales, presented by a huge cast of almost all of the performers with circus animals marching also. Whatever the theme, the common factor was that large groups of women, often with no discernible connection to the original story, appeared in abbreviated costumes ("Spec-ology" 4).

Several circuses through the years presented specs about Cinderella. For Ringling Bros. and Barnum & Bailey in 1927, aerialist Jennie Rooney played the starring role, riding in a magic coach, with floats carrying the hideous stepsisters and large groups of women riding and marching along side in very short versions of ball gowns. Additionally, aerialists on trapeze appeared as fairy godmothers. Then, for the dramatic ending, the prince entered for the shoe scene. This rendition of Cinderella's story, reiterated at many circuses through the years, drew a young audience while also offering their mothers a romantic escape story, and the men accompanying them definitely could enjoy the rows of ballet girls.

Poster advertising the appearance of 100 ballet girls in a Sells Floto spec, 1921. For the young and attractive woman, without any definite skill, the first circus job might be the one called "ballet girl." Strobridge Lithograph Co. (John and Mable Ringling Museum of Art).

Not all heroines in specs came from fairy tales. The Ringling Bros. spec for 1913 featured Joan of Arc, the program naming her while the description focused on the scene: "An inspiring, vivid picture of bewildering splendor and patriotic zeal. The magnificent coronation procession of Charles VII." Young equestrian Helen Girard appeared in a two-wheeled cart in short battle gear as the star. The procession included knights on horseback, royalty in carriages, and rows of dancing women, as usual with no clear relationship to the story. A circus historian commented on these out-of-place ballet girls, "The real French saint-warrior might have felt out of place amidst 300 girls cavorting in revels under the big top" (Jando; Draper, "Beautiful Cart Acts" 40).

Some specs featured morally questionable historical figures, appearing with large groups of scantily dressed, highly made up, "eastern" women, whose costumes often involved veils and drapes that male patrons might hope would be further removed later in sideshow dance numbers. The Barnum & Bailey spectacle *Cleopatra, Queen of Egypt* from 1912 to 1913 involved elephants, camels, seven hundred horses, and seventy-five ballet girls (Duble). Even the description of Marc Anthony's entry quickly segued to women and elephants: "The ancient Roman came in at the head of about 800 appropriately costumed young women and a score of gorgeously clothed elephants, and the great gathering that filled every nook and corner of the Garden shows by its applause that it appreciated the picture which the Ringling Bros. had arranged" ("Circus Opens"). There were not actually 800 ballet girls, but a much smaller number circling back into the parade as quickly as possible. John

Poster advertising the Cleopatra spec for the Barnum & Bailey Circus, 1912. A spec might feature well-known stories from ancient history, from the bible, from famous battles, or from fairy tales, presented by a huge cast of almost all of the performers with circus animals marching also. Whatever the theme, the common factor was that large groups of women, often with no discernible connection to the original story, appeared in abbreviated costumes. Strobridge Lithograph Co. (John and Mable Ringling Museum of Art).

Robinson's Big Ten Shows featured *King Solomon and the Queen of Sheba* from 1898 through 1904 (Smith, "Spec-ology" 51). Beautiful aerialist Eugenie Silbon starred as Sheba. In 1913, similarly dressed, she appeared as Cleopatra amidst rows of exotically eastern ballet girls.

Instead of heroines, male heroes often provided the focus, but the spec would still feature perhaps a hundred women on floats, in marching rows, on tops of elephants, and in vaguely eastern conveyances. They included Barnum & Bailey's *Nero, or the Destruction of Rome,* an elaborate affair featuring a circus day in Rome, an imperial banquet, and Nero's triumphal procession, all presented along with rows of Greek and Egyptian ladies and slaves, as literary historian Michael H. Means described the scene created by famous choreographer Imre Kiralfy: "The whole affair is, of course, to show off a dozen or so elegant chariots, three or four hundred gorgeous costumes, and every show horse, camel, and elephant carried by the circus." The spec also focused on the crowd's murderous pursuit of Thirza, a Christian maiden, saved because of Nero's lust for her. Lewd displays of Roman decadence quickly led to the dramatic burning of Rome (3–6). Similarly, Ringling's *Caesar's Triumphal Entry into Rome* in 1891 and 1892 focused on a huge parade, featuring rows of dancing girls.

Offering an apotheosis of those values, the spec for 1892 and 1893, *Columbus and the*

*Discovery of America,* created by theatrical producer Imre Kiralfy, employed a cast of 300 advertised as 1200, the dancers closely organized to come in waves, returning quickly to the stage over and over (Barker 154). This show ended the circus, occupying an hour and a half, with a parade and then an elaborate stage show that featured a war of Moors, the ascendancy of Ferdinand and Isabella, Columbus' request, his sea voyage, his landing in the new world where he was greeted by natives, and a Grand Finale of Joy. All of this plot was "performed mainly by shapely young women in lavish sequined costumes," a fact which, according to dance historian Barbara Barker, "did not seem to Imre in the least ironic" (153). The ballet corps first danced as a Moorish group celebrating the end of the Moorish War: "flights of dancers in yellow, pink, white and purple spilled from the stage of Madison Square Garden to fill the three center rings with kaleidoscopic patterns" (Barker 162). These dancers presented not just color but sensuous gyration, described in the program as "the slow, sensuous movements of oriental dances ... accompanied by the wild, weird, mysterious music of quaint instruments" (*Imre* 10). In the final dances, the ballet again filled the stage and three rings as Indian maidens, the dancers now darkened, appeared in short native costumes.

If seemingly hundreds of cast members in exotic veils and short skirts were not enough, many presentations featured odd combinations to further garner attention. Singer Lottie LeClaire, riding in a horse carriage with a wolfhound, appeared as Queen Anne, the wife of King James I, in a spec about Pocahontas, and gave a soprano performance in full dress while white pigeons descended from the tent top to the back of her horse; marching all around her were "ballet girls' darkened and costumed in the shortest of costumes as "Indian maidens." They all appeared along with the beautiful Pocahontas, who indeed had met with royalty in London in 1617, but not dressed in the scantiest of "native" clothes as in this parade and not accompanied by the fearsome braves who rode in the carriage in this spec with her and the hound (J. Davis 199–206). Aerial performances might also take place during these marches, as they did in the Pocahontas spec, their swirling presence linked to the domination and superiority of the English heroes portrayed below (Tait 13).

A mini striptease could also add to the appreciation from the crowd. Among the most popular was the spec called *Lalla Rookh's Departure from Delhi,* for Adam Forepaugh Circus in 1881. It starred actress Louise Montague, whom the circus owner had crowned as the most beautiful woman in America in a rigged beauty contest. Based on a tale from the *Arabian Nights,* "The Thief of Baghdad," the story offered perfect tropes for a spec: it concerned a princess famed for her beauty who is carried into the city during a great parade, but shielded from public sight by a swirl of veils because she is betrothed to a despotic sultan; anyone who looks on her directly must die. In the circus version, as the procession made its way into the arena, she began removing some of the veils, so that all could see part of her beauty — with more available via admission later to the sideshows.

Specs offered an amassing of women, with similar exposed arms and legs, similar veils and leotards, bright colors, decorated carriages, and animal accompaniment. Circuses spent large amounts to usher in the show with a profusion of exoticism and beauty, mesmerizing the crowd with women so unlike what might be seen in the small town, women worthy of view without doing anything but standing, walking, and swaying. Ballet girls came in waves at the viewer, apparently infinitely reproducible as they entered the tent again and again. All were in the same costumes and without individual names in programs, and they were lovely in their multitudes as they added sexual tension and excitement to any big scene in history or myth, seemingly necessary in fact for keeping the audience focused on the scene even if they had nothing to do with the plot. In the continuous marching in of women, the semblance of a thousand, the circus took such profusion beyond the Broadway chorus line and brought it to every small town. For the performers, this multitude of jobs had offered a chance of entry-level employment, which might lead to further training as an equestrian or aerialist or the chance to remain on the road with a performer husband. For the woman seeing the show, such an opportunity to be an exciting and mythic woman was right at hand, right there for the asking, with newspaper ads for these jobs touting an exotic world that required some degree of beauty as well as a willingness to hit the road. Most women across the country, of course, did not sign up, but that possibility and the nearness of the performers made this involvement seem right at hand.

# CHAPTER 20

# Statuary / Tableaux Artists

Choreographers for the most elaborate circus specs used the term "tableau" to describe the main pantomimed scenes of their performance, occurring on floats and on stages set up between the circus rings. Kiralfy's *Nero*, for example, opened "with hundreds of Romans going about their business until Nero and a few cronies in disguise steal a poor man's donkey, play some pranks on each other, and then beat their victim just for fun. The passersby instantly coalesce into an outraged crowd. When Nero throws aside his disguise, the crowd immediately falls to its knees in fear" (Means 5). This action occurs in highly stylized, pantomimed scenes, the key facts spoken by the ringmaster.

Circuses also featured another type of tableau, following a theatrical use of the term, in the creation of stilled beauty posed as though the subject of statuary or painting, another form of circus beauty there for extended gazing. In the late nineteenth century, such themed tableaux without any pantomimed action, also referred to as "living pictures," appeared frequently in theatres and burlesque halls, a freezing in time, a placement of women for examination and analysis. In the circus, these tableaux occurred on floats in parades, between acts in the three rings, and in the sideshows. Participants generally imitated a painting, sculpture, or cultural value such as beauty, in groupings that most commonly involved women only. Completely composed, tableaux appeared from behind a curtain or under a spotlight, often with ringmasters describing their import. The tableau posited viewers as busy moderns, like readers of a magazine or newspaper, quickly flipping forward, on to the next acts after a momentary look at a stilled image.

Tableaux were not invented at the end of the nineteenth century, but they reached an apotheosis then. Indeed, they have a long history in theatrical enterprise. In medieval and Renaissance masques, for example, men and women created stilled depictions of biblical scenes (Case 51). Stilled portraits, however, later abandoned their religious beginnings as well as their employment of men. In England during the Restoration, madams used living pictures of Greek statuary, the Old Masters, and the exotic Orient to display their prostitutes (Shteir 15). In 1787, Goethe attended a more exclusive style of tableau: an upper-class entertainment staged in Sir William Hamilton's Naples residence, where his mistress Emma Hart posed in a beige costume within a frame to simulate a classical painting (Faulk 147). By the 1830s, a few New York theatres and museums began offering living pictures of famous paintings and statues (Allen 92–93; Sobel 109).

By the 1890s, living picture troupes toured the country regularly. In an era of strict decency laws, regulations in New York and other cities facilitated these shows: women could be unclothed onstage if they remained stationary. In working-class venues in the United States, like Sam T. Jack's Chicago burlesque house, reference might be made to a painting or a Greek value — or women might just appear on stage in scanty garments, with small revolving stages allowing them to be seen from all angles. In imitation of burlesque and other theatres, circuses included tableaux in which women posed topless and nearly bottomless, often in white or bronze greasepaint to simulate marble. As aerialist Tiny Kline noted about these standing roles, the work could become repetitive: "It gets weary — the same music, the same scenes, day in, day out, ceasing to be anything but work; no glamour, no nothing" (74). Wives of performers, those with beauty but no particular skill, worked as statue girls, as did apprentices from the ballet girl troupe. As Tiny Kline wrote, it was not lack of skill but age that was the disqualifying factor: "Older women were not eligible ... natural bloom of youth was as essential as good looks by the circus standard" (134).

At the end of the nineteenth century, Annie Roy, who also worked as one of the first female sword swallowers with both the Ringling Brothers and Barnum & Bailey circuses, appeared as a silent stander, an albino who could pose as statuary without the white make-up. She appeared for Ringling as the "White Madagascar Princess," her description in the *Official Program* in 1893 tying her skin tone to classical themes and beauty: "In appearance Annie resembles very much the sculptured female loveliness of Grecian art. Her snow-white

Poster of Colossal Displays of Living Statues at the Al. G. Barnes Circus. Participants generally imitated a painting, sculpture, or cultural value such as beauty, in groupings that most commonly involved women only. Erie Lithograph (John and Mable Ringling Museum of Art).

hair and alabaster complexion, together with her graceful form, if clad in flowing robes of white, such as Grecian maidens wore in ancient times, would make an excellent imitation of marble." This program's description then turns the spectators' attention to sexuality and even sexual violence, helpful for titillating the audience staring at this actual woman, and the program there included her own name: "If Pygmalion had lived in the present day he probably could have found a Galatea who would have had little inclination to become cold marble, and thus drive the enthusiastic sculptor to an early grave, provided, of course, that lovely Annie Roy would not spurn the impassioned kiss, or jealous Bobby go after his gun."

Tiny Kline appeared along with Madeline Rogers, Doris Davies, and Margaret Mays, and a host of other ballet girls for Barnum & Bailey at the beginning of her career, from 1916 to 1918, until she got the training to move into other acts. These women felt like a tight group, separated from the other artists who had more skill and a higher salary. They dressed together, their trunks side by side in an outer row of the dressing tent, helping each other to put on the white and the bronze greasepaint, a messy undertaking, and standing together in statue scenes. Rogers taught Kline poses and movements that she had learned in the ballet. Kline started to learn an iron-jaw routine so that she could increase her opportunities and salary. With this circus, the only male poser was Leo Picchiani, "the perfection of the masculine physique," who appeared in greasepaint in just one pose, as Apollo (Kline 141).

As a silent presentation on a parade float, between acts of the circus, or in a sideshow, the tableau featured the woman stilled, not marching by or waving but appearing as a statue or painted object, thus creating an art form in which men rarely participated. This art gave women and men the chance to see the barely clothed woman, with the aura of Greek statuary or French painting making the presentation more acceptable. With the connection to burlesque as well as art and mythology, the tableau offered another celebration of beauty and sexuality tied to traditions of cultural worth — as well as another means for young women to secure circus work.

# CHAPTER 21

# Mostly Stationary Freaks

At the circus, the fascination with the stilled or passive woman often concentrated on the most beautiful. To entertain, she didn't have to do much beyond smiling, marching, or waving. The circus also presented another group of women worthy of the steady gaze while just standing still or sitting down. They were not presented as beautiful, however, but as abnormal and frightening; and though they stood similarly to those in tableaux, they did so not in the big top but in the sideshow. There customers viewed another extreme, not beautiful ballet girls or tableaux artists but women designated as freaks, an anti-reality, cordoned off as totally unacceptable to the "big top." One effect of this was to construct everyone else that performed therein, all the marchers and standers as well as the highly skilled equestrians and aerialists, as much more a part of the American normal.

Freaks had exhibited since the Renaissance, but it was not until the nineteenth century that an expanding middle class in increasingly urban centers, with shorter work weeks and more disposable income, helped to create their widespread popularity (R. Adams 11). P.T. Barnum perhaps best understood this fascination with difference, which he mined first at his museums, with Joyce Heth, presented as the nurse of George Washington and over 160 years old; the Fiji Mermaid; Chinese Siamese twins; and then General Tom Thumb, his wedding to Lavinia Warren widely publicized as well as his performance for Queen Victoria. At Barnum's museum and many others, in niches on the sides of a large room, crowds generally saw little people like Tom Thumb as well as a fat lady, albino girl, living skeleton, and giant. Gawking at such wondrous human beings, like watching impossibly exotic and beautiful women in parades and tableaux, provided family entertainment.

As museum acts moved into other venues in the late nineteenth century, the niches generally appeared in sideshows. "Sideshow" was a new word for the period. In the late nineteenth century, the word first meant a minor issue or subordinate matter. P.T. Barnum, himself, used the term in that way in 1855, in his autobiography, to describe his business dealings: "In attending to what might be termed my 'side shows,' or temporary enterprises, I have never neglected the American Museum" ( 344). According to the *Oxford English Dictionary,* the term appeared in 1884 in *Dickens's Dictionary of London,* edited by Charles Dickens, Jr., to mean an entertainment separate from a main show, with a separate admission.

These sideshows starring freaks soon appeared at the new amusement parks. When Dreamland at Coney Island opened in 1904, it featured a Midget City, a village built to scale for three hundred. Dreamland burned in 1911, but it was built back as the Dreamland Circus Sideshow, with ten-in-one attractions, ten freaks to see for one admission, going continuously all day, the whole taking forty-five minutes to an hour for a full viewing, a site similar to the niche room at a museum. By 1915, as many as 30,000 people came each day to see the constantly changing attractions.

With the backing of Barnum and other promoters, soon the greatest number of freaks traveled with circuses and carnivals. Especially before the first world war, ten-in-ones and other varieties of freak shows were hugely popular, their success assured by publicity. And whether the freak was a "born freak," with a perceived physical difference, like a woman with a beard, or a "made freak," like a woman with tattoos, popularity involved the right props and the careful weaving of a story. As circus historian Robert Bogdan has written, even the entertainers with "blatant physical and mental differences" needed to be "packaged to exaggerate and enhance their abnormalities in ways that made them attractions" ("Circassian Beauties" 22).

Theories abounded throughout the twentieth century concerning the attraction of all types of well-marketed freaks. In the late nineteenth century, the freak show defended itself as existing in a middle ground between scientific investigation and mass entertainment. In promotional pamphlets and talks, supposed doctors, explorers, politicians, and royalty testified to the freaks' authenticity and import, rendering this voyeurism semi-appropriate even for the middle class, for women and children as well as men (R. Adams 28).

But certainly the attraction did not simply involve educational opportunity. In the early twentieth century as today, analysts claimed that viewers experienced an improvement in their own self-image when they viewed supposedly inferior human beings. An article in the *Nation* in 1931 maintained that the circus freak could make the viewer feel normal and thus safe: "And the sideshows! Here is the boldest, the crudest, the most canny form of showmanship. We are all cripples of a sort. Each carries about with him the knowledge of some defect. One is too plump, another is not beautiful enough, one is too tall, another too short. The ugliest man in the world, the fattest woman, the bearded lady, the giant, and the pigmy — these extremes induce a sense of normality beyond words soothing to the human spirit" ("In the Driftway," Mar. 1931, 272).

As Rachel Adams claimed in *Sideshow USA* in 2001, freaks introduce the comforting fiction that there is a permanent difference between normality and deviance, but they also fascinate and attract as deviants (6). As Leslie Fiedler maintains similarly, "all freaks are perceived to one degree or another as erotic"; they provide a "flirtation with the abject realm where the human and nonhuman collide" (137).

This popularity, whatever its cause or causes, made an industry out of finding and "training" freaks. Since "the supply must be kept up," as an article on sideshows from 1897 noted, "there are men traveling in outlandish parts who yearn after inconceivable monstrosities, human and animal, as if their lives depended on the finding of them" (FitzGerald 521). Since finding the sought after physical abnormalities was not always possible, circus owners and trainers also recruited locals to feign them.

In the early 1900s, critics began looking at this freak showing as inhumane, at freakishness as disease or disability, as in a 1908 *New York Medical Journal* article reprinted in *Scientific American*, which gave anatomical explanations for "pathological rarities." These victims of "a gaping and unsympathetic crowd," this study maintained, were more properly seen as "a valuable subject of study for the scientific physician, which may add to our knowledge of development of normal types " ("Circus and Museum Freaks"). In response to such articles and resulting protests, freaks didn't appear with Barnum & Bailey from 1908 to 1913. But such criticism ultimately did not stop circus goers from wanting freaks as part of the circus experience: with other circuses keeping them, Barnum brought them back ("The Passing"). While the *New York Times* had proclaimed the death of sideshows in 1911, it also covered their return in 1913, part of a nostalgic, always similar circus ("The Circus Freak Seen").

Many of these extreme, designated freakish bodies were of course those of women, out beyond definitions of middle-class American normality, as distinct and worthy of view as those of the most beautiful. These women freaks were the subject of the male and female gaze, possessing a "strong visual and erotic impact" that Laura Mulvey labeled as "*to-be-looked-at-ness*" (715). And abnormalities, what counted and what didn't as freakish, certainly reflected gender prejudice. George Moore, for example, provided an example of a common male type, the Living Skeleton. He came from Helena, Montana, having joined a circus there at age twenty-one, choosing a life on the road instead of a future in his father's dry goods store. In the sideshow, he boxed against Fred Howe, much shorter and called The Fat Man. Moore was 6 ft. 3 in., and he weighed ninety-seven pounds at the time of their boxing; sharing the ring with the 4 ft. 2 in. and 422 pound Howe allowed Moore to appear as more of an extreme (FitzGerald 526). While such skeleton men were common, women generally did not appear as skeletons in freak shows. (Perhaps no woman could be too thin in the United States.) The individual freakish choices that were available for women all came with specific readings of gender: of what was sexual, forbidden, repulsive—and thus fascinatingly abnormal.

## Fat Ladies

There may not have been skeleton women, but there certainly were fat women, generally referred to as Fat Ladies, many more than fat men, a form of inappropriateness worthy of exhibiting. Such depictions revealed fascination with excesses of the female corpus: hideous perhaps, but hard to turn away from.

These women were part of a group appearing in almost every circus, often sitting in a ten-in-one with little people or skeleton men as though married, to create a contrast and thus hint at oddities of sexual matching and behavior. The lecturer generally inflated the woman's weight, called attention to her arms or thighs, and proffered jokes about the chairs that she had broken. If the manager felt that the woman was not large enough, he might bring in extra padding to create greater girth for the show.

Titillating sexual abnormality could arise not just from the fat lady's supposed husband, but from her child. Fat ladies often appeared with little persons pretending to be their children. In the case of Madam Carver, such a twosome was real. She did not begin exhibiting as a fat lady until after her son Willis, a little person, was old enough to join her, and they enjoyed a successful career. As her autobiographical manuscript states, she was born in New Britain, Connecticut, and went to Kansas with her husband where they embarked on a hard farming life: "A five-dollar bill did your soul good to see it, let alone to own it" (3). Her son weighed just a pound and a half at birth: "He was so small we were almost afraid to touch him" (4). They began exhibiting together when he was twelve, working at first for Dan Rice's Floating Opera House and then with Pullman & Hamilton Circus and the Sells Bros. Circus. As publicity reported, her "456 pounds compel her to use two chairs when gracefully reclining. This lady is married and is the mother of a midget son who is 15 years old and but 29 inches high, and who acts like a protector of his delicate mamma" (Anderson, "General Willis Carver"). As she says in her autobiographical manuscript describing the public construction of their appearance, "Wherever the General has appeared he has the reputation of being the smallest and most perfect man in form and feature ever placed on exhibition, and the mother among the heaviest ladies before the public, her weight being 456 pounds" (8). She was part of a special congress of fat ladies at the Chicago InterOcean Museum in 1885, joined there by her son, who as he aged sometimes also exhibited as her husband.

In these exhibits, though some fat ladies appeared with (supposed) husbands and children, noteworthy for their contrast in size, they were also depicted as childlike and jolly, silly and a bit dumb. They often wore short skirts, polka dotted dresses, and puffed sleeves; they might lick a lollypop or sit in a large version of a high chair. Their stage names reflected this depiction. Ruth Pontico, fat lady, who died in 1941 at Tampa, Florida, at age thirty-seven, was known as "Baby Ruth," her weight exaggerated in advertisements and pamphlets. She was employed during her career in carnivals as well as circuses. Other women employed "Baby" or "Jolly," creating stage names like Jolly Babe, Jolly Eva, Jolly Mabelle, Baby Betty, and Baby Irene ("Fat People").

In making excess weight into freakishness, circus sideshows told a cautionary tale, of an abnormality that kept women from becoming normal wives and mothers. These women remained as jolly children or they entered into embarrassing adult relationships, with husbands and children way too thin or small: the audience could thus see who might want such women and what they might produce if they had sex. Such stereotypical views of the fat lady's personality or marriage prospects also existed outside the sideshow tent, but inside of it everything became so much more poignant.

## Giants

Another nightmare prospect for women involved not just too many inches around but too many inches tall, causing them to tower over the majority of men. Men exhibited as giants, but the crowds, and thus the large salaries, more frequently followed women, who were much more inappropriate at a tremendous size.

Madam Carver exhibited as both giant and fat lady, but others of a thinner and taller nature took on the sole appellation of giant. Ella Ewing, reports of her height varying from 7 ft. 6 in. to 8 ft. 4 in., exhibited in world's fairs, in 1892 in Chicago and in 1904 in St. Louis, and then with Ringling Bros., with Buffalo Bill, and later with local shows. With the headline of "Ella Ewing, the Missouri Giantess," she appeared in a large canvas portrait advertised as Ringling Bros.' featured freak in 1907. The barker called out, "Come in and see the tall girl from Mizzoura. Only 10 cents, one dime! The tallest person on earth today. Ringling Brothers' greatest sideshow" (Chasteen 78). When spectators paid their dime and entered the tent, they saw Ewing first seated in a niche that combined chairs and tables, some suited to her size and some much too small; then she stood along with little persons to create a contrast and thus emphasize her height (Smith and Naunheim). The patter concentrated on the size that gave her a life as someone's daughter, kind to her parents, part of a rural world in which she read, played guitar, made butter, and milked cows, but inappropriate as someone's wife, too tall to be chosen. Other women had busy lives performing as giants and as giant fat ladies, such as Madame Cortina, with the Sell Brothers Circus in the 1880s, who often posed alone or with little people, the emphasis being either on the giant's lack of a married life or participation in an inappropriate one (Mitchell 86). As Barnum and Bailey clown Uncle Bob Sherwood commented in his autobiography, about the exhibition of a giant/fat lady with the skeleton man: "The question is often asked, 'Are normal children born from these strange unions?'" (107).

## Little People

Among the women seemingly not meant to be, beyond the realm of the normal and thus appropriate for placement in a niche, sideshows presented the too fat and too tall, and also those who were too short. Male little people often worked as clowns, their sudden appearance providing shock and fun. In the often repeated Safe Gag, for example, a clown of average height wearing a burglar's mask attempts to open a safe. Frustrated by the effort, he attaches a huge stick of dynamite to it and backs away. When it explodes, a little person dressed as a policeman pops out and chases the clown out of the ring (Gobin 86–87). Though male little people often appeared in the big top with the clown troupe, female little people did not. This aberrant sort of woman was only to be seen in the sideshow.

Like fat ladies, little people appeared as children or as part of inappropriate adult couplings. They often dressed in gingham and petticoats, wearing Mary-Jane shoes, and exhibited with names like "Dolly." These women could often be found in niches with giants and skeleton men to create a contrast. Mock weddings also provided an extra to advertise.

With little people suspended somewhere between child and adult, customers also had a fascination with watching them do seemingly normal things, a trend from amusement parks reiterated on a smaller scale within sideshows. When the amusement park Dreamland at Coney Island opened in 1904, it had a Midget City, built to scale for three hundred. The city, built as a replica of fifteenth-century Nuremberg, had everything from a theater to beach lifeguard towers to a Midget City Fire Department that responded hourly to false alarms. To accentuate the little people's size, giants walked the area (Stanton). At the 1933-34 Century of Progress World's Fair in Chicago, the Midget Village, designed after the ancient walled city of Dinkelspiehl in Bavaria, contained a small council chamber, jail, mayor's office, Eagle Hotel, and telegraph office as well as a full-size theatre. The Flora Dora Sextette, taking a name from a famous Broadway play and group of chorines, appeared regularly there (Roth and Cromie 136). Many of the seventy-two residents went on to the San Diego International Exposition, opening in 1935 with a Midget Village and a Midget Farm.

Cut-down versions of such homes and businesses also appeared in circus sideshows, with niches made to resemble living rooms and offices. There patrons might not be seeing activities that were especially abnormal: the abnormality lay in the fact that these people, too small to partake of full humanity, insisted on electing mayors, sending telegrams, and cooking supper. Here in an inside view, spectators watched an imitation of human life, a lesser version of it, amazing in the fact that it took place at all. The viewer is certainly the voyeur here, the gaze involving a high degree of intimacy — focused on women not meant to be seen in regular homes and towns. "How odd it is that they try to be like us," the spectator seems expected to say.

Some little people did variety acts to extend the crowd's interest in them, following the example of Lavinia Warren, born in Middleboro, Massachusetts, in 1841. After traveling with her cousin, who launched a floating museum of "curiosities" on western rivers, she began performing with her husband, Tom Thumb — songs, dances, impersonations, and dramatic skits — while conversing with patrons. Additionally, she worked with a magician, doing sleight of hand, advertised as a "mini-prestidigitateur." She also worked as a ventriloquist and had a trained bird act. The couple appeared in circuses, which she didn't like, but more frequently in halls, museums, and later in vaudeville theatres (Magri 10–38). Other little people followed her example to increase their entertainment value, appearing in sideshow acts in which they danced and sang, often like children. Daisy Earles, who toured with the Buffalo Bill Show in 1922, went to Ringling in 1926 along with Dolly Kramer, a German advertised as Queen of the Midgets. They sang and danced in a sideshow act with Ringling until 1956 and then with the Cristiani Circus for two years. Harry Doll appeared with women advertised as his sisters, Grace, Daisy, and Tiny, with Ringling Bros. for many years, also singing and dancing (Roth and Cromie 97). Daisy, her real name Hilda Emma Schneider, a native of Germany, came to the United States in 1922 and toured with Ringling Bros. and Barnum & Bailey for forty years. Some little people who appeared in circuses had also toured with the Leo Singer Midgets, a vaudeville troupe formed in Vienna that came to the United States at the outbreak of World War I.

Little women, appearing at the circus just in the sideshow, shocked viewers by size alone. Here was another group not within the realm of normal for American women, worthy of view only where oddities reigned, odd to see just sitting in a chair or just standing in a mock kitchen, their assumption of home and town life beyond the acceptable. The inappropriate size marked this woman as another instance of continuing childhood or another type of inappropriate bride, not eligible for normal womanhood.

## Bearded Ladies

Women who were too big, in weight or height, or too small, seemed to earn the astonished gaze; their size made them so inappropriate that they were worthy of niches at the sideshow. The Bearded Lady was another common exhibitor, an expected part of any ten-in-one. Even more than the giant, fat lady, or little person, the bearded woman seemed to step outside of regular roles for women, as someone either too modern or pre-civilized to be tolerated except as something at which to stare. Within this category very different stereotypes arose for white women and women of color, constructing them as the worst of the future and the past.

From the middle of the nineteenth century, the bearded white woman exhibited as evidence that political and social changes were leading to terrifying consequences. In the early 1850s, Josephine Fortune Clofullia, born in Switzerland, appeared in private exhibition rooms across the United States, beginning in Boston at Armory Hall: "There has not been for years so great a curiosity to be seen in Boston," declared a local journal, "and we are told that it is found difficult at times to accommodate the large concourse of persons who throng the hall to behold the bearded lady." Curiosity concerned gender trouble, as Judith Butler might label the subject: Clofullia's beard and appearance were deemed "remarkable departures from the laws of nature." The writer claims further that women's rights societies, like those that had met in Seneca Falls in 1848, would be interested in her appearance: "Heavens forefend," he comments, for "here is a member of their sex who out Herods Herod; not content with claiming the right to vote" but also "laying siege" to a distinctive trait of men ("The Bearded Lady" 268). This white bearded lady thus drew crowds not just because of a physical abnormality; her presence indicated what could happen as women stepped out from the True Womanhood lauded in the nineteenth century. The beard represented all that was unnatural about the modern woman who attempted to appropriate the most basic qualities of men.

In the twentieth century, scientific experts claimed that a woman's beard resulted from inappropriate changes that women were making to American social life and thus to the perquisites of men. "Bobbed Hair Brings Beards," from the *New York Times* in July 1924, claims that all women leaving home would soon be affected by the hirsuteness deemed by scientists to be resulting from the assumption of unnatural public roles and aggressiveness: "The women of the future may have longer beards than the bearded women of the circus today, in the opinion of Dr. Adolph Heilbron, if they continue the invasion of man's domain of activities." The *Times* quotes the *Berliner Morgenpost*, a German newspaper, in which Heilbron cited other anthropologists to increase his authority: Heilbron contends, American readers learn via the *Times*, that the number of bearded women had increased dramatically and that "families wherein generations of women bob their hair will develop bearded women as a parallel phenomenon." The New-Woman or Flapper attribute of bobbed hair, a departure from traditional values, was thus engendering much more extreme abnormalities.

Annie Jones, born in Virginia in 1865, was one of the first bearded New Women appearing in a circus sideshow instead of exhibition halls, an economic asset to her family in hard times. Soon circuses and carnivals commonly employed such women as representatives of the worst of modern life.

The popularity of such acts may have influenced Jane Barnell, born in 1871, who joined the John Robinson's Circus sideshow in 1892. But as a darker woman, with Indian blood, her beard would be used not as evidence of her New Woman status but of something else: here was woman existing completely outside of—or before—cultural control: a jungle gorilla. According to later accounts, during her childhood in Wilmington, North Carolina, when her father was out of town, Barnell's mother sold her bearded four-year-old daughter to the Great Family Orient Circus and Menagerie, a mud show with horse-drawn wagons. When this group merged with a larger show, Barnell was taken abroad, working in circuses as well as at city aquariums as the missing link, her beard growing to thirteen inches. In 1884, at the Berlin Aquarium, this troupe proposed to put her in with real apes but local authorities wouldn't allow it. When she fell ill in Berlin, the show managers left her in an orphanage, from which she later returned to the United States. When she was working on her grandmother's farm, she met a circus strongman who invited her to join John Robinson's Circus. At that time her beard was thirteen inches long. In 1903, at age twenty-seven, using the name "Johanna, the Live (Human) Gorilla," she began traveling with Barnum & Bailey, displayed next to an actual ape (Burrows).

Those bearded ladies with fuller beards and even darker skin appeared as a much more dangerous Other, a throwback to an earlier time, something more elemental and sub-human than even Johanna, the Live (Human) Gorilla. This darkened bearded woman, the beard and skin color either real or false, could be advertised by the lecturer and pamphlet as an exemplum of evolutionary theory. In his last letter to rival Herbert Spencer, Charles Darwin spoke of a "missing link" between man and ape, which would prove his theory of humans' evolutionary descent from apelike ancestors. Entertainment entrepreneurs seized on the idea of the missing link and sought a variety of hairy individuals with which they could sell acts and make money. Perhaps the most famous of these exhibitors was Krao, a Thai girl born around 1872 in Laos. She had a short beard along with a thin layer of coarse black hair that covered her body from head to toe, and she was also endowed with supernumerary teeth and hyperextensible joints. Scouts for showman G.A. Farini brought Krao to him when he sought to top Barnum's success with a Burmese hairy family. Farini exhibited Krao, eleven years old, at the Royal Aquarium at Westminster in London in 1882 and brought her to New York the following year for a dime museum tour, beginning at Philadelphia's Chestnut Street Dime Museum. In 1885 she left the museum circuit and went on tour with John B. Doris' New Mammoth Shows, a Midwestern circus, as part of the menagerie and sideshow, a star as the Missing Link (Anderson, "Krao Farini"). Given her success as an exhibitor, many sideshows featured dark women, with real or fake beards and with real or fake body hair, as biological rarity, as missing link.

The bearded white woman appeared to represent much that Americans feared by the end of the century, especially the new feminist — sporting a physical demonstration of all the trouble she might cause to men. This woman might be moving beyond cultural control in new and dangerous ways. And with the darker bearded women, sideshows claimed that women's most out-of-control tendencies reached back to pre-civilization, to the terrifying realities of women before cultural morés — and men — could get them under control.

## Strong Women

Another freak of the circus, another crossover that could shock, was the strong woman. Here again, an exhibitor terrified viewers in her unnatural assumption of a basic attribute of men.

While strong men generally lifted huge weights and pieces of equipment in their sideshow niches, these out-of-bounds women often lifted much smaller men. Zittella Flynn, a strong woman in vaudeville shows and with Barnum & Bailey, came from London in 1887 to do an act in which she carried six men ("Miss Zittella Flynn"). Madame La Blanche appeared with the Howard Damon Big Show in 1909; Ada Bell Edwards, with Forepaugh-Sells in 1910: both hoisted men above their heads. Madame Sandwina, born Kate Brumbach in 1884 in Vienna, the daughter of strength performers, lifted circus workers over her head and challenged men in the sideshow crowd to beat her at lifting weights. She took on famous bodybuilder Eugene Sandow in a well-publicized competition. They lifted the same amounts of weight until Kate hoisted 300 pounds above her head with one hand; Sandow could only raise the weight to his chest, and Kate was declared the winner. Shortly afterwards Kate adopted the name Sandwina, a feminine derivative of "Sandow," to remind customers of her triumph against the strongest of men. In years of shows with Ringling Bros. and Barnum & Bailey, Sandwina pressed her husband above her head using one arm while also lifting horses, carousels, and cannons (Pednaud). She also performed in WPA-funded circuses in the 1930s, carrying her husband under her arm and lying on a bed of nails ("WPA Circus Performance").

As some strong women lifted men, they did so in the costume of a dominatrix or goddess. Babette Tyana Brumbach, who trained as a strong woman in her family's famous European circus, came to New York from Germany in 1905 to perform with Ringling Brothers and with Barnum & Bailey (Frega 43). Billed as Mademoiselle Tyana, The Earth's Strongest Woman, she bent steel bars and drove nails through thick boards with her bare hands, lifted with her feet as many as ten men seated on a board, and hoisted a baby elephant weighing

500-plus pounds several inches off of the floor. She performed while wearing a provocative and domineering costume, of black boots, tights, and leotard with a huge feather over her head and a satin cape (Frega 51). Strength acts often deliberately invoked mythic women as separate from the normal. Sandwina appeared as Juno in a Roman chariot as well as Catherine the Great, in acts in which, oddly enough given the historical themes, cars drove across her body (Tait 38–39).

At the beginning of the twentieth century, as a woman carried her husband or lifted ten men or competed with a man in a weightlifting contest, she was certainly demonstrating dangerous and inappropriate gender traits. At a time when cities were growing and fewer women worked on farms, this strength was not what women should be able or willing to demonstrate: thus a shocking sight indeed.

## Tattoo Artists

Along with the woman who was too tall, small, strong, fat, male-like, or uncivilized, the marked, tattooed woman was a mainstay at the circus sideshow. The tattooed woman, who exhibited very differently from the tattooed man, represented another type of inappropriateness that generally remain hidden: the victim of abuse and rape. In the sideshow tent, these women did not tell their own stories. Instead, a pseudo-explorer or barker wove tales of violence and degradation that could enthrall the crowd with where women should not have been and what no normal women, living appropriately within their homes and towns, would ever have to endure.

At first, tattooed men acquainted viewers with this ancient art of native Americans and other peoples. In the 1880s, P.T. Barnum promoted Georg Constantine, whose 388 elaborate and artistic tattoos included, on his breast, two crowned sphinxes, two serpents, two swans, and one horned owl. Barnum called him Captain Constantinus, the Turk, or the Living-Picture Gallery, a term echoing a popular label for tableaux (Parry 59–61).

By 1920, hundreds of fully tattooed people traveled in circuses and sideshows. As this art form garnered interest, female tattoo artists, especially young and pretty ones, quickly became more popular than men: revealing their tattoos led to their appearing almost naked. They thus created "a sensational double whammy onstage — a peep show within a freak show," as described by Margot Mifflin in *Bodies of Subversion: A Secret History of Women and Tattoo* (18). A popular song "The Tattooed Lady," which originated in England but was adapted in the United States with special words, testified to the detailed gazing that tattooing encouraged: "All up and down her spine / Was the King's horse guard in line, / And all about her hips / Was a line of battleships, / And over one kidney /Was a bird's-eye view of Sidney, / But what I liked best, / Across her chest / Was my home in Tennessee" (Parry 68).

To attract and shock crowds, women presented many detailed inkings that juxtaposed the most basic of social values to their inked skin. In the 1890s, Emma de Burgh emphasized patriotism and religion, with an American eagle on one knee, the Union Jack on the other, and Da Vinci's *The Last Supper* on her back (Mifflin 22). In the 1920s, Anna Gibbons, exhibiting under the name Artoria, sported a baby Jesus, a Madonna, Botticelli's *The Annunciation,* and Michelangelo's *The Holy Family with St. John the Baptist.* She also had a portrait of George Washington between her breasts.

Many of these tattoo artists used exotic stage names that reflected the subject matter of some of their tattoos. Serpentina had scales; Lady Viola sported six presidents, Babe

Ruth, Charlie Chaplin, and a violin. La Bella Angora had boot laces, and the beginning of angora socks, inked onto her ankles. Dyita Salome displayed herself as "the one and only oriental beauty tattooed in 14 colours" (Mifflin 25).

To enhance an exhibitor's attraction, a barker or "explorer," but not the woman herself, often told involved fictional tales of sexual violence that made the tattooed woman into an exotic victim, as seldom occurred with tattooed men. Tattooing stories often concerned a woman who had been mistreated or raped, the tattoos a mark of her use by inappropriate savage men.

Some stories involved the markings as an indicator that the woman had been under attack but ultimately not ruined. Nora Hildebrandt arrived at Bunnell's Museum in New York in 1882 and later worked in various circuses, boasting 365 designs and claiming to have been tattooed by her father after being captured by "red skin devils," including Sitting Bull. At shows, she sold a fabricated memoir with the following tale of the tattooing as her salvation from these savages:

> One of Sitting Bull's warriors accused him [Nora's father, the two then in captivity] of trying to poison them, and the chief told the prisoner if he would tattoo his daughter he would give him his liberty — that he must tattoo her from her toes to her head.... She was tied to a tree and the painful operation commenced. He was compelled to work six hours a day for one year before she was rescued, accomplishing three hundred and sixty-five designs [Mifflin 18].

As a white woman, she had been marked emotionally and socially by being with these warriors, then marked physically before she and her father could return to the regular world, tattooed to ultimately please and save her father as well as herself but with markings that wouldn't leave her (Mifflin 18).

Many other stories concerned rape and domination of American white women by primitive dark men. These tales appealed for pity and denounced, while making mysterious and powerful, the savages that caused the disfigurement. The narrative used for May Brooks and Annie Howard, with Barnum & Bailey in the 1880s, had them journeying from Pennsylvania to the Pacific, where they were supposedly shipwrecked and then abducted by some indefinite form of island savages who tattooed every inch of them as an indicator of ownership. In some routines, such as Olive Oatman's, women were even seen behind screens, supposedly being tattooed against their will, a re-enactment of this violation ("Olive Oatman").

Other presentations were more humorous but still involved woman as object or victim. One sideshow story concerned an exhibitor who had supposedly been donning temporary tattoos every Monday through Friday for carnival and circus work. One week, in revenge for being jilted, as the story told by the barker attested, her lover chose permanent tattoos that he stamped on her back as on a box: Keep Dry, Very Fragile, Handle with Care, Strictly Private, and This Side Up (Parry 64). After the barker finished her story, she revealed all these signs to the crowd. Although here was a crazy, comic tale, it again concerned the marking as domination, this time by an American man seeking revenge for a woman's unfaithfulness.

In the exhibition of tattooed women, customers again witnessed women outside of traditional controls, supposedly left to marauding men in a bigger world beyond middle-class homes and conventions. Viewers especially flocked to tattooed performers who were attractive, young white women, much more so than to minorities or to men. For whatever violent reasons that the barker might graphically describe, they had been forced to live and sleep with savages. Although they had been rescued, they had been permanently marked by exotic abuse and rape.

## Circassian Beauties

Circassian Beauties, another popular sideshow act, featured the same themes as tattoo artists, of lesser and dangerous foreigners raping white women. The Circassian narrative involved savage Turks as rapists of the most utterly pure. Here was a complete fabrication involving racial purity and violence, a freak created by Barnum in the 1860s that became popular across the circus world (Robert Bogdan, "Circassian Beauties" 22).

This exhibit type stemmed from theories of white superiority. Johann Friedrich Blumenbach, a monogenist theorist of race, claimed that the "Caucasian," a term he introduced in 1795, was the pure race from which all others had been a degeneration, and that the purest version of that race occurred in the Caucasus Mountains, in a tribe with the whitest of skin and even white skulls, the "autochthones of Mankind" (269). P.T. Barnum made up tales concerning the perfect women of this race, direct descendents of Eve: they had been stolen by marauding Turks but rescued by Barnum's agents from slave markets and harems in Turkey. Circus barkers could thus intertwine appealing extremes, preparing viewers to see the purest of women and of whiteness, only made available to the American circus after purportedly entering the harem world of exotic Turkey, a tale of the worst sort of domination of the most pure.

In sideshows, including Barnum's, these women all seem to have actually been Americans, their markers being very white skin, big frizzy dark hair, and harem outfits, their stage names exotic choices such as Zoe Meleke and Zola Zolene. As historian Linda Frost pointed out, the big frizzy head of hair only complicated the presentation since it did not actually represent any trait of Eurasian mountain women but instead of African Americans and thus this presentation created various frightening mixtures of light and dark, purity and impurity (56–85). This group lost its appeal by 1910, many practitioners becoming snake charmers and mind readers to keep their circus jobs.

Like women with tattoos, but without any actual physical oddity, Circassian Beauties continued the fascination with the rape of white women, in this instance the whitest of the white. The telling of the tale alone imaginatively initiated the act, by combining the most frightening of male foreigners with the most pure of virgins.

## Other Dark and Exotic Foreigners

Although Circassian Beauties exhibited as the best of whiteness, almost all other exhibited foreigners symbolized the frightening, pre-civilized world, including types of women well beyond the overly tall or short, the bearded, or even the raped. In "ethnological congresses," circus goers encountered womanhood to be stared at and judged, avoided outside of the sideshow tent, as only semi-human and therefore terrifying.

Like Krao, many other exotic peoples were owned and exhibited by circuses as well as menageries and zoos. Circus agents traveled to find women and men from foreign lands, especially those with what Westerners deemed to be disfigured bodies, to create the shock of the new and exotic that pseudo-experts could describe in pseudo-scientific tones. Especially in smaller circuses, Americans often filled in as exotic, marked foreigners: makeup darkened European and white American women; exhibitors added disfiguring humps and scars. Phony Zulus were common in sideshows along with phony Borneo aborigines and head-hunters.

These exhibitions placed people from other countries in what were presumably "native" costumes and settings, with "professors" or pamphlets to explain them, thus creating an educational veneer that made such exhibits more acceptable, in sideshows and within cages in the big top. The stories that "experts" told included cannibalism, human sacrifices, head hunting, and polygamy. Producers generally created jungle-like settings, especially when the cast was truly from New Jersey, props helping to create the sense of strangeness and fear necessary for the impact sought. These presentations emphasized the culturally strange, the primitive, the bestial, the exotic — supposedly from darkest Africa, the wilds of Borneo, Turkish harems, and Aztec kingdoms. Here was the exoticism of disfigured jungle women, in various stages of undress, caged with jungle men, there to be ogled.

A sure innovator in this business was P.T. Barnum, in his museums and then circuses. The Barnum and London Circus presented its first ethnological congress in 1886. Barnum's display of Ubangis featured women with distended lips and men without them, accompanied by a sham professor who explained their culture to viewers, emphasizing that this disfigurement kept women safe from raping marauders (J. Davis 134). As the "expert" spoke, the Ubangis stood still, creating a tableau. Following Barnum's lead, other circuses came to have both real and sham versions of the ethnological congress, with authenticity prohibitively expensive for many shows.

This circus ownership of human beings stirred controversy — and, of course, audience fascination. A *Times* reporter, in a story in 1913 about Claude Hamilton, a sideshow owner, described the exotic Obongos, a vague name for Congo pygmies of Upper Welle River, Equatorial Africa. The reporter cites such ownership of human beings as part of a tradition "remembered by those of us who are out of youngsterhood." In 1907, Hamilton had bought these people from a failing show in Key West and brought them to Barnum & Bailey as the least of humanity, the *Times* reporter reiterating the harsh judgments of the show's pamphlets: "The Obongos are scientifically described as being a race of dwarfed negroes, having their home somewhere near the equatorial line in Africa, and being among the very lowest of the human race, not only in stature but in civilization" ("The Circus Freak").

The article describes Rhynie and Seam, a man and woman, about whom the reporter, referring to himself as "the *Times* man," evidences a sense of absurdity and superiority. He comments that the caged pair do not speak English and are not expected to speak intelligently in any language. They "did not talk for themselves, their only vocalizations being grunts and derisive ejaculations, both of them apparently having come to the understanding that the *Times* man was not of their liking." As the interview continues, Hamilton as "owner" describes his purchase of these people and doesn't appear to understand any questions about their right to pay or freedom:

"I bought them in 1907 in Key West from a show that was half starved. I bought the entire outfit, including these two dwarfs."

"How much a week do you pay them?"

"I paid a thousand dollars for them."

"No," explained the reporter, "you don't understand me. How much do you pay the dwarfs a week?"

"Pay them!" exclaimed Hamilton in surprise. "I pay them nothing; they belong to me."

"How do you keep them satisfied, then?" asked *The Times* man.

"Why, they are just like animals; keep their stomachs full and keep them warm and they are satisfied." Then he added quickly.

"There is just this difference between them and animals: We've got to give them so much liquor every night. 'Rhynie' takes gin, 'Seam' whiskey. If they did not get this regular allowance they would sulk and be ugly."

Hamilton criticizes these two exhibited "creatures" for only having learned the vices of civilization, and none of its virtues, since they want to be drunk all the time. He calls them lazy, just like monkeys: "Why, they won't even keep themselves clean. We have a colored maid that gives them a bath every morning." But, though Hamilton judged Rhynie and Seam as ignorant and lazy, he did recognize that given any opportunity they might react violently to imprisonment and attempt to escape: "You've got to treat them like monkeys, keep them in their place, or they are apt to forget themselves and bang you on the head with a club" ("The Circus Freak").

In these exhibits, as in the *National Geographic,* racial color often determined the degree of nudity deemed appropriate for display. Dark skin and a lack of clothing, even exposed breasts, characterized the "lady savage," available for extended perusal since the audience was seemingly attending a scientific demonstration (J. Davis 185). Such displays were of course erotic as well as instructional. In 1930, pamphleteers and exhibitors spoke about various views of beauty as they concentrated on "eight duck-lipped women" then with Ringing Bros. and Barnum & Bailey. The women's lips created "a duck-bill effect which is greatly prized among the younger set," the barker said, as he compared the woman with the biggest disk to Miss America: "In fact, Kananinbongo is entitled to be called Miss Ubangi because her disk is 8 inches in diameter" ("African Beauties"). Barkers also enjoyed telling tales of male domination and violence toward women. Barnum & Bailey advertised Americans Johanna and Moko as a cannibal man and his mate — "the *weirdest, wildest* specimens of monstrosity ever secured alive," from the jungles of Central Africa, discovered by Dr. Livingstone. The lecturer discussed Moko as a bloodthirsty primitive scoundrel, his violence extending to his mate: "His wife does all the work — should she refuse, she is tied hand and foot, and left to starve in a dark cave, or be devoured by wild animals. Moko, the Wild Man, will now sing for you his war song" (Sherwood 118).

In these sideshows, visitors might secure physical contact for an additional fee. Sold along with an exhibit of the "Giraffe-Neck Women from Burma" in 1933 was a five-cent pamphlet where readers could find out why they wore neck rings and what results of x-rays of their necks revealed (Bary). If they paid another nickel or dime, they could come up to touch the rings and hear more insider details. The handler would force the women to open their mouths and then comment not just on their necks but on their brown teeth: "They walk around in bare brown feet and are rather pretty until they smile. They chew betel nut" ("Burma Ladies").

Dark foreigners seemed worthy not just of the sideshow tent but of cages. They drew crowds when they were not just dark but disfigured, marked beyond tattoos. In their looks as well as the sexual and violent tales told about them, they represented the worst of what the world had to offer, well beyond the securities of middle-class America.

## Real Disabilities

"Real" freaks had an additional cachet, were sought by shows that could afford to hire them. Though often faked physical disabilities enthralled the crowds, there were well-known women exhibitors whose carefully presented bodily differences placed them on the edge of what could or could not be considered human, fascinating in their bizarre looks and sexual possibilities.

Josephine Myrtle Corbin, born in 1868 in Lincoln County, Tennessee, was a dipygus, double from the waist down. Below her navel, she had two of everything, two pelvises and four legs. The infant created an immediate sensation in the local Tennessee newspapers, which discussed her examination by physicians and the notice paid by medical journals. When Myrtle was about five weeks old, her father William Corbin, a Civil War veteran who was money challenged, began to exhibit her. Over the next decade, Corbin took his daughter around the country, showing her at fairs, sideshows, and dime museums. When she was fourteen, her father secured a contract for her to appear with Barnum & Bailey at the unusually high salary of $250 per week. She spent the next few years as one of Barnum's most popular acts and then left in 1886, when she married. After her children reached adulthood, at the age of forty-one in 1909, she began appearing at Huber's Museum in New York, more than twenty years after she had last exhibited. She continued to perform with Ringling Brothers and appeared at Coney Island. Even with this physical oddity, she felt the need to work up a stage presentation to secure attention, using different colors of shoes for a "soft-shoe" dance ("Myrtle Corbin"). Throughout her career, pamphlets and barkers stressed her sexual and reproductive possibilities as well as her status as a documented American oddity.

Conjoined twins Millie-Christine, "the two-headed nightingale," were also among the highest priced freaks. Well promoted, they attracted 150,000 in Philadelphia at an eight-week museum stay and 10,000 in a single day in New York (McNamara 224). At age thirty, they began traveling with circuses, first Batcheller and Doris's Great Inter-Ocean Railroad Show in 1882, a show that impressed them for its salaries and clean image. They left that show for Barnum, where they sang duets while showing themselves on a revolving stage and skipping rope (Martell 112). They also added a polka dance to their routine, after which they sang in two-part harmony and played guitars (Mitchell 82). Like Corbin, they allowed discussion of their sexuality and even physical examination "by a committee selected from the audience" to extend their popularity with the sideshow crowd (Martell 207). They eventually bought and retired to the same plantation where they had lived as slaves before the Civil War (FitzGerald 521).

Like other circus stars, many of these freaks came to the United States from Europe for greater opportunities and higher wages. Mademoiselle Gabrielle Fuller, born in Basle, Switzerland, in 1884, first joined the circus at the Paris Exposition in 1900. She then came to the United States to appear with Ringling and with Coney Island's Dreamland sideshow. She had a perfectly formed upper body until just below the waist, where her body ended. She was famed for her beautiful corseted figure, always in traditional formal garb, and for the barker's discussion of how a husband compensated when he lived with a half-woman.

These freaks shocked because of their difference from the normal, but they also brought up sexual anomalies and fears, of highly deviant women, of what might be possible beyond your neighborhood or town. Here was disgust and attraction: an extreme example of the many types of women that should not be seen beyond the sideshow.

## Exotic Dancers

Many of the same women who stood in white make-up in tableaux during the day, marched in the parade or spec, or served as assistants to magicians, also appeared in the sideshow, especially in the evening, doing exotic dance movements that included shaking all over. Certainly these women caused men to find the circus an attractive choice, both in the day with their families and at night in the girlie shows. Though such dancers had no deformity, their unusual sideshow trait seemed to be their willingness to dance with wild abandon, clothed in spangles and little else, to entrance men as normal women presumably would not.

The sideshow dancer became especially famous through the hoochy-cooch. In Paris, at the International Exposition in 1889, an Algerian Village presented exotic dancers in native costumes. At the 1893 Chicago World's Fair, in The Streets of Cairo exhibit, a belly dancer appeared as Little Egypt, her real name supposedly Fahreda Mahzar Spyropolos. According to fair publicity, she was a native of Armenia. Competing newspaper articles, however, made her a native of several American and foreign cities, and some even argued that she was a man.

Within a year, hundreds of Little Egypts were starring in circus sideshows, with their own exotic names, like Little Zelika and Little Zelima, and men danced the part as Little Egypt in drag. The costumes remained vaguely oriental: a short bolero with coin decorations, a white chemise, harem pantaloons allowing the navel to be seen, and a wide sash. The dancer's hair hung loose over her shoulders, an outward indication of abandon (Sobel 57).

While many Little Egypts were touring, circus goers also enjoyed a new bad-girl dance sensation — the shimmy — one associated not with the foreign exotic, but with what was deemed perhaps the most dangerous of American Others, the sexual African American woman. This dance originated in Haitian voodoo ceremonies that ceded power to full-body trembling, an overall shake done in one place, similar to the Nigerian *shika*. These movements appeared in the American dance Shimmy Sha-Wabble around 1900, were mentioned in the popular song "The Bullfrog Hop" in 1908, and became common in African American saloons. As the shimmy dance craze spread, white women began to do this shimmying, with and without blackface.

Mae West first saw dancers doing this movement, as she wrote in her autobiography, in two African American jazz clubs in Chicago: "They got up from the tables, got out to the dance floor, and stood in one spot, with hardly any movement of the feet, and just shook their shoulders, torsos, breasts and pelvises. We thought it was funny and were terribly amused by it. But there was a naked, aching sexual agony about it too" (64). At the next day's matinee of Arthur Hammerstein's *Sometime,* about a touring theatrical troupe, she incorporated the dance into her routine "and perfected it again and again as an encore" (64). In the film *I'm No Angel,* in which West appeared as a sideshow dancer who became a tiger trainer for a higher income at a bigger circus, she was recreating powerful dance movements that had launched her own career.

This dance came quickly to the sideshow. Tiny Kline appeared as one of a row of shimmy-shakers in various circuses, in the Oklahoma Wild West Show, and at Coney Island. After the barker hawked their attributes, as Kline recalled, they would come quickly out in costumes "composed mostly of beads — lots of beads — hanging down in fringes from the chest and hips, the purpose of the beads to accentuate the movement of those parts." As soon as they lined up, they went into a quick shimmy act — "We were to come out, give 'em a flash, then scuttle back inside" — and then those that paid could go inside for the full routine (87).

In all of these designations as freaks, women appeared in a separate area: as too fat, tall, short, hairy, male, liberated, strong, marked, abused, uncivilized, deviant, or sexual.

This list of infractions made the exhibitors of educational but certainly also of prurient interest. These freaks thus provided an opposite of the ballet or tableau girls, the antithesis of beauty and majesty, placed in isolation, not within the big top, but equally worthy of viewing — as other exotic extremes of what women were capable of being.

With the most weird and unacceptable of women thus contained in separate niches, cages, and tents, they opened up the possibility for other working women at the circus to be considered as not quite so strange and abnormal. Certainly the gaze focused on sideshow exhibitors altered the judgment of how inappropriate the performers known for their skills, such as equestrians and aerialists, might be.

# CHAPTER 22

# The Silent Assistant
# and the Magic Act

Another act during which women stood silently at the circus involved magic. Though magic acts occurred more commonly in vaudeville halls, they also found their way into the big top. Certainly magicians could not do card tricks in a three-ringed circus, but they could present dramatic large movements. Done quickly, in broad strokes, at big distances, without dialogue, circus tricks included throwing knives, shooting assistants out of cannons, and making people and animals disappear. In sideshows, magicians could do similar tricks at a more intimate distance. In both the big top and the sideshow, these acts generally involved a pretty woman, vulnerable to attack; she was not just looked at, like a ballet or statue girl, but systematically subjected to stylized torture, as she alternately stood or lay down. She was quite visibly able to withstand the knives or saws and pop back up smiling at the end.

At the circus as well as in vaudeville halls, almost every starring magician was a man and every assistant a woman. The amount of clothes on the able assistants, whose real names are difficult to find in histories of magic, might vary with the time of day and the nature of the crowd. Dressed in a short skirt or a leotard, the ubiquitous female assistant was always sexual, pliable, and mysteriously re-formable, with a made-up partial name that might emphasize her attributes, such as Lovely Lola or Vivacious Viv.

For this occupation, carnivals, sideshows, and the big top constituted a step below vaudeville, providing a place where careers began. At seventeen, for example, Harry Houdini left his family to pursue his magic career. By the age of twenty, he had been performing at dime museums in Chicago and New York. He and his wife Bess Houdini then joined the Welsh Brothers' Circus for the 1895 season, touring eastern towns for twenty-five dollars a week, Bess doing mind-reading and Harry an escape from handcuffs and a trunk as well as a wild man act, "with Houdini growling and tearing at a bit of wild meat." He especially pleased the owner when he picked a lock and got the whole troupe out of jail after the cast had been arrested for performing on Sunday (Brandon 62–63). Circus goers had little patience for coins or cards or rabbits, for anything small — they liked Houdini's trunk escape better than his handcuffs — but they did appreciate Houdini's difficult escapes as well as his interaction with Bess as scantily dressed female assistant.

Other popular magic performances at the circus included quasi-violence aimed at the smiling assistant. Magicians placed a woman's head in a guillotine and caused it to fall, with a cabbage head then rolling away. They also put a woman's head into a box and pushed a flaming torch through it. Another oft repeated trick began with a woman standing across the stage or circus ring from her partner. Blindfolded or facing backwards, the magician threw knives at this woman as target, coming quite close to key body parts, acting shaky or drunk to build the tension. Another favorite involved a large vise in which a woman could be stretched and flattened.

Of all these potentially violent tricks, one of the most popular was sawing a woman in two. This illusion, described in Albert A. Hopkins' manual *Magic: Stage Illusions and Scientific Diversions* in 1897 and introduced in theatres by P.T. Selbit, dominated music halls, vaudeville theatres, circuses, and county fairs for several decades. The trick might involve one of several types of equipment: a box large enough to hold two similar looking women, one who went in and one who came out; a box in which a woman could avoid the path of the blade in a small area at one end while fake feet dangled out of the other end; or a trick blade that collapsed inside of the box and caused no damage. At the end of most versions of this trick, although not of all, the woman reappeared put back together; thus the violence ended in a miraculous reconstitution and reappearance. When famous magician Howard Thurston did the trick, both in vaudeville and with the Sells Brothers Circus, with special equipment built for a "bright cartoon version of a crime," he brought members of the audience up to hold the head and feet, which protruded throughout the entire trick (Steinmeyer 285). Then he began sawing; the lady screamed; and the volunteers fled the stage, as he had asked them to do. At the end, she came out unharmed and gestured grandly to the crowd.

Another popular magic trick which appeared to place women at physical risk involved an aerialist skilled at flying through the air as well as landing in a net. A Canadian, the Great Farini, invented the human cannonball. From a large cannon, seemingly loaded with gunpowder, he launched the first person, George Loyal, in 1875, the magician appearing to light the flame and the assistant to passively ride. Two years later, in 1877, a fourteen-year-old acrobat, Rosa Richter, appearing as Zazel, took off from one of Farini's cannons at the Royal Aquarium in London in a scarlet costume and pink tights (Gossard, *A Reckless Era* 104). First Farini asked for silence, and Zazel signaled her readiness "in a small, sweet voice." Then he seemed to light the powder, smoke issued out, and the key action began: "The next thing the audience saw was a flash of red flying from the cannon across the cavernous hall, where it landed squarely in a huge safety net. Frightened and enthralled, spectators held their breath until Zazel stood up and smiled" (Paquet 31). Zazel came to the United States two years later to be shot from the cannon in featured acts with the Yankee Robinson Circus, the Sparks Circus, and then Barnum & Bailey. In the United States, as in England, there was special power in the sight of a vulnerable young woman thus launched: men were much less commonly shot through space. But some of these projectiles were actually female impersonators, their opportunity coming from appearing as women. These performers included Lulu, Queen of the Trapezists, "a young man that had a feminine face and body and dressed like a girl," who beginning in the 1870s performed with the Howes and Cushing Circus ("Act: Thrill": Pfening, Jr., "Human Cannonballs" ).

Farini's early cannon made use of rubber springs to launch human cannonballs into the air, and the distances they could reach were fairly limited. By the 1920s, however, performers began relying on a new cannon that used compressed air and could launch a woman

Zazel, the Human Cannonball, at the muzzle of her cannon (Circus World Museum, Baraboo, Wisconsin).

all the way across a three-ringed tent. Magicians also added fire-crackers, and not just smoke, to create an extra layer of excite-ment and thus keep the act before the public through the years. Using this mechanism, Victoria Zacchini, called Miss Victory, The Human Projectile, worked in indoor circuses in Chicago into the 1940s.

While the cannon act might involve a circus aerialist, other magic acts engaged equestrians in odd appearances and disap-pearances. Early in her career, Dorothy Herbert worked with Howard Thurston, both in the circus and vaudeville. At the end of his act involving birds, rab-bits, and various props, Thurs-ton fired a gun, workers released a cloud of white smoke, and then a crate fell to the stage, leaving Herbert on a horse dangling in mid-air. "I never did quite un-derstand how the stunt worked," she later declared. One day, the crank that should have gotten the horse and rider down sud-denly broke: "There we hung, all through the third act. Needless to say, those below were nervous throughout the balance of the show. When the show was over, I was very happy to get back on the ground" ("Herbert's Horses" I. 9).

In magic acts presented in vaudeville halls and at the circus, making the pliable assistant disappear became fashionable by the beginning of the twentieth century. Joseph Buatier De Kolta created the original Vanishing Lady Illusion, which he performed first at the Egyptian Hall in London beginning in the 1880s. He began by unfolding a newspaper on the stage to convince the audience that there was no trapdoor and then positioned a chair on top of it. His female assistant sat on the chair, and he covered her with a long silk shawl. As he gestured, throwing his arms apart, the shawl and the lady vanished, and she never reappeared, a feat met with great cheers from the audience (Steinmeyer 111–13). Magicians in United States quickly copied this trick, bringing their own props and patter to the disappearance and often adding a re-appearance. Von Arx, an American-born magician actually named Charles Nicol, performed the Throne of Mystery Illusion, in vaudeville and circuses, in which a woman seated in an ornate chair suddenly disappeared into thin air and didn't return. Some disappearing acts ended not with the woman remaining gone or reappearing but with a surprise replacement. Lafayette, a German famed for his spectacular showmanship, thrilled American and European audiences with his Lion's Bride, a trick especially suited to performance at a circus: his assistant disappeared and then turned into a lion (Steinmeyer 11).

In vaudeville halls and circuses, with so many shows touring, audiences regularly saw beautiful women at highly stylized risk; the scenes routinely involved fires, torture chambers, saws, knives, swords, steel rods, vices, cannons, and guillotines, the excitement enhanced by the assistants' short skirts, by dramatic gestures, and by suspenseful music.

In magic acts, the assistant is not the magician, but instead the subject of the magic, generally not worthy of a complete name, yet she demonstrates great presence of mind and body control throughout the act. Like women in specs and statue acts, she remained silent, moving as part of a designated routine, but she garnered attention as an individual as they did not. Here is woman pliable and manipulated by the male magician, thus in the most traditional of secondary roles, but also quite worthy of note. As a body contortionist, aerialist, or equestrian, she visibly brought her own skills to bear, a harbinger of the magic that women would create in many acts within three rings when they would be more fully in control of their own movements.

# CHAPTER 23

---

# Equestrians

Beyond the variety of women who stood in the big top and sideshow, who represented extremes of beauty and of depravity, and beyond those whose moves were constructed as the product of another's magic, audiences encountered highly skilled performers, women who either came from circus families or who made their own way into a difficult business. The extremes of ballet girl and freak garnered interest as women more beautiful and more hideous, and thus more exotic and sexual, than anyone on view in the average town. They appeared to begin and end the show and to entice within a separated tented area. But the stars of the main show were women renowned not primarily for their features but for their advanced level of training, skill, and risk, generally beyond what had been seen before by the viewing crowd, a demonstration across three rings of apprentices and experts in the most highly demanding of careers.

One of these groups consisted of equestrians. At early circuses, in England and the United States, equestrian shows featured the horse, as people estimated what horses similar to those they might purchase could do. Acts in which women rode sidesaddle on those horses, sat in carts that horses pulled, or held ropes while horses reared and jumped would continue through the decades, but becoming much more popular would be bareback riding that featured the rider, her tricks of standing and dancing on the horse's back taking on more notice than the horse. In bareback routines, the skill examined was the rider's. The best women equestrians, famed for their graceful, athletic, and dangerous feats, had well-known names like those of movie stars.

## "High School" Riders — Focus on the Horse

In a high-school or *haute ecole* act, riding sidesaddle or driving in a carriage, the performer instructs her horse to execute a series of intricate steps and kicks, along with rearing, dancing, and waltzing. Generally women wore full skirts as they rode sidesaddle on high-school horses. As equestrian Elizabeth Hanneford Clarke pointed out concerning the European circus of her childhood, facts that were similar in the United States, "women rode fully clothed — no skimpy costume in England and Ireland before the turn of the century" (Smith, "Elizabeth Hanneford Clarke" I.26).

Across circuses and decades, high-school riding involved repeated tricks, often taught by older performers either at the circus or in off-season schools. Carousel riding involved a series of tight turns and circles, of one horse or several synchronized, apart from each other but doing the same maneuvers. Windmills, with up to twelve riders, included great circles, with the horses changing places while maintaining the overall form. Garland Manoevres featured canes twelve to fifteen feet long, held by two riders and shifted as their horses did intricate turns. Other acts involved moving within large hoops and maneuvering with hats and other props (Draper, "Beautiful Cart Acts").

The high-school performance also included jumps up and down, popularly known as "airs above the ground," done by the horse with and without riders, in a group and singly. Complex jump moves revealed the horses' agility and training: in the *courbette*, for example, the horse balances on its hindlegs and jumps, keeping its forelegs off the ground; in the *capriole*, the horse leaps into the air, pulling in his forelegs while kicking out with his hindlegs. Today's "World Famous Lipizzaner Stallions" demonstrate this style of riding.

Many American women came to these routines with a history of riding horses on farms—and with a need to support themselves. As clown Emmett Kelly wrote of these women's preparation, "A farm background is a valuable asset to a girl who wants to be a circus performer. She has grown up with animals and she knows about working in all kinds of weather and she doesn't expect the tour to be a plush picnic" (199). Farm girl Bette De Clow, for example, was born in Pennsylvania in 1901. Her father died when she was three weeks old, and she grew up in the home of her grandparents, who kept ponies as a hobby. When her grandfather died in 1917, her grandmother disposed of the animals; several went to Cooper Brothers Circus—and Bette went with them, to a place where she could use and extend the skills she had developed on the farm and thus earn her living. There Bette made her debut in the circus parade and in a posing act with a pure white horse. The following year, she was with the Christy Brothers Circus in Texas, billed by that time as a famed high-school rider, leading horses through the waltz, an elaborate series of turns, and straight-up jumps ("Accident Took").

Like De Clow, many other women started their riding careers in the town parade or spec, and then went on with additional training to high-school careers. In 1903, Helen Girard appeared in a spec as Joan of Arc and also stood in a tableau dressed in all white with white greasepaint makeup, on a white horse. While appearing in both, she began riding sidesaddle and securing the training needed to work in high-school acts. Her specialties included an act in which two fox terriers ran in and out between the spokes of her cart while nine riders did a cake walking routine, a stately movement featuring "an exaggerated extension of the horse's foreleg" (Draper, "Beautiful Cart Acts" 40).

Besides learning the turns and jumps, high-school equestrians developed their own unique combinations to secure the audience's attention. With Ringling Bros., in 1892, Allie Jackson, called Queen of the Side-Saddle for her act with her thoroughbred horse, Mizpah, did high-school tricks and gaits, after which her horse retrieved like a dog, the only retrieving horse in the world as he was billed, with her husband Lew Sunlin throwing large items across the ring and the horse coming back with them. Before Jackson retired in 1904, her horse Mizpah was also a great hit for his "hoochie-koochie," a version of the shaking dance done with "reckless abandon and evident delight." To an interviewer, Jackson declared that she "almost worships her horse and that she is really ashamed to risk wrecking his morals by letting him do the oriental steps but that the people seem to want it and she has to submit" ("Louis F. Sunlin").

As some of the most famous equestrian stars focused on high-school acts, their skills led them from circuses to Wild West shows. High-school rider Emma Lake, whose parents were circus owners, took a job with Buffalo Bill's Wild West in 1887, riding sidesaddle. As another artist who appeared as Queen of the Side-Saddle, she listed herself as Emma Hickok (even though Wild Bill Hickok was not her father but her step-father). In the Wild West show, she rode a horse that stood on two legs and did intricate square-dance steps and drills (Enss 35; Roach 81).

## Bareback Riders

By the beginning of the twentieth century, high-school riding was becoming old school, with spectators showing less interest in seeing how a horse could turn and dip. With each decade, the equestrian show instead became more and more the bareback show. Unlike high-school riding, bareback uses the horse's back as a platform from which the rider performs; thus it entailed a switch in attention from the horse to the rider, the horse becoming "essentially a reliable platform" on which the action occurs (Draper, "Beautiful Cart Acts" 40). In these acts, women appeared in brightly colored short costumes or body stockings, with sheer tights, dramatic capes, and headdresses. Though circus goers attended to these costumes, they also witnessed a high level of skill — the woman's skill much more than the horse's.

Some of the riders did acts based on acrobatic moves, perhaps with dramatic attention getters that would further draw the audience to the horse and rider. In 1903, Ella Bradna came to the United States with Barnum & Bailey upon its return from a five-year tour of Europe, James A. Bailey, managing director of the show, having seen her act in the London Hippodrome (Eckley 92). Bradna, in short skirts and tights, danced, tumbled, and balanced on her white horse's wide back, creating an act based on ingenuity and beauty. She also did acrobatic floor movements in the center ring, going back and forth from floor to horse. This act followed her entrance into the ring "gowned in white and riding a white winged horse," surrounded by other riders who released doves that "nestled in her arms" ("Mrs. Ella Bradna").

Other bareback riders used the broad back of the horse for intricate ballet dancing. Louise or Lulu Davenport, the youngest child of famed rider John Davenport, Sr., was often compared in publicity and articles to Anna Pavlova, a ballerina well known for her performance in *The Dying Swan*. As a critic noted, "Louise, in her fascinating gowns, did the Russian dancer one better when she executed pirouettes and the 'pas-seul' and tripped lightly on her toes on the backs of swiftly moving steeds." A Wilmington, Delaware, newspaper described her in May 1913 as the highest paid circus rider in the world, having successfully combined ballet movements with the double forward somersault and single backward somersault (Draper, "The Davenport Family" 27).

Other bareback equestrians did routines based not on classical beauty or dance but on acrobatic movements combined with physical risk. Linda Jeal, born in 1852, was a member of a well-known group of riders, including her sister Elena, an adopted daughter Dallie Julian, and Linda's niece Nellie Ryland, all appearing with many circuses over long careers as stars. The attention given Jeal came not just from expert riding but from the kind of trick that could scare and enthrall the audience in the big top. Jeal did extremely well the physically demanding tricks aspired to by other bareback riders: "Her stamina in the bare-

**Miss LINDA JEAL,**
"Queen of the Flaming Zone."
ONE OF THE FEATURES OF P.T. BARNUM'S GREATEST SHOW ON EARTH.

Poster of Linda Jeal for P.T. Barnum's Greatest Show on Earth, 1880. She was known as "the Queen of the Flaming Zone." Courier Co. (John and Mable Ringling Museum of Art).

back riding act with mounting and dismounting at full speed, bursting the balloons and going over the hurdles was so extraordinary that many believed that she must be a man" (Draper, "Linda Jeal" 32). But it was a special, and especially dangerous, trick that made her reputation and persona: "In her 'flaming zone' act she rode 'Pluto,' her specially trained horse, through a hoop of blazing petroleum…. This intrepid bareback rider went through a complete circle of flame bursting from a hollow iron tube which was filled with oil that flowed out through small tubes feeding the flames" (31). This trick involved a busy crew as well as Jeal: "While cage boys with asbestos gloves held three flaming hoops, she went through them while galloping her horse" (32). The trick earned Jeal the epithet of Queen of the Flaming Zone. She built her act and career from 1870 to 1879 with smaller shows such as Ryland's Oriental Circus and then went to work for Barnum & Bailey, for whom she presented the flaming zone act until 1894. Another rider, Adelaide Cordona, called the Empress of the Flaming Zone, whose pictures on posters were interchangeable with Jeal's, did a similar act from 1881 to 1887 for Sells Brothers and then various Barnum & Bailey–owned circuses (G. Riley 24).

Another well-known daredevil bareback star of a slightly later period was May Wirth, who stared in her adopted parents' circus in Australia, her startling gymnastic moves a key to her routine. Born in 1894 as May Emmeline Zinga, she learned gymnastics and contortion from her father Johnny Zinga, a circus gymnast. When his wife left him with their three youngest children in 1901, he offered May to the Wirth circus family, and they educated her with their own children, teaching her acrobatics and the tight wire (St. Leon 5). At age ten, in 1904, she began training as a trick rider; by the next year, she could do flip flops all the way around the ring on the bare back of a horse. Starting in 1910, she performed a feet-to-feet forward somersault on horseback, the only woman to do so. While still in Australia, she also learned to jump from the ground to a horse's back.

Wirth debuted as a bareback rider in Europe in 1911, joined the Barnum & Bailey Circus in 1912, and had her center-ring debut with Ringling Bros. the next year. In 1912, the Barnum & Bailey program announced, as the *New York Times* quoted, "the first appearance in America of the world's greatest bareback rider, exhibiting feats of equestrianism never attempted before by a woman." At Madison Square Garden that year, she did a forward somersault from her knees on the horse's back, the only woman to perform the trick in public. By 1913, with Ringling, she did a somersault from the back of one horse to the back of another running in tandem, the first public exhibition of this trick, which she next complicated by doing it blindfolded ("Circus Opens").

Her challenging performance changing with each year, Wirth perfected the back-backward somersault on a single horse, beginning by facing the tail of the horse and then doing a half-twist and flip, landing face front, all with the horse galloping. And she set a world record with somersaults, seven in one turn around the ring (Dickinson 17). By 1917, for the show's climax, she attached two twenty-inch market baskets to her feet, jumping from the floor and not a spring board onto the back of a running horse. "With this feat of strength as well as her forward somersaults and somersault from one horse to another," as historian Wilton Eckley wrote, "she was stopping the show" (88–90). Eventually she did this trick blindfolded. Wirth also perfected tricks that involved lying flat along the horse's side while it galloped and passing underneath it to the other side, a graceful and dangerous movement that seemed to emphasize her sexual as well as gymnastic presence: "She could dash around the ring on, over and under the horse, clinging ... with loosened, tangled hair floating to the winds with the form of a Venus." She performed this act repeatedly and quickly all around the ring, dressed in a short skirt, a low-neck blouse, with a giant bow in her hair, stopping the show (Draper, "May Wirth" 16–17).

Many other bareback riders created their own unique acts. With Barnum & Bailey at the Garden in 1895, for example, Quicka Meers did a bareback serpentine dance that the *New York Times* labeled as "decidedly original" ("The Tank's). In a spangled leotard, she used her doublejointed limbs to move like a cobra as the horse rushed forward. Other tricks that engaged audiences involved comedy. Lulu Davenport, for example, performed for Ringling Bros. doing an intricate bareback routine and also appearing as an old rube country woman, seemingly falling off her horse and climbing back on, losing her boots and glasses in the humorous process. "With the versatility of the great artist," circus historian John Draper claimed, "she changed from a dainty young equestrienne danseuse to a hick character and she made good on both roles" ("The Davenport Family" 27). Another of the greatest stars was Dorothy Herbert, her own act formed around the increasing challenge of her moves. Fans thrilled to her blindfolded jumps over hurdles of fire, her galloping ride while standing on two horses and controlling eight others, and her appearance as Mazeppa.

Equestrian acts appeared frequently during the circus program, in all three rings, with stars like Jeal, Bradna, Wirth, and Herbert filling the center ring while other equestrians performed on their sides. They were American stars: known to circus attendees, imitated by younger riders who rode with them in practice sessions — highly successful American workers who were women.

The movement from sidesaddle to bareback shortened the costume, but it also changed the presentation of the woman rider. In the bareback act, she appeared as a symbol of sexuality but also of skill and courage. Professional bareback riders, groups like the Jeals or single performers like May Wirth, presented not just passive beauty or adornment, as did so many ballet girls or magicians' assistants or even high-school riders. For one of the stars of the main show, the bareback rider, beauty certainly helped, but it was the woman's skill and risk that riveted the crowds.

# CHAPTER 24

# Trainers of Wild Animals

Through the years, many women did silent posing from the backs of exotic animals and in all manner of conveyances drawn by them. In the late nineteenth century, as her first assignment, Lilly Mondena Martin, wife of well-known trainer Stewart Craven, rode on an elephant as an Egyptian princess in a circus spectacle, then in a gilded chariot drawn by a dozen Shetland ponies, with sons of the circus owner as her slaves, waving large bamboo fans during the procession. Riding on an elephant, a scantily dressed woman like Martin provided a contrast to a large, potentially dangerous beast, her small size and vulnerability emphasizing its hugeness and power and creating sexual tension. Tiny Kline recognized that circus goers much preferred women as riders even if they seemed less able than men to engage the animals in tricks: "Elephants are downright drab looking, but a girl dressed in colorful raiment adds vividness to the act. She is agile and strikes pretty poses when mounting, whereas a man would only sell the tricks he taught the elephants" (173).

The backs of animals could also be found inside of pools, the woman adding to the attractiveness of the presentation there, as seal trainer Captain Charles Adams recorded in 1930: "Twenty years ago, with every vaudeville bill, circus and park showing trained seals and all the acts much the same, I revised mine completely, abandoning stunts for feats of intelligence, and adding an attractive young woman, who swims with them and feeds them under water in a glass tank" (60). Though equestrians like Edna Bradna and Dorothy Herbert owned and trained their own horses, in other animal acts women were less commonly the owner or trainer or even the skilled performer, but instead the beautiful ornamentation. Circuses owned these animals, and menagerie bosses controlled them. But into the twentieth century, as women became the focus of the equestrian act in the movement from high-school riding to bareback, they also moved, with exotic and large circus animals, from decoration to trainer, a highly dangerous and thrilling demonstration of expertise.

## To Become a Trainer

Though women traditionally rode elephants in the parades and spec, they had a difficult time getting the opportunity to do more than ride. Lucia Zora wanted the chance not just to parade on elephants but to train them, yet she found that goal not so easy to achieve:

"I was thwarted by two excellent reasons. One was that the menagerie was under the command of a man who neither desired women trainers nor believed that any feminine performer could possibly develop herself into a position of control over wild beasts. The other was that the show, in the vernacular, 'went broke'" (8). When at a second circus in 1900, Zora again made her request.

The circus managers voiced their amazement, as she described their reaction: "A woman actually was going to attempt to handle 'the big herd'! That was news! All for the simple reason that it never had been done before." Immediately, as she recalled, these men accosted her with a list of the disabilities under which she supposedly suffered. "A woman, by instinct, is timid," she was told, and furthermore women lacked the requisite knowledge, concentration of thought and effort, and assertive personality to control large beasts (28).

In her autobiography, Zora stated the arguments that she made in response, thus defending the place that she ultimately made for herself and advocated for other women. Any trainer had to be dominant, she certainly agreed, or else the elephant would shirk during performance. And the handling of the bull hook, with its attached whip, could be difficult if the woman (or man) lacked strength: the elephant needed not a "faint pop" to attend to a command, she believed, but a "violent crack of the lash, although that lash never touches him" (29). All the criticism that she heard fit the stereotypes of the times, but did not deter her: "Half a hundred dire things were predicted for me — all of which I considered, but gradually, one by one, cast aside.... I felt sure of myself. I was one hundred and sixty pounds of strong bone, muscle and sinew, of a type better described as masculine strength" (29). Even with all this determination, Zora still had to rely on the persuasiveness of her husband, Fred Alispaw, superintendent of the Sells-Floto menagerie, to get her opportunity.

After Zora began training elephants as well as performing with them, she did not argue with managers who wanted to keep her full involvement with the animals a secret. As an example of their discourse, she recorded what a show owner said to important visitors to the dressing tents in Albuquerque: "'Course she doesn't do much,' he announced — for our secret had been guarded carefully — 'but then it makes a good flash — a woman handling a bunch of elephants. Besides that, she looks the part and — huh, here she comes now!'" As she noted further, in that show in Albuquerque, this woman who "doesn't do much" had just finished the "lay down under a herd of elephants, had reclined upon a carpet while every elephant in the herd stepped over her, then halted, and returned to a position over her body, this time backward; she had stood on the head of an elephant as it reared from a position on all fours to a standing one on its hind legs; she had been whirled madly about in an elephant's trunk" (39).

This tendency to hide the fact that the woman performer trained the animals and did not just serve as a beautiful adornment continued through the decades. In the circus fan magazine *White Tops,* in the article "Jodie Talks, Elephants Listen" in 1990, the author argues that elephants had always been handled by men, women having been added just to "dress up the act." Only "in recent years," the article claims incorrectly, had women become trainers since African elephants "seem more subject to a woman's touch" than had the Indian elephants used more commonly in earlier decades. One of the trainers here described as a new phenomenon, Joanne, or Jodie, Craigmile, had "created a stir when she came into her own" in the 1980s by handling an African elephant.

In the late nineteenth century and more commonly in the twentieth century, women began training other types of wild animals, though they often still appeared to the crowd like the act's decoration. With her husband Emil, Catherine Pallenberg presented a trained bear act from the 1920s to the 1940s. They were the first to teach a bear to ride a bicycle, with a huge front wheel and seat eight feet high, the first to teach a bear to walk a tightrope ("Trainer Reaches Top"). As they did the act, as Earl Chapin May wrote, Catherine wore "silken tights, a silver cloth gown, an elaborately embroidered Russian costume whose cost is in the neighborhood of $2,000," looking more decorative than controlling though the couple actually worked the animals together ("Why Women Dominate" 9).

## The Big Cats

With the elephant or bear, it might not be clear who had done the training, and thus a man could be publicized as the trainer, the woman as adornment. But such a construction was much harder to maintain when women in the twentieth century began to work alone with big cats, since whoever entered a ring or cage with tigers and lions was clearly not just parading with these animals but controlling them. Since women could not then be advertised as just an accessory, another gendered representation became common, of the women as both controlling and controlled, in the grips of a motherly or even sexual relationship with cats.

When women first entered lion and tiger cages along with men, they appeared there as decoration, as in magic acts or elephant rides. The first such act occurred in the Adam Forepaugh Show in 1891, with a man and woman publicized as Colonel Edgar Daniel Boone and Miss Carlotta, working with lions as well as with two hounds. For this act, a cage rolled up to a steel ring's entrance, pushed by a big elephant, and opened dramatically. Then three lions entered the ring, where they formed pyramids on pedestals, played on a seesaw, rode a tricycle, and held ropes for the hounds to jump over. In publicity, Boone was described as a descendent of "Kentuck's famous pioneer," this ancestry explaining his bravery: "Col. Edgar Daniel Boone is the name of the man who is at present astonishing the people of this country by his performance with five full grown ferocious lions ... the colonel is a Kentuckian by birth, and a direct descendant of Kentuck's famous pioneer." The 1891 route book of the Forepaugh Show gave the epithets of Lion King and Lion Queen to these circus stars, but claimed that the "colonel" provided "the most astonishing exhibition of man's supremacy over the brute creation," here the man controlling the wild animals (Culhane 167). Though the husband and wife worked together, Carlotta, her actual name Millie Boone, appeared in ads as the beautiful assistant who trained the dogs.

Over time, even though women began in big-cat acts as assistants, they moved into solo performance, for which they took charge of the animals and accepted all the risks. One of the first of these women was lion trainer Eugenia de Lorme Ames, who appeared from 1858 to 1866 with various circuses — G. N. Eldred's, Robinson & Lake, and John Robinson's. She next worked for her husband Clark in his Ames' Southern Menagerie in 1866 and his New Orleans Circus and Menagerie in 1867. His New Orleans show, described in his advertising as "A Colossal Aggregation of Olympian Sports and Nature's Wonders" boasted "a score of beautiful ladies, a legion of male artists, a duo of lion tamers, a most extensive menagerie of rare wild beasts of nearly every known species and of every geographical range from the frigid to the torrid, a herd of trained horses, and clowns, musicians and comedians." As one of the lion tamers, Eugenia performed by herself and with a partner, the duo equally described as "male and female, the personification of miraculous and incomprehensible courage and fortitude."

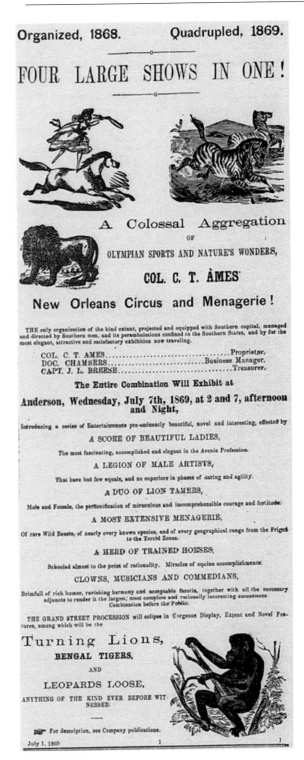

Organized, 1868.    Quadrupled, 1869.

# FOUR LARGE SHOWS IN ONE!

### A Colossal Aggregation
OF

OLYMPIAN SPORTS AND NATURE'S WONDERS,

## COL. C. T. ÀMES'

## New Orleans Circus and Menagerie!

THE only organization of the kind extant, projected and equipped with Southern capital, managed
and directed by Southern men, and its perambulations confined to the Southern States, and by far the
most elegant, attractive and satisfactory exhibition now traveling.

COL. C. T. AMES............................................Proprietor.
DOC. CHAMBERS.........................Business Manager.
CAPT. J. L. BREESE...............................Treasurer.

The Entire Combination Will Exhibit at

**Anderson, Wednesday, July 7th, 1869, at 2 and 7, afternoon
and Night,**

Introducing a series of Entertainments pre-eminently beautiful, novel and interesting, effected by

A SCORE OF BEAUTIFUL LADIES,

The most fascinating, accomplished and elegant in the Arenic Profession.

A LEGION OF MALE ARTISTS,

That have but few equals, and no superiors in phases of daring and agility.

A DUO OF LION TAMERS,

Male and Female, the personification of miraculous and incomprehensible courage and fortitude.

A MOST EXTENSIVE MENAGERIE,

Of rare Wild Beasts, of nearly every known species, and of every geographical range from the Frigid
to the Torrid Zones.

A HERD OF TRAINED HORSES,

Schooled almost to the point of rationality. Miracles of equine accomplishment.

CLOWNS, MUSICIANS AND COMEDIANS,

Brimfull of rich humor, ravishing harmony and acceptable facetia, together with all the necessary
adjuncts to render it the largest, most complete and rationally interesting amusement
Combination before the Public.

THE GRAND STREET PROCESSION will eclipse in Gorgeous Display, Extent and Novel Features, among which will be the

Turning Lions,
BENGAL TIGERS,
AND
LEOPARDS LOOSE,
ANYTHING OF THE KIND EVER BEFORE WIT-
NESSED.

For description, see Company publications.

July 1. 1869                    1

In the twentieth century, many other women performed alone with big cats. Mademoiselle Marguerite, a lion trainer, appeared with John Robinson's Ten Big Shows in 1911. In 1901, she had begun working as a lion tamer in Frankfurt, Germany, issuing a challenge to the mayor to come into the cage and drink champagne with her, a publicity stunt for a liquor manufacturer that she repeated in other European and in American cities, a well-advertised challenge to local men that they did not accept ("Champagne in a Lion's Cage"). Margaret Thompson and Margaret Ricardo trained pumas and showed them in several American circuses (Stark, Letter, 28 May 1933). Jules Jacot performed in The Bride and the Beasts, an opening spectacle for the Sells-Floto Circus in the early 1930s. In this show, she appeared as Sahadamese, the Virgin Sacrifice, "fed to the lions" in the center arena. This trainer of tigers and lions, who raised them from infancy, as Earl Chapin May wrote, "happily subdues eight mountain cats who play opposite her in this drama, puts them through their paces and retires, intact, amid proper applause" ("Why Women Dominate" 7).

Often circus owners presented women with odd arrays of felines and other animals, thus adding to the shock of the sole woman's appearance within a cage of cats. Working with trainer Essie Fay and in several circuses, Olga Celeste learned to present several combination animal acts: elephant and pony; wolf and collie; a baby bear with two dogs; two blue Dane dogs with lions and bears; and lions, pumas, and leopards. In the fall of 1910, she began

Newspaper advertisement for the C.T. Ames New Orleans Circus and Menagerie. Over time, women took charge of the big cats as solo performers. *Anderson Intelligencer* (Anderson, S.C.), 1 July 1869 (Library of Congress Prints and Photographs Division).

training animals and appearing in shows at the new Selig Zoo, a home in Los Angeles to the seven hundred animal species that director William Selig used in films, a site at which he shot many jungle scenes (Taber).

While women might gain an opportunity by working with odd arrays of animals, they also drew on their own extremes of personality and attraction to get a chance to launch a big-cat act. In 1937, at Ringling Bros. and Barnum & Bailey in Madison Square Garden, one new attraction was Maria Rasputin, as she was advertised and described in the *New York Times*: "Daughter of Imperial Russia's World-Famous Mad Monk and Confidant to the Late Czar" ("A Study in Concentration"). After her husband died of tuberculosis in Paris in 1926, Rasputin found work as a governess to support her two young daughters. She then became a cabaret dancer in Bucharest, and next a performer for Ringling Bros. During the 1930s she toured as a lion tamer, billing herself as performing magic over wild beasts just as her father dominated men. At the beginning of World War II, after being mauled by a bear in Peru, Indiana, she stayed with the circus until it reached Miami, Florida, and then began work as a riveter in a defense shipyard. She became a United States citizen in 1945 (Alexander 297).

While some women secured a position working with cats through a novel assortment of animals or through their own novel biographies, others gained an opportunity through representations that powerfully separated these cat trainers from the men. Circus historian Janet M. Davis has argued that the image of a gentle woman handling beasts was constructed as an act of sexual arousal and tension, a combination of woman and animal that took sexual attraction further than did equestrian or elephant riding (101). While men always appeared as vanquishers of big cats, a very different kind of depiction arose for the women who began appearing alone with lions and tigers.

As we have seen, circus posters introduced the difference in depiction that continued in the show. They often featured the woman trainer alone with big cats, in a crowd of animals, very close to them, thus vulnerable and titillating in fluffy, impractical garb (though most actually wore protective clothing in the ring). In contrast, posters of men showed them in safari or military garb, armed with chairs, whips, and guns, the tigers and lions cowering behind them. Male trainers in parades as within the ring wore khaki or formal wear, with certainly no hint of a sexual connection to the cats.

## Mabel Stark

One of the greatest circus stars in the 1910s, 1920s, and 1930s, Mabel Stark, most fully embodied this tradition of a sexual connection of women to tigers, not just in posters but in her act itself. Stark first went to a circus at age eight, in Princeton, Kentucky. Then she began teaching her dogs to do tricks, her desire to join the circus, as she later wrote, causing her mother to grab her by the ear, yank her down a set of stairs, and paddle her. She went to nursing school in Louisville after her parents died and then on to California. Without skills, Stark could only get a job as a sideshow hootchie-cootchie dancer, with the Parker Carnival in 1909, using a Greek last name given in several versions, one being Aganosticus (Hough 425).

Stark began working her first animal act, a routine with trained goats and not cats, with the Al G. Barnes Circus in 1912 (Hough 42). She quit and went with the Con. T. Kennedy Carnival, which she quit at midseason and then returned to the Barnes Circus, which would only sign her as a horse rider in the parades. She tried riding a bronco to get attention, but she had not given up on her goal of working with big cats.

Part of her difficulty in getting a job as an animal trainer certainly involved gender. Stark recognized another separation, of cat men and their cats away from what they called the hay animals, like elephants, horses, zebras, and camels. Trainers definitely did not want to give a chance to a young woman, especially not one that had worked with goats, dogs, and horses. When the Barnes Circus closed for the season in December 1913 in Venice, California, Stark stayed there to try to ingratiate herself with the cat trainers and overcome their prejudices. Finally Al Barnes told her, as she later recorded his dialogue, "You're little and blonde. You'd look good in the ring with those big brutes. But I can't take the chance. Your people would sue me if you were killed" (Stark and Orr 50). Stark assured him that she was an orphan; he finally had her sign a release and told the trainer to help her because "a little girl and three big tigers ought to be a good drawing card" (Stark and Orr 58). Her salary then went from twenty to fifty dollars a week.

Even though Stark sought an act with tigers and Barnes assured her that she would get a tiger act soon, Barnes continued to book her as a novelty act, not as a serious trainer of tigers but as a woman, like Olga Celeste, who extended her own oddity by performing with a varied group of animals, which she sometimes could not control. Stark worked in a ring with both lions and tigers, coaxing three lions, as she later recounted, to mount onto the backs of horses. In one such show, a large lion "turned and grabbed me in the thigh. There was a horrid ripping sound as his powerful fangs sank into me" (Stark and Orr 72).

At the Al G. Barnes Circus, after much persuading, Stark moved to an act with just tigers in 1914, for which she trained the animals. She created an immediately popular act, in which tigers sat erect on pedestals, arranged themselves in a pyramid, played with balls and other props, and rolled over on the floor in unison. In 1916, in an attempt to keep her on this show, the owner gave Stark the tigers that she had been training. She kept pressing him for more, for seven when she had five, but he didn't want the additional expense. When she threatened to go with another circus, he got additional cubs for his star performer, to ultimately make a total of twelve. These tigers included Rajah, who would become her star animal. By the mid twenties, Stark's act with this tiger "was the best known cat-act in the American circus" (Hough 426).

After Stark proved herself with Barnes, she had to do so again when she sought to move to Ringling Bros. and Barnum & Bailey. This organization also had reservations about hiring a woman to work with cats, as Stark wrote in a letter to her biographer, Earl Chapin May: "The idea of having a woman about the animals did not go so good as such had never been on that show, and they had me pictured as a temperamental hell cat but finally I won them over" (Letter to May, 28 May 1933). She ultimately signed with Ringling Bros. in 1922 for double the money and left her tigers with Barnes, though she came back there after several seasons when Charles Ringling took the tiger act out of his line-up as too violent. In 1930, when the Ringlings bought the Barnes Circus, Stark was offered the job as head trainer and performer with Ringling, the circus no longer so concerned about violence, and she took the job. Stark also trained cats for films: about *King of the Jungle*, a Tarzan-like story starring Buster Crabbe in 1933, she wrote, "no tigers went on the set unless I was with them" (Letter to May, 29 May 1933).

In her public discussion of her tiger act, and in letters to and interviews with Earl Chapin May, Stark offered gendered discussions of her performance and life. Not just at the beginning but throughout her career, she told him, she had faced the challenge of trying

to overcome prejudice: "Because I was a woman and grew tired of hearing men trainers say that a woman could not do this or that, I broke a twelve tiger act sixteen years ago and began wrestling tigers eight years ago. And now I am going to have my twenty tiger act — the biggest tiger act in the business!" (May, "Why Women Dominate" 2–3).

She married twice without love, Stark told May, to launch her career the first time and to please a circus owner the second. Her first husband, head trainer Louis Roth at Barnes Circus, whom she met in 1912, "was billed as the world's greatest trainer, his methods were on the same line as mine." Roth, she further asserted, "used a lot of patience and done a lot of talking to his animals when training." He offered her two lions from his act — "this he did not have to do and

Mabel Stark at work. "Because I was a woman and grew tired of hearing men trainers say that a woman could not do this or that, I broke a twelve tiger act sixteen years ago and began wrestling tigers eight years ago. And now I am going to have my twenty tiger act — the biggest tiger act in the business!" (Circus World Museum, Baraboo, Wisconsin).

none of the others would have ever gave up any animals from their acts" — because he saw her dedication: "he soon learned that he could rely on me" (Letter to May, 28 May 1933). She agreed to marry Roth not because she loved him but because she needed his help to get "an edge over the others." She told May that she was constantly with him anyway to help him keep from drinking. But Roth went on to other shows and they divorced: "I married to help the show and I loved the tigers better than he." Her second husband, Al Drivin, came on the show as an accountant, "a good looking man." Al Barnes made Drivin an assistant manager and encouraged Stark to marry him, hoping that marriage with a manager would help keep her with the show. After their marriage, however, Drivin did not stay with Barnes for long because of money irregularities, though he kept coming back to Stark to borrow money. She didn't want any trouble with him after she went to Ringling Bros.

**Mabel Stark at work.** "After his [her third husband's] death I can find no pleasure or happiness anywhere except with the tigers so here I am" (Circus World Museum, Baraboo, Wisconsin).

because of the morality clauses in the contract. Friends helped him get a job with Ringling, however, with Stark afraid to speak against him as he traded on her name, and he began forging checks there. She ultimately divorced him (Letter to May, 28 May 1933). In her letters to May, Stark wrote further about these men's failures and the price of ambition, about choices that she had felt compelled to make: "I had firmly made up my mind to go to the top. Regardless of the price I might have to pay when I had to sell my own soul and which I did in the end.... I still love the tigers best. They may snarl back at me but they never cause me to be sneered at or talked about, tigers only tear flesh — which heals — but men hurt characters, break hearts, spirits, and souls — and my spirit is easily broken or perhaps I should say pride in myself and work" (Letter to May, 28 May 1933).

Part of her problem with both men stemmed from their jealousy about her professional success: "I have learned that husbands do not want the public to think that a wife is above them or can do anything that they can't do." Both husbands also resented her contact with the other animal trainers: "I am the only woman employed in the training quarters. This brings me in company with the working men as caretakers seven days a week from 7:30 morning to 4:30 evening. I even have my lunch with them. My husbands — Roth and Drivin — were jealous of animal men — they said I paid more attention to the animal men that I did to them, which was true, for I have a man's job and am in company with the men all the time." Her close relationships with other crew members, which she judged as a necessary part of her career, caused both men to always be "nagging and arguing." She felt happy and contented with her tigers, she claimed further, but "with husbands I was never happy" (Letter to May, 17 May 1933).

Stark's third husband, Art Rooney, whom she met in 1922 when he worked as an assistant menagerie boss, she found to be different. He did not need to demonstrate his superiority: "He was the only one I ever loved enough to give up the tigers for but he never tried to take any credit from me." As she claimed further, Rooney was the only one who "always seemed to be proud of me and my work." She loved him and met no one else, she said, after he died in 1931: "After his death I can find no pleasure or happiness anywhere except with the tigers so here I am" (Letter to May, 28 May 1933; "You Can't").

Though Stark certainly succeeded in a primarily male world, she did so through a gendered act and public discussion of it. Stark viewed herself as entirely different from a male trainer and repeatedly contrasted herself with a particular man "who thought he was the king of all trainers [and who] began the very first thing to try and put fear in the beasts by throwing seats and trying to beat them" (Letter to May, n.d.). This man was Clyde Beatty, who often staged fights among his forty lions and tigers, so that he could seem to beat them into submission with gun, whip, and chair. Beatty reveled in the publicity caused by a visit to the show in 1931 by the SPCA, there to chastise him for his fierce methods (Coleman). The advertising and book-jacket copy for his autobiography, *The Big Cage*, published in 1933, struck the same tone of fierceness and bravado to which Stark objected: "Forty lions and tigers in a 32-foot arena, snarling snapping, biting — a steel cage chock full of angry cats — and in their midst a single man fighting them all off with nothing but a kitchen chair and a flash gun — this is a spectacle that will never fail to bring every spectator in the big tent to the edge of his seat." In this popular autobiography, Beatty seemed to enjoy quoting Carl Hagenbeck, a famous European animal trainer: "Those cats will get Beatty. The act is too dangerous" (268). After telling many stories of life-threatening attacks in this book, he declares in his devil-may-care manner: "People with a fondness for statistics ask me how many chairs I use in fending off attacks in the arena in the course of a season. My records show that I used — 'consumed' would be a better word for most of them were utterly demolished by my playful pets — sixty-three chairs last year" (268–69). He refused, he wrote, to deal with any lions or tigers raised in captivity for the wild animals are "more formidable than their cage-born brethren — stronger, more ferocious, and better supplied with primitive passion" (4). Beatty also publicly declared women to be as untrustworthy as tigers: they could be as dangerous and impulsive as wild cats — but they did not have the fortitude needed to control wild animals and thus he didn't allow them near his act. (See C-8.)

Beatty's movies helped build his fearsome image. A lion named Nero mauled him in 1932, on the Hagenbeck-Wallace Circus, an accident much discussed in the press ("Trainer Seriously Hurt by Lion"). In the film version of *The Big Cage* (1933), co-starring Mickey Rooney and Andy Devine, one of Universal Pictures' most popular releases that year, Beatty fought this lion again, a fact emphasized in previews and other publicity. In the serial *The Lost Jungle* (1934), Beatty appeared as the brave and fierce lion trainer, involved in many adventures: commandeering a dirigible, surviving a jungle crash, capturing lions and tigers, overcoming dangerous rivals, and rescuing his sweetheart and her father from an uncharted island filled with wild animals.

In comparing herself with Beatty as the quintessential male trainer, both in correspondence with May and in newspaper interviews, Stark presented strongly gendered contrasts in training methods. She depicted herself as believing in encouragement and repetition, in firm but kind work with animals, traits she also attributed to female teachers of young children and to mothers. She claimed that any woman has more patience than a man, is willing to give more time and try more methods. She equated her slow and kind approach to the patience women demonstrate with babies and that men would not: "A man would never fool away hours teaching a baby to walk or sit alone ... tigers need that same time and patience." She maintained to May that she first watched closely what the cats did naturally as cubs, like whirling or jumping or playing with balls, and built an act on those proclivities. With tigers that she raised almost from birth, she used what she called her "sugar method," choice bits of meat as reward for performance instead of the whip as punishment (May, "Why Women Dominate" 5). In daily practices and in performance, she maintained, the best sort of control involved the trainer's knowledge and strong will and kind presence, not physical strength or brutality: "Trainers who try to beat animals into submission always get into trouble" (Stark and Orr 18).

In her letters to her biographer, as she prepared the account of her career that she sought to make public, she gave more details of this method and thus further analyzed the violent tendencies of male trainers like Beatty. "A man wants to be the big bully boss," she argued, and if the animal did not do exactly what was wanted, "he never tries to coax the animal, in most cases he uses brutality, a whip or a club." That bullying created the need for constant attacks with the whip to get the animals to follow commands: "Most men trainers do their work by force; a tiger won't stand a lot of clubbing and hurrahing." Thus the trainers' violence led to further violence, a constant acceleration of aggression, since a tiger "will not sit and take a whipping" but instead will jump at the trainer or try to get away (Letter to May, 4 Feb. 1934). "I find a tiger yields to my voice better than a man's," she asserted. "A tiger yields to kindness quicker than force" (Letter to May, n.d.).

In her act, Stark worked with several images of femininity, connecting with the audience through them. Her presence emphasized her vulnerability, as male trainers like Beatty would not do. Her persona appeared naïve, too trusting, always at risk of death, not in control as a male trainer might appear. Early in the act, she faced the audience, turning her back to the tigers, at which time they would make angry pawing motions to which she seemed oblivious, causing audience members to shout warnings and come to their feet, protective of the small woman seemingly in need of their help. Then a tiger attacked and seemed to crush her to the ground, going for her throat, another part of the act that male trainers didn't employ. She fought back, wrestled with the beast, triumphed, and then came to her feet and took a bow. Then the audience understood that what they had seen was an act, one made more dramatic through her small size and seeming lack of control.

Over time, this crushing and wrestling scene came to take up most of Stark's act and to reiterate other fears about the small blond woman with the beast, casting her as within the clutches of an animal at least as dominating as Fay Wray's King Kong in the 1933 film. The act developed into a stylized sex scene during which audience members could not tell what they saw. She described the action, as it involved her tiger Rajah, to Earl Chapin May: "Rajah got his satisfaction in the act. Rolling on the ground he would come in and go to his seat. When I turned and called him he would come up on his hind feet and put both feet round my neck. Pull me to the ground, grab me by the head, that is why I wore a padded helmet, you know a male tiger grabs the female by the neck and holds her and growls till the critical moment is over. So in this fashion Rajah grabbed me and held me. We kept rolling over till he was through and while the audience could not see or discover what Rajah was doing, his growling made a hit" (Letter to May, 29 May 1933).

When Stark attempted to market her life and career in 1933, she could not do so even though she did interest Earl Chapin May. By that time he had written several books about the circus, fiction like *Cuddy of the White Tops* as well as nonfiction such as *Behind the Seams of a Circus*, both in 1924. In 1932, he published a popular history, *The Circus from Rome to Ringling.* When in 1930 he co-wrote the story of Winfield Scott O'Connor, a famous jockey, socialite, and criminal of the 1920s, his name appeared in the title: *Jockeys, Crooks and Kings: The Story of Winnie O'Connor's Life as Told to E.C. May.* His plans for the Stark book seemed to include not just her motherly training methods but a discussion of the faults she found in men who would rob women of their independence, her use of sexuality in her act, and her desire to train and own her own animals.

In 1933 and 1934, the story of a "feminist" animal trainer, a label that both Stark and May used in their letters, did not seem to be wanted. Book editor Oscar Graeve at the *Delineator* wrote to May in September 1933 that "'Tiger Girl' sounds much too lurid for us." John Farrar, then an editor with Duffield and Green, wrote of this proposed *Tiger Woman* as introducing readers to too difficult a person and story: "The lady's personality is unpleasant to me" (Farrar to Chapin, n.d.). May ended up with a manuscript of 90,000 words that he couldn't sell. His movie scenario did no better. In May of 1933, he wrote Nina Lewton, head of MGM's New York story department, saying that "the love element and the recurring conflict between men trainers and Mabel Stark are susceptible to indefinite development," but he encountered rejection from MGM as well as RKO, Warner Bros., and Fox Film. As he made these attempts, he was trying out various film titles: *Tiger Girl, Tiger Woman,* and then the more evocative *Tiger Lover, The Private Life of the Tiger Woman,* and *Love Affairs of a Tiger Trainer.*

At the same time, May tried to market an article that might lead to interest in the larger project, but even an article version proved hard to place: *Cosmopolitan, Redbook, McCall's,* and *Ladies' Home Journal* found the material too provocative . Finally May toned down his material and placed pieces with the *Pictorial Review, NY Herald Review, American Magazine,* and *Elks Magazine,* his subject the oddity of a lady tiger trainer, her bravery and dedication to her craft, and nothing more controversial. He hoped this more acceptable approach would lead to a contract with the Literary Guild or the Book of the Month Club, but no book offers were forthcoming.

After May finally gave up on a book or movie project, screenplay writer Gertrude Orr, who worked on films for children such as *Little Men* (1934), presumably collaborated with Stark on *Hold That Tiger,* marketed as an autobiography. In 1935, Orr had written a children's book about Stark called *The Tiger Lady: The Life of Mabel Stark, Noted Animal Trainer.*

Published in 1938, in a limited printing from a small press in Idaho, *Hold That Tiger* concentrated on accidents and shows and not on Stark's feminism, love life, sexual display with the tigers, or judgment of other trainers, indeed not on any of the controversial topics that had presumably been in the May book (Dickinson 82–83). Robert Hough, who created a fictionalized version of Stark's life in 2001, found *Hold That Tiger* to be "highly sanitized and highly inaccurate" and perhaps written, like the children's book, with assistance from the Ringling press department, not from Stark herself (427).

For the woman who wanted to work with big cats, elephants, or bears, getting the chance to do so was much more difficult than with horses. Women were not supposed to be training large, ferocious animals. Beginners certainly could not purchase them, and so they had to get help from menagerie bosses often loath to give them a try: Mabel Stark had to marry one. With these animals, women generally appeared as sexual decoration, doing a dog act near the big cats; riding the elephant in the circus parade with the male trainer walking nearby. But in the early twentieth century, women began working as wild animal trainers and performers, perhaps first as the assistant or partner, but also in the ring by themselves. Gendered representations often led to opportunity: women provided pretty accompaniment to male trainers; they were more vulnerable to attack or more motherly with the animals; they might be the object of bestial sexual attraction. Even though they often had to rely on the gendered renderings available to them, just as women riding bareback appeared in costumes that would attract viewers, these cat trainers created careers based on careful training, daily practice, courage, patience, showmanship, and calculated risk.

# CHAPTER 25

---

# Aerial Artists

Though equestrians and animal trainers could introduce spectators to women's hard work, courage, skill, and risk as well as their beauty and sexuality, perhaps nothing else did so like performing in the air. "Many Victorians lived prim and circumscribed lives," according to social historian Laura Byrne Paquet, "and they thrilled to the death-defying bravery of flying acrobats." She added that "when the performer attempting feats was a scantily-clad young woman, the combination of terror and sexual attraction was simply too much to resist" (73). The marvel of a woman flying through the air seemed to rivet the circus audience as little else did: the circus performance reached its apotheosis in the air as women approached the heavens, clearly soaring above every tradition and barrier.

Male acrobats first brought aerial acts to the United States from France. French rope-walker The Great Blondin, or Jean-François Gravelet, crossed Niagara Falls on a rope in 1859, a stunt he repeated several times, with theatrical variations: in a sack, on stilts, blind-folded, pushing a wheelbarrow, carrying his manager on his back, sitting down midway across to cook and eat an omelet. Frenchman Jules Léotard, who debuted in Paris, invented the trapeze that same year. His act involved leaping from one swinging trapeze bar forward to grab hold of a second and then a third. The Siegrist Brothers brought the trapeze act to North America in 1861, as did the Hanlon-Lees Brothers, who introduced the excitement of a group of performers on a long line of trapezes (Tait 11).

Although the trapeze act, like many others, began with men, by 1880 "female performers were the most highly paid aerialists," perhaps because of the added excitement of women at mortal risk (Tait 2). Ada and Maude Sanyeah, both called Madame Sanyeah and both advertised as the Most Daring Woman in the World, declared themselves the first women in the United States on the trapeze. The feats of both women shocked the audience, as the *New York Clipper* noted in 1870: "So daring and so apparently dangerous as to be really unpleasant to those of a more sensitive nature … beyond all computation of human strength as to be truly marvelous" ("At the Circus: Madame Sanyeah"). English performer Zuelila, who worked for many American circuses, claimed to be the first woman to perform with a partner and to do the "leap for life" from one swinging rope or trapeze to another (Tait 2–17). Many other women performers soon followed with their own complex tricks on trapeze. Lupita Perea did a sensational half-somersault forward, catching a swinging trapeze by her heels. The four Darling Sisters, who came to the United States from Europe, worked together on a quadruple trapeze.

Many other types of aerial acts also emphasized thrill and risk. "Static rope" referred to an act in which at the top of the arena the performer hung from a rope or rings, suspended by her jaw, hair, arms, or legs, and performed a wide range of movements including balances, drops, and swirls. The difficulty on a static rope is in making every move look effortless — and holding on. An especially dramatic static rope act involved the artist holding onto a rope or bar with only her jaw. Mademoiselle Granville, an aerialist with the Great International Menagerie and Circus in America in 1874, advertised herself with the epithet the "lady with the jaws of iron." Monsieur and Mademoiselle LeStrange appeared as "human butterflies" hanging by their teeth. In 1879 Emma Jutau began doing the iron-jaw spin, turning her body around in the air as she held on by her clinched jaw (Kline 319). She then streaked down a cable while hanging by her teeth, reaching seventy-five miles per hour and creating an intense sense of excitement.

Another tremendously popular aerial act, wire walking or tight wire, involved the art of maintaining balance while walking along a tension wire between two points, by either using a balancing tool, such as an umbrella, fan, or balance pole, or walking"freehand," using only one's body to maintain balance, a risk that could further enthrall the crowd. Artists worked with an array of props out on the wire to balance and to enhance the entertainment value: spinning plates, juggling clubs, pushing wheelbarrows with children and pets as passengers, and climbing ladders. Instead of the tight or high wire, some aerialists worked the slackwire, with which the tension on the wire is provided by the performer and her props. Victoria Codona began performing with her family in Mexico, in 1904, as a dancer on the slack wire (Parkinson 11). As the slackwire went up and down precariously, a movement that the aerialist could emphasize, audiences thrilled to the balance act and to the possibility of a deadly fall.

Performing in all of these aerialist acts, women demonstrated the same agility and strength as men. Like the men, the women had musculature clearly on view: "The developed muscular bodies and physical power of accomplished female aerialists," as trapeze historian Peta Tait asserted, "were unprecedented elsewhere in society until the late twentieth century" (3). Their costumes began as longer skirts but soon became the fitted leotard that got its name from the act's inventor. On the trapeze, women performers could seek to dramatically combine the sexual with physical risk: star performer Bird Millman especially knew how to mine this territory. In fact she appeared as "the Eva Tanguay of the Wire," the epithet involving the name of a vaudeville singer known for her gauzy veiled costumes and very short skirts. Millman wore fluffy costumes, looking cute and sexy, often carrying a balloon and singing popular songs from the high wire. Her flirtatious, whirlwind act was thus described: "She danced! ... Laughed aloud as she bounded in the air with dancing toes that came down to whirl and waltz and pirouette so fast across the silver thread that it took your breath away!" (Paquet 32).

Tiny Kline, who as she got past entry-level assignments did trapeze work as well as a loop-the-loop act from a ring on which she balanced upside down while swinging over and over, commented on the changing, more sexual dress in both equestrian and aerial acts. As a bareback rider, she had profited from the publicity and the criticism that occurred when she wore a very skimpy costume: "Yes, they found my bare legs shocking the first year I rode Roman. I was ridiculed: 'What decent female would appear without tights?'" When she appeared in trapeze acts, she went for an even skimpier costume that would rivet the crowd: "Now my costume was truly shocking: 'A bare midriff, for shame!' But I risked all their criticism for the success of the act which was based originally on the Oriental dance, the theme of whirling carried out in various phases" (240).

In aerial acts, the focus was not just on the costume but on dramatic, visual risk. With the risky and new always sought, trapeze artists and wire walkers, like equestrians, felt the pressure to try out the ever more dangerous. In 1897, sixteen-year-old Nellie Jordan of the Flying Jordans became the first of either sex to complete a triple somersault from a trapeze bar, sixteen years before a man did the trick (Paquet 32). Her adopted sister Lena, who performed the same trick, was examined by New York medics who very publicly declared that she was indeed a woman and not a young man in costume ("The Flying Trapezes" 26–27). Rita Dunn, called the Queen of the High Wire in the 1920s, worked with her husband for sixteen years, always motivated in their risk-taking by their desire to keep the crowd's attention, as indeed they did, as the fan magazine *White Tops* reported: "Hundreds gazed, not daring to speak, during their thrilling exhibition. They worked on a wire stretched between two steel poles 80 feet up in the air. No net was used by these daring performers" (Lowry). Like Lena Jordan, Madame Rita faced "public indecision as to her sex"—because of her bravery and fortitude.

People thrilled not just to the risk taken by women aerialists but also to startling juxtapositions. Circus writer Diana Starr Cooper, for example, described a static rope act that started with a belly dance and ended on an elephant: "The glamorous belly dancer reaches up, catches a pair of rings, is swept up into the air high above the arena. The lights go out, except for a single silver spot fixed on her. This is the first of several times you will see someone in the air, flying, and you are transfixed, every time. You crane your head back, your mouth drops open a little. She swings, one spot of flying light in the dark expanse near the roof. Then the music soars, she plummets earthward, the full lights pour on to show that she has landed, sitting beautifully, *on an elephant.* WHERE DID THAT ELEPHANT COME FROM?" (30).

Startling and clearly dangerous aerial tricks, done with and without the protection of a net, caused this performance type to dominate in newspaper stories of accidents and potential accidents. Discussion in the press, as in Hugh C. Weir's "The Women of the Circus," in *Hampton's Broadway Magazine* in 1909, emphasized the possibility of death with specific details of what could happen: "The mistake of an inch means death to the girl in the blue tights. She is swinging head down, and the swaying man in the trapeze holds her ankles firmly—below them stretches the hard, dull surface of the tan bark, a sheer drop of thirty-five feet. There is no safeguarding net." Jennie Ward, the article says further, "risks her life twice each day ... with a drop of twenty-five feet certain if she over-balances herself by so much as an inch" (799). As a child, Ward had begun performing with her brother; she was twelve when they debuted at the Parker Brothers Carnival Company and began building an act that soon involved sixteen performers, at least nine of them women. They joined Ringling Bros. in 1908, performing on swinging ladders suspended from the top of the tent as well as double trapeze, one trapeze hanging above another from which aerialists performed a series of contortions, flips, drops, and catches. The act was performed without a net or safety device of any kind, the risk of the deadly drop thus magnified, as the patter of ringmasters emphasized: the flyers might fall ... they fell last year during a simpler routine ... only inches separate life from horrible death (Gossard, "The Flying Wards").

On the trapeze and other aerial devices, women often pretended that they were closer to the death-causing accident than they actually were. Tiny Kline exited the trapeze platform by way of a breakaway act, causing thrills because of the seeming look of disaster: "What the spectator sees is that I take hold and bite on a mouthpiece while up in the air, letting go my hold on the rope—my weight on the teeth. Something breaks. Zoom! And down I

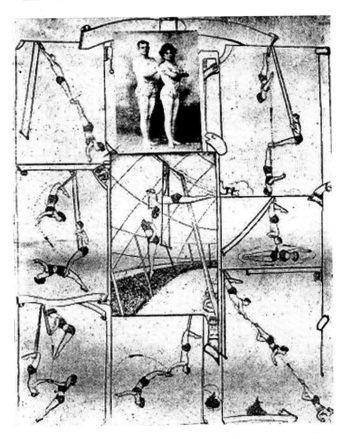

Drawing of Ward Aerial Act, from their letterhead, 1912 (Library of Congress Prints and Photographs Division).

come. 'An accident!' is the impression it creates. But just before I reach the floor, I am really hanging by my teeth from a thin wire the mouthpiece is attached to, which is trimmed so that I clear the floor by an inch or two" (45). The impression of an accident excited the circus crowd, she well understood, as mere competency might not.

Of all those defying death on the high wire, Bird Millman was among the best, a premier performer with Ringling Bros. and Barnum & Baile. Born Jennadean Engleman in Colorado in 1890, Millman spent her childhood traveling in small circuses with her parents, who were wire-walkers and trapeze artists. She first appeared at age six in a trained pony act while her father was teaching her wire work and iron jaw. She started performing on the wire at age twelve, the first American woman on the high wire without pole or parasol. In 1904, the Millman Trio, parents and child, entered big-time vaudeville, playing Keith's Union Square and Hammerstein's Roof Garden in New York. In 1913, Millman became a center-ring performer with Barnum & Bailey, where she remained after its merger with Ringling Bros. In 1919 and 1920, the side rings remained vacant during Millman's performance.

Bird Millman sold her act to the public on personality as well as great skill and speed. She did a waltz, a one step, a cakewalk, and a Hawaiian dance, gesturing at the audience as she performed intricate dance steps and ran back and forth on a wire thirty-six feet long — the usual length then eighteen — the longer length enabling her to build up greater speed. Millman's moves were accompanied by an eight-member chorus, and she sang with them in the act (Eckley 112–14). Through the years she wore a similar costume: "Her entrancing figure, clad in skin tight, one piece tights did much to enhance the beauty of the act" (Robie 46). Millman did not rely on novelty or hair-raising stunts; rather, she was acclaimed for her unusual speed and seemingly effortless grace (Robie).

Of all aerial performers the greatest was perhaps Lillian Leitzel, born in Germany in 1892. She created a thrilling aerial act, one that especially combined bodily risk with bodily attraction. She got her start with the Leamy Ladies, the aerial troupe in which her mother performed. As circus historian Robert Lewis Taylor described it, the troupe's rigging and act were "so complex that its like has never been seen again. At one point, the whole gigantic

Lillian Leitzel in the air. She was perhaps the greatest of the aerial performers in the best years of the circus (John and Mable Ringling Museum of Art).

rig revolved in a brisk circle, while one of the ladies rode a bicycle to propel it and her cohorts performed almost unbelievable acrobatics from trapezes suspended beneath" (225).

Then, on her own, Lillian Leitzel created an act that took place on a rope extended from the top of the tent. First, she ascended on a series of roll-ups, "her body in a horizontal arc, to a pair of Roman rings on which she swung and twirled as airy and incorporeal as a hummingbird flitting among the blossoms." Then, from a rope loop, with all other activities in the tent stopped, she threw her body up and over her right shoulder to make a circle, like a propeller, from a rope loop, a snare and bass drum dramatically accompanying. She might do 150 swingovers in a performance; her record was 249 (Taylor 217). As Earl Chapin May noted in *The Circus from Rome to Ringling*, the appeal of the circling, what he called basically "an ugly thing," lay in her appearance and personality: "If any one but Leitzel had done this act it would have been coolly received as a jerky demonstration of physical endurance. Others who essayed the one-arm giant swing or plange proved this fact conclusively. But little Leitzel, by no means a beauty, was histrionic from her golden hair to her tiny toes. Smartly walking into the big-top, she focused the attention of 15,000 persons. She held them by merely striking an attitude. She won them completely by her performance because she surrounded an ugly thing with supreme artistry" (271). Claiming that Leitzel had that "It" of stardom, Robert Lewis Taylor wrote that, beyond the talent on the rope and wire, she had "an ability to make men rabidly anxious to perpetuate the race ... her eyes held a rich glint of devilry that made men itch and grow pale" (234). "To say that she glorified in her power over men," historian Wilton Eckley asserted, "would be something of an understatement. She relished having them fawn over her; it was her way of enjoying life" (179). Part of the bodily attraction, certainly, was scarcity of clothes, necessary for doing the acts safely and for attracting an audience: she came out in capes and gowns and did an undressing number down to leotard and tights in the air.

Besides fostering individual achievement, aerial acts also offered the possibility of men and women together in large groups, working at high speeds, in complex synchronized flying movements. A poster from the 1890s advertised the five Silbons doing head-first dives from perch to perch, on flying rings, their tricks including double somersaults and involving "Great Displays of Muscular Strength." On the same bill the Siegrist Troupe did single and double somersaults in mid-air while rapidly flying from one trapeze bar to another — their heads covered with sacks. After merging in 1892, the Silbons and Siegrists continued doing a finale act for Ringling until the 1920s. with new performers joining and leaving to create other similarly named troupes.

In such groups, women were generally a third to a half of the performers, working as catchers as well as flyers (Tait 29–30). Eugenie Silbon spent thirty-seven years as a catcher, appearing effortless in demonstrating the skill and strength with which she caught both male and female aerialists. Born in San Francisco in 1879, she married Englishman Eddie Silbon in Guatemala City. As one of the twelve members of the combined Silbon-Siegrist troupe, Eugenia rehearsed a single trapeze act and then worked on a double and triple trapeze as the main catcher after the troupe joined the John Robinson and Franklin Brothers Circus in 1896. In 1898, the troupe sailed for England, joining the Barnum & Bailey Circus there.

In 1903, in the center ring of the Barnum & Bailey Circus, Eugenie Silbon served as one of two catchers, suspended in the center of the double rigging, facing opposite directions, and caught seven other performers flying from pedestals at each end. For the 1916–17 season, the troupe built rigging in the shape of a giant Maltese cross, with leapers passing each other at right angles in mid-air, fourteen performers participating, among them Eugenie as principal catcher.

The Silbon-Siegrist troupe remained with the Barnum & Bailey Circus until its merger with Ringling Brothers at the end of the 1919 season and then continued with the combined Ringling Bros. & Barnum & Bailey Circus through the 1931 season. The troupe spent thirty-three years with one circus, a record unequalled by any other feature act (Smith, "Eugenie Silbon").

In the air, acts especially riveted the crowd when they starred women, their sexuality, strength, skill, individual movements, and closeness to death thrilling to the crowd. Some women reached the heights of success, as Bird Millman and Lillian Leitzel did. But every circus featured women aerialists several times during the program, in all three rings, clearly as strong and skilled as male performers. The song "Flying Trapeze," written in 1874, said of a woman who left home and began performing with the dashing man, "She floats thro' the air with the greatest of ease" (Broadside Ballad). On the trapeze, the high wire, the slackwire and other aerial apparati, daring young women indeed did float and fly "thro' the air with the greatest of ease," and the country avidly watched them do so, admiring their beauty as well as their strength, skill, and bravery, their movement above all that contained American women on the ground.

# CHAPTER 26

# Bike/Car Tricksters

While women and men thrilled spectators throughout the years with their aerial acts, another death-defying trick, presented primarily at the beginning of the century, involved just women performers. As Americans encountered the shock of first bicycles and then automobiles with women at the controls, an added element of extreme physical risk could make their pedaling or driving into a circus act. Especially with the woman advertised as French and dressed in a leotard or gown, these acts involved driving as a transgressive act, imbued with sexual attraction, physical risk, and appropriation of mechanical instruments meant for men.

When in 1902 the Barnum & Bailey Circus returned from a five-year European tour, James Bailey found Ringling supreme and began to scramble to add new features to his show. A bicycle leaping a gap and looping the loop, branded as French tricks with his star women given French names, became a new circus act intended to increase business. Like watching the performance of horses in earlier generations, seeing what a bicycle could do interested Americans as this vehicle grew in popularity; John Kemp Starley's 1885 Rover Safety Bicycle, manufactured in England, appeared as the first recognizably modern bicycle, with two similarly sized wheels. Soon cycling clubs, along with long-range touring and racing, appeared on both sides of the Atlantic (Herlihy 235–37). Very quickly, women began riding these independent vehicles though fashion, medical, and ethical experts disapproved at first, labeling this hobby as too independent and indecorous, indicative of the New Woman running amuck. Even by 1894, the *Ladies' Standard Magazine* still felt the need to defend the practice and its effects on body and mind: "The head doctor of the New York Hospital on Fifteenth street states that no case has ever come under his notice where any organic weakness or derangement could be traced to bicycling" ("The Bicycle and Health"). With this article appears a picture of the ankle clips that could allow the woman to ride safely without shortening her skirt. By the turn of the century women rode bicycles more commonly, but circuses could still shock viewers with their dangerous tricks upon them, an act type not presented with male riders.

For Bailey, Mademoiselle D'Zizi did a bicycle leap, called "Spanning Death's Arch," in which she took off pedaling from a platform eighty feet high, went down an incline, turned a somersault in the air, and then leapt over a herd of elephants for added effect. Other shows soon added similar routines as well as new feature moves. For the Wallace

Shows, Mademoiselle French, an appellation making her supposed country of origin clear, rode a bicycle on a tight wire and then zoomed down a ramp to begin a long jump.

In this use of modern technology, with the additional thrill and abnormality of a woman at the controls, the vehicle in question soon went from the bicycle to the automobile, a more dangerous and startling mechanism for women. At the beginning of the century, car ownership increased quickly, but women behind the wheel remained a rarity. Even by 1915, the *Houston Automobile Directory*, for example, listed 7,732 auto owners, including 425 women, just 5.5 percent of the total (Scharff 25–26). Automobile manufacturers used well-publicized cross-country trips by women to tout the dependability of their cars — which performed well even with a woman behind the wheel. In 1909, Alice Ramsey, a twenty-two-year-old Vassar College graduate from Hackensack, New Jersey, became the first woman to drive across country, as a publicity stunt for the Maxwell-Briscoe Touring Company. Newspapers carefully reported on her fifty-nine-day voyage (Ruben).

In 1905, Barnum & Bailey helped invent a circus enthusiasm for vulnerable women in dangerous cars by featuring L'Auto-Bolide, the Dip of Death, in which Mademoiselle Mauricia De Tiers of Paris, alternatively named Mademoiselle Octavie LaTour, looped the gap in an automobile, creating a sensation at Madison Square Garden. For this ride, the star began her descent from a tower, streaking down a runway to a wooden receiving track, with a gap between the two of about twenty feet. According to the press release, the ride engaged "you," the viewer, fully:

> As the car descends the incline it gathers velocity. You are dimly conscious that its speed is so terrific as to be beyond comparison with anything you have ever seen. An express train is seemingly slow beside it. You think of a pistol shot; a speeding arrow; a meteor. It is all three in one. Before you can realize it, the car has descended the incline, turned upside down and still inverted, has shot into space. Twenty feet away, across a veritable chasm of death, is a moon-shaped incline.
> Your breath comes fast. You gasp. Your heart seems to stop pulsating.
> Will the auto strike the incline?
> Will it be upright? [quoted in Culhane 160].

The car wheels seemed to be coming off the runway, but smaller wheels in the axle actually guided the car down. The receiving track was three times as wide as the throwing runway, and its angle and distance insured that the car would arrive at the right place after it turned a flip in the air.

This act, featuring women in careening cars, received a huge amount of press and audience interest. On April 8, 1905, the *New York World* quoted Mademoiselle LaTour at length, indicating that viewers sought ever increasing risk and excitement and that she would readily take on the next challenge to maintain their attention:

> At present, I am courting death each day in La Tourbillon De La Mort, the supposed limit of human daring. But this act of plunging down the steep incline in an automobile that turns a back somersault in midair and lands on a runway is not really the limit of human daring. It is only the most perilous act that human imagination has so far devised for human daring. But it is the limit for only a moment. Hundreds of inventors are hard at work trying to perfect a machine that will make a double turn.... For hair-breadth as the escape must seem, the probability of accident must be really small. No one wants to see people die. The game is one of mettle not of death. So get your minds fermenting; give your imagination free play; and invent the real limit of human daring. Show us how to fly to the moon; direct the way to Mars; point the signboards down the roads of human daring. And I for one will go [quoted in Culhane 160].

Her act, even without the moon or to Mars, brought "every heart to a stand still for four seconds" ("New, Bigger Circus" 1905). Soon "the roads of human daring" led to a backwards somersault in the air with LaTour at the wheel.

This act quickly went from New York and Barnum & Bailey to circuses across the country, still with the rider vaguely French. Mademoiselle Reinal did the "Dip of Death," a similar act, in the Frank A. Robbins Circus in 1906. The Hagenbeck-Wallace Circus advertised a "Hurling, Whirling, Twirling, Automobile Driven by an Intrepid Woman" in newspapers across the country that same year.

In the Dip of Death, the combination of bicycles or cars, huge looped tracks, the possibility of a crash, and the oddity of the foreign woman driver engaged circus goers. At the end of the act, off of the bicycle or out of the car came the French mademoiselle, resplendently or scantily dressed, vulnerable yet transcendent and free. In this act was another transgression, like women on high wires — moving beyond the regular earth and the bounds of normality. With the final bow, coming out of a situation fraught with violent possibility, women proved themselves miraculously in control of the newest mechanical conveyances that had been intended only for men.

# CHAPTER 27

## Sharpshooters

Another astonishingly transgressive circus act involving women shooting guns. Like working in a tiger cage, on a high wire, or on the loop-the-loop, shooting at inanimate and live targets involved substantial skill and risk—and the crowd became fully engaged with the unexpected and amazing as women took aim. As was true of tiger training, the opportunity to be a sharpshooter came along with participation in gendered presentations of performance. Women shooters could both soothe and shock a crowd, as pioneer women or as the latest of frightening, independent New Women. In fact, women with guns could especially rivet an audience if they seemed to be jealously capable of aiming at each other.

Best known of these shooters, Annie Oakley began in vaudeville with her husband Frank Butler. In 1881, they signed with the Sells Brothers Circus for a forty-week engagement. The two welcomed the steady pay and honed their skills in the circus tent, which afforded a bigger shooting range than a vaudeville hall, but they soon grew tired of the incessant, difficult travel.

For better working conditions, they applied with Buffalo Bill Cody, with whom Oakley performed for most of the next seventeen years. Cody's Wild West show spent the summer of 1886 on Staten Island, where almost 360,000 people attended the performances. In May of 1887, the show headed to London, his well-publicized visitors including Queen Victoria and the Prince of Wales. In 1893 Cody set up shop right outside of the world's fair in Chicago, on two large lots across from the main entrance, many visitors thinking they were on the fair site. Oakley continued to tour with Cody until 1901, crisscrossing the country by train while firing, in her estimation, more than 40,000 shots in a single year, and then appeared with other shows such as Young Buffalo Wild West. She retired in 1913.

In each town, Cody used the presence of the small and conservatively dressed woman to ease the audience into the sound and risk of shooting. The general manager of the show, John M. Burke, described her position in the program as making all that would follow more acceptable for families:

> It was at first thought that so much shooting would cause great difficulty. It was said that horses would be frightened, women and children would be terrified. It was then that Col. Cody devised the idea of graduating the excitement. Miss Annie Oakley was secured. She comes on very early in the performance. She starts very gently, shooting with a pistol. Women and children see a harmless woman there, and they do not get worried. Gradually she increases the charge in her rifles until at last she shoots with a full charge. Thus, by the time the attack on

179

the stage coach comes the audience is accustomed to the sound of shooting ["How the Wild West"].

Oakley was animated, doing her acts rapidly, on stage for rarely more than ten minutes, a startling entrance and a star that the crowd was excited to see. In her accelerated presentation, always in motion, she aimed from over her shoulders, and backwards with mirrors, shooting an apple off a dog's head and the ash off a cigarette that her husband held in his teeth (Kasson 4; G. Riley 52).

Oakley's presentation at both the circus and Wild West show relied on biography to further her image as a solid, unintimidating woman. Publicists stressed that she grew up in poverty in Ohio, both in an orphanage and with her mother. When she was fifteen, a grocer told her he would buy the small game that she could shoot with a Parker sixteen-gauge shotgun that he gave to her. She did so

Lillian Smith, dressed to perform. At the age of seven, she became bored with dolls and asked her father for a "little rifle" instead (Buffalo Bill Historical Center).

well that she helped her mother pay off the mortgage on their home and began entering and winning shooting contests. When she began touring with her husband in 1876, performing on the variety circuit, their act emphasized their marriage and partnership. She thus described herself as always involved in shooting as a family activity, for the support that it could bring to others, like a western woman taking on ranch work for her family. Throughout her life, Oakley thus equated her willingness to shoot a gun with an older code of pioneer days, as though she were a western woman braving difficulties, forced to be strong.

Part of the selling of Oakley came not just from her assumption of a pioneer-woman persona but from the very public creation of a rival, thus two women with rapidly firing guns — two constructed as perhaps choosing to fire on each other. On Staten Island in 1886, a fifteen-year-old sharpshooter named Lillian Smith, a Californian, joined Cody's show and quickly became Oakley's well-publicized rival. She soon constructed her own tale and persona, as The Champion Rifle Shot of the World, a more aggressive, flirtatious, brash woman than Oakley as well as younger (G. Riley 39). At the age of seven, as her publicity maintained, she became bored with dolls and asked her father for a "little rifle" instead. She performed in San Francisco at age ten, and soon her father made a five thousand dollar wager that no one could beat her. She challenged Doc Carver, one of the era's best-known marksmen, to a competition in St. Louis, and he never showed up, a moment that publicists later constructed as demonstrating his fear. In this story, we have a woman not choosing marksmanship to support her family, but to keep herself from boredom and to beat men. This brash New Woman loved to challenge male shooters and publicly vied with the traditional pioneer figure that was Oakley.

Cody's show featured competitions between the two shooters, the true nature of their relationship not known, but a publicly exhibited animosity involving guns created a great publicity opportunity. Even the nature of their

Annie Oakley, dressed to perform. In the sharpshooter act, women presented circus nostalgia as they appeared as pioneers; they also shocked audiences as they seemed to be moving too quickly, aiming at their husbands and at other women with whom they competed in a seemingly out-of-control shooting spree, the most modern of skilled and dangerous women (Library of Congress Prints and Photographs Division).

guns became part of the rivalry, Oakley using a shotgun, a symbol of the old West, for her rapid delivery of pellets and Smith a rifle for her slower and more stylized act featuring decorated targets and flirtatious gestures.

In London, where Oakley and Smith performed before Queen Victoria, they also shot against each other at a Wimbledon shooting competition, press coverage in England and the United States following Oakley's victory and Smith's tempestuous reaction to it. In various English and American cities, Smith, constructed as the more boisterous and outlandish of the two, would very publicly walk out and quit, their competition seeming to involve shooting as well as their contractual relationship with Cody. Both Oakley and Smith entered contests at American shooting clubs, generally the first women to enter and thus a source of press attention, with it seeming possible that they might shoot each other.

As they publicly emphasized their rivalry and differences, Oakley and Smith also appeared in contrasting costumes. Sharpshooters generally dressed conservatively, as westerners, in long skirts, very different from bareback riders in short skirts and tights. Lillian Smith's western gear was quite feminine, especially when she appeared opposite Oakley: she wore highly decorated dresses and bonnets of the 1890s, in light colors and floral patterns. Annie Oakley, however, dressed in western buckskin, often highly decorated and fringed, her long hair generally down and on her shoulders. Cody called her "Missie" and the promotional materials called her a "little girl" from the West, not a flirt in ruffles but a steadfast pioneer.

Within the Wild West show and the circus, shooting remained of interest as an act type for women, crowd interest driven by their skill and by the shock of their engaging in a typically male activity. Though more women sharpshooters worked in Wild West shows than in circuses, many had careers that involved circus big tops and sideshows, Wild West shows, and rodeos, where women often rode and shot. Fanny Sperry Steele worked an act with her husband; they both shot rifles at an array of targets, and then Fanny "shot china eggs out of her husband's fingers and a cigar out of his mouth" (Enss 54). May Manning Lillie, who with her husband Gordon organized a Wild West show with many circus elements, appeared during her twenty years with this show as the Princess of the Prairie and The New Rifle Queen (Enss 41). Circus and Wild West show owners often pitted two women stars against each other for extra exhilaration, two warring for a man in the tradition of Oakley and Smith, thus emphasizing the danger of women with guns even as these stars wielded them expertly. In the sharpshooter act, women presented circus nostalgia as they appeared as pioneers; they also shocked audiences as they seemed to be moving too quickly, aiming at their husbands and at other women with whom they competed in a seemingly out-of-control shooting spree, the most modern of skilled and dangerous women.

# CHAPTER 28

# Clowns

With so many risky roles for women in the circus, like shooting guns, walking on high wires, dancing on horseback, and wrestling with tigers, the one judged ultimately as the most unnatural and unacceptable might seem surprising since it involved no real physical risk. In this most transgressive of acts — clowning — women remained a minority, and a myth continued that this profession included no women at all. In appearing as clowns, women became open satirizers of American traditions, thus abandoning past expectations and traditions through a means more powerful than climbing aboard a horse or to the top of the tent. As clowns, they laughed quite openly at American homes and towns.

Throughout the decades male clowns appeared dressed as women in the broadest of humorous costumes and movements, the audience fully aware of the gender switch and the satire, as described in the *New York Times'* coverage of Barnum & Bailey in Madison Square Garden in 1905: "In this 'fool's paradise' there was every conceivable kind of joke played. The favorite of the crowd was a male clown dressed up as an old Irish woman, who patiently wheeled a perambulator around the arena, meanwhile feeding the passenger, a suckling pig, from a milk bottle" ("New, Bigger Circus"). In 1938 in a *New York Times Magazine* article entitled "Slapstick as an Art," a list of famous gags included male clowns dressing in exaggerated form as women — attempting without success to look beautiful and lure a mate, deal with bad babies, cook a gourmet dinner, repair the plumbing, or fight with a drunken husband. These "female" clowns wore balloons and other accoutrements as well as huge amounts of lipstick and wild wigs in what recreation specialist Michael M. Davis labeled as their "grotesque drag representations of the female body" (M. Davis, Introduction 11).

Some of these acts featured fairly developed plots as they concentrated on stereotypically absurd women. Charles Baldwin, in the 1890s, played the role of "a seaside landlady whose rascally boarder has gone off without paying her." The landlady appeared with all the accoutrements of satirized age and gender: "Notice the dowdy bonnet, the alternate teeth blackened out, the thin hair, the ancient knitted shawl, and, above all, the expression and the tear! To see and hear the 'Weeping Wonder' give vent to his 'emotions' is a most screamingly funny experience. And when his audience roar with merriment, his plaint grows louder and more hysterically extravagant, culminating in a far-reaching screech of impotent wrath" (FitzGerald 528). Male clowns, of course, also satirized presumably male behavior, as they attempted to rob a bank, stuff ten friends in a tiny car, or train a dog/clown. But women did not seem appropriate as satirizers of either women or men.

With the oft repeated acts generally not involving women clowns, writers who discussed the career generally preferred to posit that they didn't exist. In an article on the great clowns of the 1920s and the 1930s, in the *Saturday Evening Post* in 1942, the writer covers William Koss, Emmett Kelly, Eagle Otto Griebling, Poodles Hanneford, Lou Jacobs, and the Fratellini brothers, with many pictures and much discussion of their appeal, but with no mention of any women clowns. The only woman pictured or discussed in the article, in fact, is an acrobat whom Lou Jacobs is shown as hugging (Kelley, "Along Clown Alley"). Even recent books and articles agree that women did not appear as clowns until the last few years, and they give reasons for this lack of participation. In *Serious Play: Modern Clown Performance* in 2009, for example, Louise Peacock speaks of female clowning as a recent development.

For a hundred years, articles and books about clowning have given reasons for women's lack of participation, usually citing their insecurity and vanity, which make them unwilling to perform in outlandish costumes. An article from 1896 argued that women did not want to appear gangly and ugly: "Perhaps, as is more likely the case, there are no sufficiently brand new women who are willing to sacrifice the swiss skirts, the satin coats and the pink and white make-ups for ugly calico bloomers, pointed caps, and a layer of white paint that sinks their identity" ("The Latest New Woman"). In 2009, Louise Peacock argued similarly that women were reluctant to look unattractive or to reveal themselves without a character to play as in the theatre: "Perhaps the difference lies in the fact that when actresses make themselves look ugly, they do so to perform a character distinct from themselves. When a clown performer makes up as his or her clown persona, he/she is undergoing a transformation which reveals hidden facets of his or her personality to the audience." Such satire and self-revelation, she claimed further, were particularly problematic for women because of their insecure position in society, "making fun" being difficult for the disenfranchised: "Status is only readily given away by those whose status in society is secure. Hence the fact that most famous clowns in western society have been white men (the only exception is the Cuban clown, Chocolat)" (78). These writers thus cede responsibility for their lack of participation to the women themselves.

But throughout our time period, regardless of public declarations, women were indeed performing as clowns, albeit as a minority, even though in each decade publicity portrayed a woman as the "first" or "only." Amelia Butler, for example, appeared with James M. Nixon's Great American Circus in 1858. Other women clowns included Irene Jewell Newton with Conroy's Great American Circus in 1893; Maude Burtoli with Burtsch's New All Featured 25c Shows in 1896; Miss del Fuego, a singing and dancing clown, with the Robinson & Franklin Circus in 1896 and then with Barnum & Bailey in 1898 and the Great Van Ambrugh Circus of 1908. In 1895, the *New York Times* labeled a Miss Williams, actually Evetta Mathews, twenty-five years old, as "the only lady clown on earth" ("Why Miss Williams"). Several women clowns appeared in 1896 along with Mathews, doing tumbling and silly singing while wearing a combination of the sexy and ridiculous — a "décolletée bodice, mammoth knickerbockers, and infinitesimal hat" ("Peep behind the Scenes"). Again in 1897, Barnum & Bailey featured three women clowns, entering with the parade, tumbling together and doing tricks ("Great Fun"). Emma Barlow worked with Barlow Bros. Circus in 1899 and went from there to vaudeville, doing song and dance.

In 1901, Agnes Adams sang and jested with the ringmaster in Frank Adams' Southern Railroad Show. Eva Williams clowned in Murphy and Nickey's Wagon Show in 1908. Fanny Rice, a vaudeville comedian, signed a contract with Ringling Bros. as a clown in 1908. "Dinky" Darrow clowned with Sells-Floto in 1909. Laura Silver, with the Silver Family

Show, sang and clowned from 1900 to 1907. In 1917, the Barnum & Bailey show had two women clowns and one young girl, the funniest of all the clowns according to the *Times* ("15,000 New Yorkers"). The Two Rosells appeared with the Al G. Barnes Circus in 1917. In an article in *Popular Mechanics* in 1927, continuing the publicity focus on the "first" and the "only," Earl Chapin May referred to Loretta LaPearl, "a fair young woman with luminous eyes" as "the only woman circus clown" ("With the 'Merry Joeys'" 596). She worked along with her husband Harry La Pearl. With humorous gestures and movements, Loretta played the clarinet both in the circus street-parade band and under the big top, interacting humorously with the regular musicians as she satirized a high-society orchestra in a mock dramatic costume featuring a "green coat with golden epaulets and broad hat with a high cockade" (596). Grace Fairburn worked for the Clyde Beatty Circus in the 1930s and 1940s; Mary Koster sang clown songs with Robbins Bros. in 1938. Irene Eastman, singing clown, traveled with the Cole Brothers World-Tour Shows.

Bessie Castello, from an equestrian family, quit riding in 1935 and then began appearing in the St. Louis Police Circus, as a character clown, and was such a hit that Roy Rogers contracted her for a thirteen-week tour with his troupe. Castello, by then a grandmother, impersonated a little girl who had lost her father at the circus, and she prowled through the seats, screaming for "Daddy" to the amusement of spectators. Louise Craston (or Cranston) Adams, born in 1899, was a daughter of Joe Craston, a well-known English equestrian and clown. As a child, performing as Lulu, she appeared in England with her father in his clown act and then developed her own act with her brother and sister, called the Crastonians, in 1923. At age twenty-five, after she married her husband Albertino, she presented a comedy duo with him. They performed for Ringling Bros. and Barnum & Bailey from 1939 to 1941.

With prejudice against women as clowns and a seeming lack of them, some women presented themselves as making a shocking feminist choice in embracing this career option and ability to satirize, an advertising hook that worked well. In 1895, press releases and newspaper articles tied Evetta Mathews' choice of clowning to women's emancipation and labeled it as brand new: "There were plenty of women trapeze performers, bar performers and tightrope performers, and even strong women who could hold half a dozen people on their shoulders. These fields seemed to be pretty well occupied, so Miss Mathews got advanced notions of emancipation and determined to invade a new field and become a clown. There never had been women clowns." And she presented herself firmly as choosing a career by which she could be self-sufficient and equal: "I believe that a woman can do anything for a living that a man can do," she told a *Times* reporter, "and do it as well as a man" ("Very New Woman").

In many articles about Mathews, she stressed that her choice had seemed shocking even within a circus family. Of twenty-two children, three became clowns, the other two who made this choice being men ("Why Miss Williams"). Because the choice of clowning was more exotic for a woman than riding horses or doing a wire act, as she said, "All my people laughed at me when I told them I was going into the ring as a clown." Their negative judgments — made concerning a part of circus work by circus performers — did not stop her. The articles went on to say that ultimately she had proven to her family and herself that she had chosen well: she had steady work with less chance of injury than with an acrobatic or aerial performance and she had creative license to plan her own skits and moves: "I am paid for my ideas" ("Why Miss Williams").

As a feminist clown in 1895, Mathews appeared as part of the New Woman circus constructed by Barnum as a special ring and attraction: "Evetta, as she is billed, is a plump little woman with an abundance of life and energy and she has all of the New Woman's fads: she rides a bicycle, swings Indian clubs and does everything else that a man does to keep herself in proper trim." She is called "a brand new woman, a man scoffer, a twentieth century girl." In this newspaper coverage of Williams/Mathews, as for so many other women clowns, she becomes a satirist of traditional mores but the one and only, an anomaly, not a participant in any sort of trend: "The men in the clown business rather enjoy Miss Williams's antics, but they do not regard her as a serious competitor or believe that any other women are likely to follow her example" ("Why Miss Williams").

Within the circus program, Mathews' acts reflected her presentation as the surprisingly aggressive New Woman. One involved the surprise of a clown in the audience, wearing a cloak and bonnet, sitting by a young man there to see the show. She called out to the ring-master through a megaphone, pretending that she wanted a job with the circus and that the young man had offered her money not to go, not to make that foolish choice, causing confusion of course in the chosen stranger. Finally she tossed the coverings aside and entered the ring as a clown: as a woman who had already made the shocking choice, beyond the appeals of any one young man, a routine that certainly would not work with a male clown. Later she re-entered the ring, dressed in white face and outlandish clothes, and, after making sure that the audience recognized her, began a comic tumbling act as though fully engaged in the inappropriate job of clowning ("Why Miss Williams").

Although James Bailey sought the shock of Mathews as New Woman and although she continued as a clown in his circus, he placed severe gendered restrictions on what she could do. Even as women appeared on trapeze wires and in cages with lions and tigers, they did not get access to full physical clowning: "Evetta says that she is handicapped in that she is not allowed to tumble and somersault like ordinary men clowns. She can tumble and twist like a rubber doll, and she is an expert contortionist. But Mr. Bailey doesn't approve of this." Though she could not tumble and somersault because of Bailey, even though women were doing similar moves in the air and on horseback, she delighted "the children with her grimaces, her dances, her frolics, her mimicry and her merry laughter" ("Very New Woman"). This article does not give Bailey's reasoning, but it may have concerned the irreverence of clowning, its satire of cultural mores, and its nearness in space to the spectators.

This stern judgment of the woman as clown continued, as did the prejudice that only the odd — feminist, difficult, ugly, unnatural — woman would take on such a role. In an article from 1939, for example, the choice of clowning is attributed to a woman's inability to look as good as other women in the circus. Clowning thus appears as a form of giving up on what women were supposed to look like and do. The article gives no attention to clown Louise Cranston Adams' act or training, but to the fact that this "plain" woman wore eyeglasses, not appropriate for a ballet girl, which she had first tried to become. The writer continues by claiming that she no longer needed to don the layers of makeup that it took for her to attempt to be pretty: the "idealizing makeup" had been "scraped off and scrapped" and replaced with easier-to-install greasepaint: "A red daub landed between eyebrows shaped like croquet hoops. The nose was painted like a red heart. And the traditional tear streaks were appended to the eyes. And that, the circus man concluded with authority, was the way Lulu would appear" ("Circus Remodels").

Though women faced prejudice about being clowns and about the acts they could undertake, and though their presence was continually effaced, some were learning the full cadre of clowning skills. Loretta LaPearl found falling full length upon the floor a hard trick to learn: she thought that she had broken her back when she first did it, but she quickly learned to make her rounded shoulders take most of the blow. She also practiced making a loud clap at the exact moment that her partner put his hand up to her cheek and seemed to slap her: "Towners always laugh if they think a clown is being mistreated in some way. But the clown slap is really a bit of sleight of hand." As LaPearl told Earl Chapin May, clowns learned in the first and second year of training to use slapsticks and then moved to the bigger punch of a detonating cap: she learned to detonate the cap near her hand and not on it or on the person whom she seemed to hit hard ("With the 'Merry Joeys'" 597). With her skills increasing, LaPearl began to participate in not just singing bits but skits involving fights and accidents, physical comedy (loved by audiences) that might poke fun at domestic harmony, cooking, child-raising, and family trips to town, the kinds of scenes in which circus managers had been loath to place women and in which they generally preferred for men to play them.

In the case of clowning, the separation by gender, indeed the tradition that only men worked as clowns, did not stem from physical ability. And to some extent, it did not involve reality since women did clowning throughout the period. But critics, managers, and audiences did seem to find it controversial for women to appear as satirists, poking fun at family traditions, and to engage in skits that might include entrance into the stands and interaction with circus goers. Like stand-up comedy through many decades, clowning was deemed the purview of men. But, even these stereotypes and prejudices did not keep women from entering the business where they supposedly were not. Even more controversially perhaps than entering the tiger cage, women entered the cast of clowns and made fun of American culture and of gender stereotypes, working without beauty as a priority.

# CHAPTER 29

# Circus Managers/Owners

In circuses, most women worked for male managers and owners. But just as women appeared in many acts where they might not be expected, as tiger trainers, sharpshooters, and aerialists as well as clowns, they also ran some shows. Another type of surprising working woman — following an example set by Petsy Astley, who owned the first modern circus along with her husband in 1768 in London — made a living as the boss, a chance more likely with smaller shows and before circus consolidation in the 1920s and afterwards.

Agnes Lake's career as circus performer and owner mirrored the path of many working women, involving their marriages, children, economic needs, and aging. Born on a farm in Lower Saxony, just east of the Netherlands, she often made up a history of being from France for a more romantic origin. She was part of an influx to the United States between 1833 and 1843 of nearly 200,000 Germans (Fisher and Bowers 22; Roberts).

At nineteen, like other unmarried women, she was expected to keep house for her brothers and father and accept their choice of a husband. In 1846, she saw Bill Lake at the Great Western Circus, four blocks from her home, working with a dog act, and she married him that year, an escape from her family and a semi-arranged marriage within the local community. They eloped, no approval forthcoming from her family, and Agnes began training as an equestrian so that she could remain with him on the road. After working with many outfits, the Lakes sought to move into management. In 1859, with John Robinson, Bill Lake launched the Great Southern Menagerie and Circus, touring from Ohio through the South with bareback riders, a small menagerie, a performing zebra, and Eugenie de Lorme, a lion tamer (Fisher and Bowers 89). In the spring of 1863, the Lakes went out with their own Lake & Company's Great Western Circus, with Agnes starring as an equestrian and helping to manage the show (Fisher and Bowers 95).

After Bill Lake was killed in Granby, Missouri, in 1869 by a man he had stopped for sneaking into a performance without paying, Agnes took over management of the circus, working with her daughter Emma, a fine equestrian. On her own, Agnes continued within the industry that she knew. She wrote that she began her stint as the sole manager with the following words to her employees: "If any of you think I am incapable, all I ask is that you will give me two weeks' notice and I will endeavor to fill your places. I am determined to keep the show on the road and I shall succeed." The performers remained, joined by famed equestrian Wooda Cook who performed a back somersault on a galloping horse; her act involved twelve riders, ten of whom were women, including Agnes and Emma. Over the years, Agnes Lake used the oddity of herself as manager as a publicity item, declaring in her ads and programs that this circus was "under a woman's management," a fact, exciting in its oddness, that indicated a clean, family entertainment (Fisher and Bowers 178). In 1872, Lake combined with other owners to form the Great Eastern Circus, touring almost entirely by railroad, with a balloon ascension as a pre-show entertainment.

After the 1872 season, Agnes Lake retired and invested in a printing business in Cincinnati, but then she lost money in the panic of 1873 and joined the Great Eastern Circus in 1874 as a manager and equestrian ringmaster. She married Wild Bill Hickok in 1875, when he was thirty-nine and she was fifty, and then again quit circus work ("Mrs. Lake-Hickock Dead"). After he was shot in the back of the head in a Deadwood saloon, she returned to the circus in 1878, touring with her daughter and training horses to once again earn her living. In 1880, they were with Barnum & Bailey. Agnes' last year on the road was with the John Robinson Circus in 1882 (Culhane 93; Fisher and Bowers 287).

Other women found in a small circus the means of securing a living for themselves and their families. From a town near Mobile where she was born in 1844, Mollie Bailey joined the Bailey's Family Circus when it came to Tuscaloosa, the owners no relationship to her. She was in Tuscaloosa attending a ladies' academy, her report card testifying that she was excellent in dramatics and tableau work. She joined up so that she could marry the circus proprietor's son James (Gus) Bailey, "a young man, slender and with the halo of greatness about his head," without her parents' permission. Indeed, she had not been given permission to even see the circus (Culhane 84). When the Civil War began, he entered Hood's Texas Brigade and she became a Confederate nurse and an army spy, while also singing for the troops. After the war, with three daughters, they joined a Mississippi River showboat company, with her singing and his leading the orchestra.

With four sons and four daughters, her husband's health failing, Bailey started her own little show in 1879, which she called A Texas Show for Texas People, fighting difficult odds as she began touring primarily in Texas, Oklahoma, and Kansas. Her show traveled with seven wagons for thirty years and then went on the rails in 1905 when she was able to purchase Pullman cars, nine years after the death of her husband.

At the circus, Bailey served as host, a popular figure returning each year to the same towns, where she had little competition, often performing at lots that she had bought so that she could avoid rental fees and hassles with landlords. She advertised with signs saying "Aunt Mollie's Coming." Bailey also became a huge donor, giving free admission to needy children and the funds for thirty-two churches. As the circus fan magazine *White Tops* testified, "she was a real institution in a hundred Southern communities." Poet Frank W. Ford even described this popular presence in a poem:

> It was cotton-picking time down in Texas
> And the leaves of all the trees a golden brown.
> The children and the old folk all were happy
> For the Mollie Bailey show had come to town ["Mollie Bailey"].

The show, advertised by advance men on posters as "a scintillating aggregation of the world's greatest talent. Stupendous and mammoth," featured primarily Bailey's children. Some of her children stayed with the circus after she retired to Houston in 1914, where she had her winter quarters during the circus years; she died there in 1918, and the circus closed in 1920. The Circus Fans Association in Dallas chose to take the name of "the South's foremost woman circus owner" and thus became Mollie A. Bailey's Top ("The Mollie Bailey Texas Top").

While Lake and Bailey ultimately managed circuses on their own, other women spent long careers in management along with their husbands. For fourteen years Claude W. Webb and his wife Pauline Russell Webb toured with their Russell Brothers Circus, one of the more successful truck shows before World War II. Webb began in show business in the early twenties as the proprietor of a small show featuring a large snake. After he married Pauline Russell, they started the Russell Brothers Circus, wintering in Missouri. Their route in 1934 led into the Midwestern states and down into Texas, Oklahoma, Arkansas, and Louisiana. In 1936, the show also went for the first time into the Northeast. By 1937, the Webbs toured extensively with a forty-truck show. In 1938 and 1939, in harder economic times, the Webbs still kept their well-managed show out all year, perhaps the only truck show to accomplish the feat.

For this show, Pauline Webb served as personnel manager of a cast that she constantly sought to improve. In charge of hiring and of planning the program, she put on an impressive show, with many acts by women performers, including a fine horse exhibition by Hazel King; elephants tricks under the direction of Genevieve Hughes and Bobbie Wariner; Quints of the Air, "a lovely and graceful aerial presentation in which five girls perform in unison, followed by a brief interlude by the clowns"; a bicycle loop act by Mademoiselle Rebra; trained dog acts by Maxine Frederick and Betty Willis; Miss Aerialetta, "one of the very foremost aerial gymnasts of the day"; the iron-jaw slide by Bertha Conner, billed as Reckless Violetta; exploits on the Roman rings by the Willis Sisters and Maxine Frederick; high-school horses presented by Irene Ledgett and nine other women riders; and Aerial Ballet, "ten girls on ladders around the track to the accompaniment of serpentines, cloud swings over the end rings, and a loop over the center." The sideshow featured Princess Mahrajah, mentalist; Pearl White, iron-tongued girl; Madame Ve Ara, magician; and a large number of cooch dancers (Thayer, "C.E. Webb's").

Though management was certainly a less common career option for women than performance, they did become animal trainers, personnel managers, general managers, and owners of shows. The presence of the woman as manager or owner, in fact, could be a drawing card, a new feature worth coming to see, with women owners sometimes creating their own special relationship with the towns in which they toured, as did Mollie Bailey. For these women, management certainly provided an opportunity for an extended career in the circus, beyond the years of performance, and for supporting a family: another surprising feature of the circus as work space.

# CHAPTER 30

# Toward the End of a Career

To obtain successful circus careers, women sought every opportunity; they bargained for better contracts and higher salaries; and they dealt with the hard work of daily practice and ever more challenging routines. But a performing career, its joys and its adversities, would be over all too soon. Many performers did not want to accept that the time to leave had come, as equestrian Bunni Bartok Perz described in her poem "Yesterday's Star":

> Doesn't she see, it's really too late?
> Her glory has passed. The time has come,
> To move over and make room for the young.
> Everyone says she was the best by far.
> But there is nothing sadder in the circus than "YESTERDAY'S STAR"! [55].

Though circus stars, like athletes and actors, had to face the end of their reign at the top, they had several options to pursue once their performance years were over.

In equestrian acts and families, older performers often moved into the role of ring-master. In March 1915, when the Hanneford family came from England to the United States, opening with the Barnum & Bailey Circus in Madison Square Garden and then joining the combined Ringling Bros. and Barnum & Bailey in 1919, Elizabeth Hanneford, who turned forty-five in 1915, appeared as ringmaster and her children, Lizzie, George, and Poodles, as the stars. As Fred Bradna's autobiography described Elizabeth in this role, she was capable always of "snapping up the pace" since she was "unexcelled in the art of holding public attention." Her appearance and movements stressed the grandeur of the horses and riders: dressed "in the latest Parisian evening gown and stunning jewels, crowned by an ostrich-plume tiara," Bradna wrote, Hanneford moved "with dance steps and graceful gestures" (78–79).

Other women stayed with the circus in support roles. Maud Millette, trapeze artist, left the ring in 1932, at age forty-one, and began to do wardrobe repairs. She "turned over the trapeze work in the family to her daughter, Mildred, then 16." When she was interviewed in 1936, she answered the reporter's question about missing the center ring: "'Yes,' she mused, without giving her fingers a moment's rest over the hat-laden table. 'I do miss it. I guess I still have a yen for it'" ("Circus Wardrobe"). During World War II, Millette left the circus and began working as a welder in defense plants in New Britain, Connecticut ("Under the Marquee" 39).

Another possibility was to leave the circus but use circus skills in a related occupation. After equestrian Bessie Castello retired, first from circus riding and then from the Roy Rogers Circus, in which she appeared as a clown, she went to the John Benson Wild Animal Farm at Nashua, New Hampshire, in the spring of 1936, as a riding instructor and animal trainer (Smith, "Bessie Castello"). Many other performers who worked with animals gave riding lessons or took jobs at animal parks or with film companies after they retired from the circus.

Some fully retired circus stars saved enough money for a very comfortable retirement, including Lew Sunlin and his wife, equestrian Allie Jackson. Before their full retirement in 1904, they first became trainers at the circus, he of elephants and she of horses. The couple lived well in retirement because they had invested in property in Grand Rapids, Michigan, one of their greatest sources of wealth being extensive rock quarries there that they sold to amusement developers ("Louis F. Sunlin").

Many who retired enjoyed the regular reunions of visiting with performers when the circus came to town. When the daughter of Elizabeth Hanneford, Elizabeth Hanneford Clarke, retired, first from performing on horses and then from her own stint as ringmaster and trainer, she lived in retirement in North Hollywood, California, but when there was a circus around, she and her daughter, Ernestine, and son-in-law, Parley Baer, took off: "Our automobile," she told a reporter, "can find a circus lot all by itself if there's a show within a hundred miles." When the Clarkes arrived on a circus lot, they sparked a homecoming celebration since they knew so many people in the business (Smith, "Elizabeth Hanneford Clarke" I.26; II.28).

Many women, though, did not have in retirement the financial resources of Elizabeth Clarke or Allie Jackson. Nettie Burk had been a famous bareback and trick rider for Barnum & Bailey, earning up to $250 a week with her own troupe of trained dogs and horses. She left the circus to marry a bartender, an "unhappy match," and he died a few years later, but she was too ashamed to try to return to the show. She worked at various jobs until she was sixty-eight. Faced with starvation, she sought help from the Actors' Fund, which beginning in 1882 collected donations to provide assistance to retired entertainers. She died at ninety in 1932, "crippled by rheumatism and age" ("Woman Circus Star").

As was true of so many workers, before Social Security and without employer-funded retirement plans, many circus performers had difficulty moving into retirement, their income determined only by what they had saved. And the career might end quickly for the circus performer, for this was a business based on physical ability more than youth and beauty and one injury could signal the last performance. From the circus, generations of American women workers moved into retirement, often a hard transition to make.

# Conclusion

After 1940, a world war and television would alter the long American circus tradition. Though at the turn of the twentieth century nearly a hundred different circuses toured the United States, in 1956 the number was thirteen, the majority owned by the combined Ringling Bros. and Barnum & Bailey Circus. In that year, John Ringling North took down his canvas tents and began performing only in city arenas (Sweet and Haberstein 583–84).

In the circus, over the sixty years of its greatest American popularity, ubiquitous depictions of it in popular media, such as newspapers, magazines, fiction, and film, created extremes of imagery, constructing in this entertainment form and career path the promise — and threat — of a life outside normality. Both the positive and negative depiction, whatever its intention, riveted the American gaze toward what women might be and do.

Here was a glorious and dangerous visitor to every state, but also a site of employment for thousands of women, who complicated the literature of circus with their own versions of their motivations and self-image, of the contractual status of their work, of the formation of a circus act, and of life on the road. Though only some of these women engaged in feminist political causes like suffrage, they all involved themselves in the practical feminism of a career, and their own stories provide a complication to and contrast with other public imagery. Women's freedom could mean the freedom to have a quick adventure and fall in love, as in so many romance novels, but it could also indicate freedom to leave family and the hometown, to move from place to place, to seek training and career advancement, to take the risks that would impress a crowd, to sign contracts and bargain with employers, and to reach the highest levels of fame. With the narratives of circus performers overlaid on those of newspaper and fiction writers, American women could consider the romance and danger of a different sort of life by examining the tales told not just by outsiders but by insiders, who were exotic, certainly, but also busy and successful women workers.

Beyond romantic and realistic depictions, of course, was the real thing: the circus came to town and did so regularly. Here were not Hollywood stars seen from a screen or vaudeville performers seen only by the few, but performing women first appearing on colorful posters and then walking right through town. After the parade, they performed in two shows in which they might constitute half of the cast, the crowd's involvement essential to all that they did. And while the circus day gaze centered on the performers, it also reached to the women in the stands, possibly planning to join the performing women in a circus cast or to make their own way in the world.

In watching the circus, spectators did not just see women performing in similar acts: they saw women in an array of act types with different messages to convey. At the circus the least skilled and youngest seemed to be just standing or walking around: they marched in elaborate parades and specs; they stood in greasepaint in tableaux; they sat astride elephants guided forward by male trainers. While the most young and beautiful seemed worthy of the gaze, so also did the most hideous and bizarre, the wonder being in the existence of both extremes. Like gorgeous and close-to-naked tableau performers, freaks often did little more than sit and stand, warning of the worst that women could be once they abandoned the normal bounds of the right size, the right facial hair, the right skin, and the right genitalia.

Though the circus certainly reiterated the status of women as silent, beheld for bodily distinctions, those occupying that status were not the big-top stars. The beauty of equestrians, cat trainers, and aerialists might receive attention, but stardom required distinctive skills that evolved from years of practice and hard work. Equestrians became well known for their individual act types as bareback dominated over high-school riding, revealing women's abilities to craft unique demonstrations of artistic and athletic skill. Cat trainers like Mabel Stark exploited stereotypes of motherhood and sexuality but did so in a highly dangerous job in which they excelled by their own knowledge, stamina, and control. While men following the lead of Jules Léotard brought aerial acts to the United States, it was women who came to thrill the crowds by seeming to walk and leap among the stars. Women also came to be circus stars by manipulating traditionally male machinery such as cars and guns. And even though Americans thought of men as the appropriate agent of satirical comedy, and every generation advertised the first woman clown, women also appeared in clown troupes, making fun of American life along with their male counterparts.

Between 1940 and 1945, the female labor force grew by 6.5 million, or 50 percent. Numbers and percentages went down in the fifties and then increased with each decade. As a percentage of the total group of women, 33.9 percent worked in 1950, 37.7 in 1960, 43.3 in 1970, 51.5 in 1980, and 62.2 in 2010 (Toossi 22). As women moved into a working life, they would certainly not all swing from trapezes or face tigers. But the circus had already proved to be a site for so many developments that would reoccur across careers in the second half of the twentieth century. As women came into the work world, they were greeted by extreme reactions and depictions that involved many careers besides the circus. Work, like college for women, appeared repeatedly, in an array of media, as a youthful adventure or quick route to love and marriage. Conversely, it was a negative development indicating that women were out of control, indeed that they were evil usurpers of male prerogatives. But in autobiographies, interviews, letters, and speeches, circus's women workers themselves had more detailed and complex tales to tell about their choices, ultimately discussing their reasons for careers, their contract negotiations, the daily realities of their jobs, and their fight to obtain training, opportunity, and advancement. In examining the history of women's labor, leading to 62.2 percent of American women now involved in fulltime work along with 73.2 percent of men, we can learn from an earlier generation of circus stars, real American women workers seen across the nation who dealt with the depicted and the real, with stereotypical gender expectations, and with so many realities of a competitive industry as they reached to the highest levels of skill and success.

# Works Cited

In this bibliography, Parkinson Library refers to the Robert L. Parkinson Library and Research Center, Circus World Museum, Baraboo, Wisconsin.

"Accident Took Bette Leonard out of Circus — Not out of Her." *Bandwagon* 18 September 1948: 48+. Print.

"Act: Thrill." The Circus in America. The Institute for Advanced Technology in the Humanities at the University of Virginia. Web. 1 October 2011.

Adams, Charles F. "Trouping with Seals." *Saturday Evening Post* 24 May 1930: 60+. Print.

Adams, Katherine H., and Michael L. Keene. *After the Vote Was Won: The Later Achievements of Fifteen Suffragists*. Jefferson, NC: McFarland, 2010.

_____, and _____. *Alice Paul and the American Suffrage Campaign*. Urbana: University of Illinois Press, 2008.

Adams, Katherine H., Michael L. Keene, and Jennifer C. Koella. *Seeing the American Woman, 1880–1920: The Social Impact of the Visual Media Explosion*. Jefferson, NC: McFarland, 2012.

Adams, Katherine H., Michael L. Keene, and Melanie McKay. *Controlling Representations: Depictions of Women in a Mainstream Newspaper, 1900–1950*. New York: Hampton, 2009.

Adams, Rachel. *Sideshow U.S.A.: Freaks and the American Cultural Imagination*. Chicago: University of Chicago Press, 2001. Print.

"African 'Beauties' Here to Join Circus." *New York Times* 1 April 1930: 28. *Proquest Historical Newspapers*. Web. 10 September 2011.

*Al G. Barnes Circus Official Route Book*. 1915 and 1922. CHS: Circus Historical Society. Web. 12 August 2011.

Alcott, Louisa May. *Under the Lilacs*. Boston: Little, Brown, 1877. Print.

Alexander, Robert. *Rasputin's Daughter*. New York: Penguin, 2006. Print.

Alger, Horatio. *The Young Acrobat of the Great North Circus*. New York: Frank F. Lovell, 1888. Print.

*Alice's Circus Daze*. Dir. Walt Disney. Perf. Lois Hardwick. Walt Disney, 1927. Film.

Allen, Robert. *Horrible Prettiness: Burlesque and American Culture*. Chapel Hill: University of North Carolina Press, 1991. Print.

Anawalt, Mary Louise, "Snapshots." *White Tops* February 1928: 5. Print.

Anderson, Elizabeth J. "General Willis Carver." Phreeque.com. Web. 24 September 2011.

_____. "Krao Farini — Darwin's Missing Link." Phreeque.com. Web. 24 September 2011.

Artaud, Antonin. "On the Balinese Theater." *Selected Writings* Ed. Susan Sontag. New York: Farrar, Straus and Giroux, 1976. 215–27. Print.

*At the Circus*. Dir. Edward Buzzell. Perf. The Marx Brothers. MGM, 1939. Film.

"At the Circus: Madame Sanyeah." *New York Clipper* 3 December 1870: 275.

"The Ballet at the Circus." *New York Sun* 29 March 1903: 4.2. Print.

Barker, Barbara. "Imre Kiralfy's Patriotic Spectacles: 'Columbus, and the Discovery of America' (1892–1893) and 'America' (1893)." *Dance Chronicle* 17.2 (1994): 149–78.

Barnum & Bailey's Greatest Show on Earth, Program, 1908. University of Southern Mississippi Digital Collections. Web. 11 July 2011.

"Barnum & Bailey's Greatest Show on Earth, 1895 Route Book." *Barnum & Bailey Route from 1891 to 1900*. CHS: Circus Historical Society. Web. 20 July 2011.

Barnum, P.T. *The Life of P.T. Barnum, Written By Himself*. New York: Redfield, 1855. Print.

Barry, John D. *The Congressman's Wife.* New York: Smart Set, 1903. Print.

_____. *The Intriguers: A Novel.* New York: Appleton, 1896. Print.

_____. *Mademoiselle Blanche.* New York: Stone and Kimball, 1896. Print.

Bary, Howard Y. *Strange Customs and Weird Beliefs of the Padaung "Giraffe-Neck Women."* Pamphlet. 1933. Vertical File, Giraffe-Necked Women. Parkinson Library. Print.

"The Bearded Lady of Geneva." *Gleason's Pictorial Drawing-Room Companion* 23 April 1853. Vertical File, Sideshow. Parkinson Library. Print.

Beatty, Clyde, and Edward Anthony. *The Big Cage.* New York: Century, 1933. Print.

Beecher, Henry Ward. "Popular Amusements." Lecture VI. *Seven Lectures to Young Men on Very Important Subjects.* Indianapolis: Cutler, 1844. 167–95. Print.

Bell, Betty Boyd. *Circus: A Girl's Own Story of Life under the "Big Top."* New York: Brewer, Warren and Putnam, 1931. Print.

Bell, Pearl Doles. *Gloria Gray: Love Pirate.* Chicago: Roberts, 1914. Print.

_____. *Her Elephant Man: A Story of the Sawdust Ring.* New York: McBride, 1919. Print.

_____. *The Love Link.* New York: Watt, 1925. Print.

_____. *Slaves of Destiny.* New York: Grosset and Dunlap, 1926. Print.

"Beyond Nancy Drew: A Guide to Girls' Literature." Sallie Bingham Center for Women's History and Culture. Duke University Libraries. Web. 22 August 2011.

"The Bicycle and Health: What Physicians and Riders Say in Its Favor." *Ladies' Standard Magazine.* April 1984. Women's History. About.com. Web. 14 September 2011.

*The Big Cage.* Dir. Kurt Neumann. Perf. Clyde Beatty, Mickey Rooney, and Andy Devine. Universal, 1933.

Bird, Caroline. *Enterprising Women.* New York: Norton, 2009.

Blumenbach, Johann Friedrich, et al. "On the Causes and Ways by Which Mankind Has Degenerated, As a Species." *Anthropological Treatises of Blumenbach and Hunter.* New York: Longman, Roberts, & Green, 1865. 207–76. Print.

"Bobbed Hair Brings Beards, German Warns Modern Woman." *New York Times* 13 July 1924: E1. Women's History and Culture. Duke University Libraries. Web. 22 August 2011.

Bogdan, Robert. "Circassian Beauties: Authentic Sideshow Fabrications." *Bandwagon* May-June 1986: 22–23. Print.

_____. *Freak Show: Presenting Human Oddities for Amusement and Profit.* Chicago: University of Chicago Press, 1988. Print.

Bolin, Winifred D. *Feminism, Reform and Social Service: A History of Women in Social Work.* Minneapolis: Minnesota Resource Center for Social Work Education, 1973.

*Bostock's Circus Fording a Stream.* S. Lubin, 1903. Film.

Bouissac, Paul. *Circus and Culture: A Semiotic Approach.* Bloomington: Indiana University Press, 1976. Print.

"Boy, It's Grand, Gorgeous Circus!" *Los Angeles Times* 2 April 1931: II.5. Print.

Bradna, Ella. "From Wealth to the Big Top for Me." Vertical File, Ella Bradna. Parkinson.

Bradna, Fred. *The Big Top: My Forty Years with the Greatest Show on Earth.* New York: Simon & Schuster, 1952.

Brandon, Ruth. *The Life and Many Deaths of Harry Houdini.* New York: Random House, 1993. Print.

Brinkley, Alan. *The Unfinished Nation: A Concise History of the American People.* 4th ed. Vol 2. New York: McGraw-Hill, 2004. Print.

Broadside Ballad Entitled "Flying Trapeze." The Word on the Street. National Library of Scotland Digital Library. Web. 9 August 2011.

Bryan, J., III. "Big Shot of the Big Top." *Saturday Evening Post* 24 August 1940: 18–36. Print.

*Buffalo Bill's Parade.* William N. Selig, 1903. Film.

"Bullets of Codona Fatal to His Ex-Wife." *New York Times* 1 August 1937: 4. *Proquest Historical Newspapers.* Web. 12 September 2011.

Burke, Kenneth. *A Grammar of Motives.* Berkeley: U of California P, 1999.

"Burma Ladies Add a Few Circus Rings." *New York Times* 15 April 1933: 16. *Proquest Historical Newspapers.* Web. 10 July 2011.

Burrows, Erin Naomi. "By the Hair of Her Chin: A Critical Biography of Bearded Lady Jane Barnell." Masters Thesis. Sarah Lawrence College, 2009. Print.

Butler, Judith. *Bodies That Matter: On the Discursive Limits of "Sex."* New York: Routledge, 1993.

_____. *Gender Trouble: Feminism and the Subversion of Identity.* New York: Routledge, 1999.

Carmeli, Yoram. "Circus Play, Circus Talk, and the Nostalgia for a Total Order." *Journal of Popular Culture* 35.3 (2001): 157–74. Print.

Carver, Madam (no first name given). *Life and Travels of Madam Carver and Her Midget Son, General Carver.* Vertical File, Madam Carver. Parkinson Library.

Case, Sue-Ellen. *Feminism and Theatre.* New York: Methuen, 1988. Print.

"Cat Man: Clyde Beatty." *Time* 29 March 1937. Web. Time Magazine Archives. 4 October 2011.

"Champagne in a Lion's Cage." *Marlborough Express* 24 September 1901: 8. PapersPast. Web. 22 October 2011.

*Charlie Chan at the Circus.* Dir. Harry Lachman. Perf. *Warner Oland, Keye Luke,* and *George Brasno.* Twentieth Century–Fox, 1936. Film.

Chasteen, Barbara. "Ella K. Ewing, Missouri Giantess: 1872–1913." Masters Thesis. Northeast Missouri State University, 1977.

Cheong, Kim. "Betty Broadbent — The Tattooed Venus." *Angels of Ink*. Web. 28 July 2011.

"Children of the Sawdust." *New York Times* 14 January 1872: 3. *Proquest Historical Newspapers*. Web. 10 September 2011.

Chindahl, George L. *A History of the Circus in America*. Caldwell, ID: Caxton, 1959. Print.

*The Circus*. Dir. Charles Chaplin. Perf. Charles Chaplin, Merna Kennedy and Al Ernest Garcia. Chaplin Studios, 1929. Film.

"Circus and Museum Freaks — Curiosities of Pathology." *Scientific American* 28 March 1908: 222. Print.

"Circus Arrival Due Here Soon." *The Times-Picayune* (New Orleans) 20 October 1927: 18. American Historical Newspapers. Web. 20 November 2011.

*Circus Co-Ed*. Dir. Leslie M. Roush. Perf. Budd Hulick and The Clarkonians. Paramount, 1940. Film.

"Circus Combines Beauty and Beast." *New York Times* 29 April 1927: 25. *Proquest Historical Newspapers*. Web. 10 September 2011.

"Circus Crowd Flees While the Tent Burns." *New York Times* 12 May 1906: 1. *Proquest Historical Newspapers*. Web. 10 June 2011.

"Circus Deb." *Chicago Sun Parade* 7 December 1941. Vertical File, Gloria Haight. Parkinson Library. Print.

"Circus Fall Fatal to Lillian Leitzel." *New York Times* 16 February 1931: 11. *Proquest Historical Newspapers*. Web. 1 April 2011.

"Circus Folk Mourn 'Best-Liked' Freak." *New York Times* 19 April 1926: 7. *Proquest Historical Newspapers*. Web. 8 September 2011.

"The Circus Freak Seen off Guard as a Human Being." *New York Times* 6 April 1913: SM11. *Proquest Historical Newspapers*. Web. 7 September 2011.

*Circus Girl*. Dir. John H. Auer. Perf. *June Travis, Robert Livingston*, and *Donald Cook*. Republic, 1937. Film.

"Circus Girls to War on Foreign Invasion." *New York Times* 12 January 1914: 9. *Proquest Historical Newspapers*. Web. 10 December 2011.

"Circus Life Attracts Her." *New York Times* 5 December 1899: 7. *Proquest Historical Newspapers*. Web. 10 September 2011.

"Circus Lore Is Told by Famous Clown." *New York Times* 6 April 1932: 24. *Proquest Historical Newspapers*. Web. 10 June 2011.

"Circus Opens in Gorgeous Colors." *New York Times* 22 March 1912: 9. *Proquest Historical Newspapers*. Web. 8 February 2011.

"Circus Poster Exhibition Sensationally Brings to Life America's First Colossal Entertainment Industry." News Archive. John and Mable Ringling Museum of Art. Web. 30 Sept. 1912.

*The Circus Queen Murder*. Dir. Roy William Neill.

Perf. Adolphe Menjou and Donald Cook. Columbia, 1933. Film.

"Circus Remodels New Lady Clown." *New York Times* 5 April 1939: 33. *Proquest Historical Newspapers*. Web. 10 September 2011.

*A Circus Romance*. Dir. Carl Gregory. Perf. *Muriel Ostriche* and *Riley Chamberlin*. Thanhouser, 1914. Film.

*A Circus Romance*. Dir. Charles M. Seay. Perf. *Muriel Ostriche* and *Edward* Davis. Equitable, 1916. Film.

"Circus Scout Finds New Thrills for the Big Top." *Popular Science*. March 1937: 38–39+. Print.

"Circus Seats Fall and 100 Are Hurt." *New York Times* 12 August 1906: 1. *Proquest Historical Newspapers*. Web. 10 January 2011.

*Circus Street Parade*. Lubin, 1903. Film.

"Circus Wardrobe Enthralls Keeper." *New York Times* 8 April 1936: 25.

"Circus Will Open in Garden Tonight." *New York Times* 8 April 1932: 23. *Proquest Historical Newspapers*. Web. 5 February 2011.

"Circus's Valkyrie Awaits Challenge." *New York Times* 11 April 1934: 25. *Proquest Historical Newspapers*. Web. 3 January 2011.

Clausen, Connie. *I Love You, Honey, But the Season's Over*. New York: Holt, 1961. Print.

*Clown Princes*. Dir. *George Sidney*. Perf. *George "Spanky" McFarland, Darla Hood*, and *Carl "Alfalfa" Switzer*. MGM, 1939. Film.

Cockerline, Neil C. "Ethical Considerations for the Conservation of Circus Posters." *WAAC Newsletter* 17.2 (May 1995). Web. 1 Oct. 1912.

Codona, Alfredo (as told to Courtney Ryley Cooper). "Split Seconds." *Saturday Evening Post*. 6 December 1930: 12–13+. Print.

_____. "Taking the Fall." *Saturday Evening Post* 28 February 1931: 12–13+. Print.

"Codona Kills Self, Shooting Ex-Wife." *New York Times* 31 July 1937: 30. *Proquest Historical Newspapers*. Web. 7 March 2011.

Codonas in Dual Tragedy." *Los Angeles Times* 31 July 1937: I.3. Print.

Coleman, Sydney H. "A Circus Act Modified." *New York Times* 25 April 1931: 13. *Proquest Historical Newspapers*. Web. 10 September 2011.

Contract for the 1931 Season, Ringling Bros. and Barnum & Bailey Circus, signed by Lillian Leitzel, November 1930. Vertical File, Lillian Leitzel. Parkinson Library. Print.

Cooper, Courtney Ryley. "The Keeper of the Bulls." *Saturday Evening Post* 6 May 1922: 17–18+. Print.

Cooper, Diana Starr. *Night after Night*. Washington, D.C.: Island, 1994. Print.

Cox, J. Randolph. *The Dime Novel Companion: A Source Book*. Westport, CT: Greenwood, 2000. Print.

Coxe, Antony Hippisley. *A Seat at the Circus*. New York: Macmillan, 1980. Print.

Culhane, John. *The American Circus: An Illustrated History.* New York: Holt, 1990. Print.

*Dangerous Curves.* Dir: Lothar Mendes. Perf. Clara Bow, Richard Arlen, and Kay Francis. Paramount, 1929. Film.

Darlington, Edgar B. P. *The Circus Boys Across the Continent, or Winning New Laurels on the Tanark.* Philadelphia: Altemus, 1911. Print.

_____. *The Circus Boys in Dixie Land, or Winning the Plaudits of the Sunny South.* Philadelphia: Altemus, 1911. Print.

_____. *The Circus Boys on the Flying Rings, or Making the Start in the Sawdust Life.* Philadelphia: Altemus, 1910. Print.

_____. *The Circus Boys on the Mississippi, or Afloat with the Big Show on the Big River.* Philadelphia: Altemus, 1912. Print.

_____. *The Circus Boys on the Plains, or the Advance Agents Ahead of the Show.* Akron: Saalfield, 1920. Print.

Davis, Janet M. *The Circus Age: Culture and Society under the American Big Top.* Chapel Hill: University of North Carolina Press, 2002. Print.

Davis, Michael M., Jr. *The Exploitation of Pleasure: A Study of Commercial Recreations in New York City.* New York: Russell Sage Foundation, 1911. Print.

*Day at the Circus.* Dir. Edwin S. Porter. Edison, 1901. Film.

Dayton, Dorothy. "Circus Folks a Quiet Lot." *New York Sun* 20 April 1932: 37. Print.

Deering, Mary S. *An Average Boy's Vacation.* 2d ed. Boston: Young, 1878. Print.

DeMott Robinson, Josephine. *The Circus Lady.* 1925. New York: Arno, 1980. Print.

_____. "Exercise as Rest for Woman Who Gets Tired." *New York Times* 20 January 1918: 60. *Proquest Historical Newspapers.* Web. 10 July 2011.

Dickinson, Emily, and Martha Dickinson Bianchi. *The Life and Letters of Emily Dickinson.* Boston: Houghton Mifflin, 1924.

Dickinson, Kenneth. "Women, Society, and the Circus." Masters Thesis. Baylor University. December 1997. Print.

Draper, John Daniel. "Beautiful Cart Acts in the Circus." *Driving Digest Magazine* 92 (1995/96): 40–45. Print.

_____. "The Davenport Family of Riders." *Bandwagon* November-December 1990: 22–29. Print.

_____. "Linda Jeal and Her Equestrian Kin." *Bandwagon* May-June 1987: 30–38. Print.

_____. "May Wirth." *White Tops* Mar.-Apr. 1979: 16–18. Print.

Duble, C.E. "A Tour with the Barnum & Bailey Greatest Show on Earth Season 1913." *Bandwagon*, January 1947. CHS: Circus Historical Society.

Dudden, Faye E. *Women in the American Theatre: Actresses and Audiences, 1790–1870.* New Haven: Yale University Press, 1994.

Dwight, Timothy. "On Revivals of Religion." Sermon XIV. *Sermons* Vol. 1. Boston: Peck, 1828. 226–43. Print.

Eckley, Wilton. *The American Circus.* Boston: Twayne, 1984. Print.

Edgerton, Harold E. "Circus Action in Color." *National Geographic* March 1948: 305–324. Print.

"'Elastic Skin Joe' Takes His Life at Circus Because the Tattooed Woman Jilted Him." *New York Times* 14 July 1927: 6. *Proquest Historical Newspapers.* Web. 10 July 2011.

"Elephants, Peanuts and Freaks Again." *New York Times* 23 March 1913: C7. *Proquest Historical Newspapers.* Web. 15 September 2011.

Eldridge, C.W. "La Belle Irene." *Tattoo History from A to Z. Tattoo Archive.* Web. 22 December 2010.

"Enlist Suffragists for a Circus Holiday." *New York Times* 1 April 1912: 7. *Proquest Historical Newspapers.* Web. 8 August 2011.

Enos, Gene. Letters between Gene Enos and Al Ringling. MS. Vertical File, Gene and Mary Enos. Parkinson Library.

Enss, Chris. *Buffalo Gals: Women of Buffalo Bill's Wild West Show.* Guilford, CT: Globe Pequot, 2005.

*Equestrian Acrobats.* Dir. David Miller. Perf. Pete Smith and the Cristiani Family. MGM, 1937. Film.

"Fall from Trapeze Kills Girl in Circus." *New York Times* 13 August 1932: 17. *Proquest Historical Newspapers.* Web. 10 January 2011.

"Fat Lady Is Dead at Coney Island." *New York Times* 28 November 1940: 25. *Proquest Historical Newspapers.* Web. 21 September 2011.

"Fat People." Vertical File, Fat Women. Parkinson Library. Print.

"Fat Women." *New York Times* 6 October 1881: 4. *Proquest Historical Newspapers.* Web. 5 January 2011.

Faulk, Barry J. *Music Hall and Modernity: The Late-Victorian Discovery of Popular Culture.* Athens: Ohio University Press, 2004. Print.

Feld, Rose C. "Plucky Nellie Revell Writes a Cheery Book." *New York Times* 6 January 1924: XX8. *Proquest Historical Newspapers.* Web. 1 February 2011.

Fiedler, Leslie. *Freaks: Myths and Images of the Secret Self.* New York: Simon and Schuster, 1978. Print.

Field, Louise Maunsell. Rev. of *The Lost Girl,* by D. H. Lawrence. *New York Times Book Review,* 27 March 1921: 22+. *Proquest Historical Newspapers.* Web. 7 March 2011.

"15,000 New Yorkers out for the Circus." *New York Times* 30 March 1917: 11. *Proquest Historical Newspapers.* Web. 30 August 2011.

Finn, Frank S. *The Boy Clown.* New York: Beadle and Adams, 1878. Print.

Fisher, Linda A., and Carrie Bowers. *Agnes Lake Hickok: Queen of the Circus, Wife of a Legend.* Norman: University of Oklahoma Press, 2009. Print.

FitzGerald, William G. "Sideshows, III." *The Strand Magazine* 13 (1897): 521–28. Print.

"5,000 See Acrobat Injured at Circus." *New York Times* 13 April 1935: 17. *Proquest Historical Newspapers.* Web. 15 September 2011.

Flint, Richard W. "American Showmen and European Dealers: Commerce in Wild Animals in Nineteenth Century America." *New Worlds, New Animals: From Menagerie to Zoological Park in the Nineteenth Century.* Ed. R.J. Hoage and William A. Deiss. Baltimore: Johns Hopkins University Press, 1996. 97–108. Print.

"The Flying Trapezes." *Bandwagon* (July-August 1965): 26–28. Print.

"400 Entertain Tody Hamilton: Gov. Hughes Speaks at Dinner to the Veteran Press Agent Again." *New York Times* 3 March 1907: 12. *Proquest Historical Newspapers.* Web. 4 November 2011.

Frank, Barney. *Improper Bostonians: Lesbian and Gay History from the Puritans to Playland.* Boston: Beacon, 1999. Print.

*Freaks.* Dir. Tod Browning. Perf. *Wallace Ford, Leila Hyams,* and *Olga Baclanova.* MGM, 1932. Film.

Frega, Donnalee. *Women of Illusion: A Circus Family's Story.* New York: Palgrave, 2001. Print.

Frost, Linda. *Never One Nation: Freaks, Savages, and Whiteness in U.S. Popular Culture, 1850–1877.* Minneapolis: University of Minnesota Press, 2005. Print.

Gates, H.L. *Here Comes the Bandwagon.* New York: Grosset and Dunlap, 1928. Print.

"Gene and Mary Enos: Perch Pole Performers." *Daily Bulletin* 9 March 1917: 16–17. Print.

"Giraffe, A Rarity in America." *Chicago Tribune* 1 September 1895: 43. Print.

Glenn, Susan A. *Female Spectacle: The Theatrical Roots of Modern Feminism.* Cambridge: Harvard University Press, 2000. Print.

Gobin, Lindsey. "Small Isn't All: A Study of Little People." Masters Thesis. The University of Findlay, 2005. Print.

Gossard, Steve. "The Flying Wards: The Greatest Aerial Flying Return Act in the World." *Bandwagon* November/December 1986: 5–19.

_____. "Gene and Mary Enos." *Bandwagon* September/October 1987: 15–21. Print.

_____. *A Reckless Era of Aerial Performance: The Evolution of Trapeze.* 2d ed. Normal, IL: Steve Gossard, 1994.

Granfield, Linda. "Something Wicked This Way Comes." *The Circus, 1870–1950.* Ed. Noel Daniel. Los Angeles: Taschen, 2008. 25–36. Print.

"The Great Circus Parade." *New York Times* 20 March 1892: 8. *Proquest Historical Newspapers.* Web. 2 September 2011.

"Great Fun at the Circus." *New York Times* 2 April 1897: 7. *Proquest Historical Newspapers.* Web. 25 September 2011.

Hackett, Marjorie. "Lewis Brothers Memories from Marg Hackett." Vertical File, Marjorie Hackett. Parkinson Library. Print.

Herbert, Dorothy. "Herbert's Horses." Part One. *Bandwagon* November/December 1988: 4–23.

_____. "Herbert's Horses." Part Two. *Bandwagon* January/February 1989: 19–30.

_____. "Herbert's Horses." Part Three. *Bandwagon* March/April 1989: 20–33.

Herlihy, David V. *Bicycle: The History.* New Haven: Yale UP, 2006.

Hingston, Edward P. *The Genial Showman, Being the Reminiscences of the Life of Artemus Ward.* 1870. Barre, MA: Imprint Society, 1971. Print.

*Historical Statistics of the United States: Colonial Times to 1970.* Part I. Washington, D.C.: U.S. Department of Commerce, Bureau of the Census, 1975.

"Homeliest Woman Risks Circus Fame." *New York Times* 14 April 1929: 15. *Proquest Historical Newspapers.* Web. 24 March 2011.

Hopkins, Albert A. *Magic: Stage Illusions and Scientific Diversions, Including Trick Photography.* New York: Munn, 1897. Print.

"Horseback at the Circus: Showman's Seventh Sense Says Public Once More Prefers the Bareback Rider." *New York Times* 30 March 1919: 51.

Hough, Robert. *The Final Confession of Mabel Stark.* New York: Atlantic, 2001. Print.

"How the Wild West Show Has Developed." *New York Times* 7 April 1901: 26. *Proquest Historical Newspapers.* Web. 27 June 2011.

Huey, Rodney A. "An Abbreviated History of the Circus in America." Circus Federation. Web. 17 August 2011.

*I'm No Angel.* Dir. Wesley Ruggles. Perf. Mae West and Cary Grant. Paramount, 1933. Film.

*Imre Kiralfy's Sublime Nautical, Martial and Poetical Spectacle, "Columbus and the Discovery of America," for the First Time Now Produced in Connection with the Barnum & Bailey Greatest Show on Earth.* Buffalo: Courier, 1892.

"In the Driftway." *Nation.* 23 April 1924: 480. Print.

"In the Driftway." *Nation.* 11 March 1931: 272–273. Print.

Iwen, Marg. "The Robinsons of Zanesville, 1893–1900." *Bottles and Glass* (Winter 2004): 2–7. Print.

Jackson, Kenneth, ed. *The Encyclopedia of New York City.* New Haven: Yale University Press, 1995. Print.

Jando, Dominique. "The Birth of American Popular Culture: The Circus, 1870–1950." Taschen. Web. 18 September 2011.

"Jodie Talks, Elephants Listen." *White Tops* January-February 1990: 34. Print.

Kasson, Joy S. *Buffalo Bill's Wild West: Celebrity, Memory, and Popular History.* New York: Hill and Wang, 2000. Print.

Kelly, Emmett. *Clown.* Cutchogue, NY: Buccaneer Books, 1996.

Kelley, Francis Beverly. "Along Clown Alley." *Sat-*

*urday Evening Post* 7 November 1942: 22–23+.
Print.

———. "The Land of Sawdust and Spangles: A
World in Miniature." *National Geographic* October 1931: 463–516. Print.

———. "The Wonder City That Moves at Night."
*National Geographic* March 1948: 289–305. Print.

"Killed by Circus Woman." *New York Times* 16 April
1910: 1. *Proquest Historical Newspapers.* Web. 27
February 2011.

*King of the Jungle.* Dir. H. Bruce Humberstone and
Max Marcin. Perf. Buster Crabbe, Frances Dee,
and Sidney Toler. Paramount, 1933. Film.

Kisling, Vernon N., Jr. "The Origin and Develop-
ment of American Zoological Parks to 1899." *New
Worlds, New Animals: From Menagerie to Zoological
Park in the Nineteenth Century.* Ed. R.J. Hoage
and William A. Deiss. Baltimore: Johns Hopkins
University Press, 1996. 109–25. Print.

Kline, Tiny. *Circus Queen and Tinker Bell: The Memoir of Tiny Kline.* Ed. Janet M. Davis. Urbana:
University of Illinois Press, 2008. Print.

"The Latest New Woman: She Is a Big Factor in the
Circus of 1896." Vertical File, Women Clowns,
Parkinson. Print.

Lawrence, D.H. *The Lost Girl.* 1920. Ed. John
Worthen. Cambridge: Cambridge University
Press, 1981. Print.

———. *The Rainbow.* New York: Modern Library,
1915. Print.

———. *Women in Love.* New York: Private Printing,
1920. Print.

"Legless Woman Gone. Husband Mystified." *New
York Times* 24 July 1925: 13. *Proquest Historical
Newspapers.* Web. 11 March 2011.

Leitzel, Lillian. "Random Recollections," as told to
Paul Brown. MS. Vertical File, Lillian Leitzel.
Parkinson Library.

Lengel, Laura, and John T. Warren. *Casting Gender:
Women and Performance in Intercultural Contexts.*
New York: Lang, 2005. Print.

Letter to President William McKinley from Annie
Oakley. *The U.S. National Archives and Records
Administration.* Web. 29 July 2011.

"Liner Brings Ashes of Lillian Leitzel." *New York
Times* 4 April 1931: 31. *Proquest Historical Newspapers.* Web. 20 November 2011.

"Lizzie Whitlock, Fat Lady, Dies." *Coldwater*
(Ontario) *Courier.* Vertical File, Circus Women.
Parkinson Library.

*The Lost Jungle* Dir. *David Howard* and *Armand
Schaefer.* Perf. *Clyde Beatty, Cecilia Parker,* and *Syd
Saylor.* Mascot, 1934. Film.

"Louis F. Sunlin." Circus Biographies, Obituaries.
CHS: Circus Historical Society. Web. 22 August
2011.

Lowanda, Julia. "How Circus Women Enjoy Life."
*Sunday Leader* (Eau Claire, WI) 17 June 1906. Vertical File, Circus Women. Parkinson Library. Print.

Lowry, Velma. "Rita Dunn Called High Wire Queen
for Daring Aerial Performances." *White Tops*
May/June 1984: 18. Print.

Lynch, Kathryn, and Michael S. Sims. *Zanesville.*
Charleston: Arcadia, 2006. Print.

"Madame Victoria Dead: The Funeral of the Heav-
iest Woman in the Country." *New York Times* 5
September 1885: 1. *Proquest Historical Newspapers.*
Web. 14 March 2011.

Magri, M. Lavinia. *The Autobiography of Mrs. Tom
Thumb (Some of My Life Experiences).* Ed. A.H.
Saxon. Hamden, CT: Archon, 1979.

Martell, Joanne. *Millie-Christine: Fearfully and Won-
derfully Made.* Winston-Salem, NC: Blair, 2000.
Print.

May, Earl Chapin. *Behind the Seams of a Circus.* New
York, 1924. Print.

———. "Bigger and Better But Still the Same." *New
York Times* 9 April 1933: SM10+. *Proquest
Historical Newspapers.* Web. 7 April 2011.

———. *The Circus from Rome to Ringling.* New York:
Duffield and Green, 1932. Print.

———. *Cuddy of the White Tops.* New York: Appleton, 1924. Print.

———. *Jockeys, Crooks and Kings: The Story of Winnie
O'Connor's Life as Told to E.C. May.* London:
Scott, 1930. Print.

———. "Keeping the Circus in Motion." *Popular Mechanics* March 1926: 387–92. Print.

———. "Why Women Dominate Wild Animals."
Earl Chapin May Collection. Parkinson Library.
Print.

———. "With the 'Merry Joeys' of the Tent World."
*Popular Mechanics* April 1927: 595–99. Print.

McConnell, John H. *A Ring, a Horse, and a Clown:
An Eight Generation History of the Hannefords.* Detroit: Astley and Rickette, 1992. Print.

McGann, Susan. *The Battle of the Nurses: A Study of
Eight Women Who Influenced the Development of
Professional Nursing, 1880–1930.* London: Scutari,
1992.

McMurtry, Larry. *The Colonel and Little Missie: Buf-
falo Bill, Annie Oakley, and the Beginnings of
Superstardom in America.* New York: Simon &
Schuster, 2005. Print.

McNamara, Brooks. "'A Congress of Wonders': The
Rise and Fall of the Dime Museum." *Emerson So-
ciety Quarterly* 20 (3rd Quarter 1974): 216–32.
Print.

Means, Michael H. "Imre Kiralfy meets Barnum &
Bailey—and the Circus Spec is Never the Same
Again." *The Many Worlds of Circus.* Ed. Robert
Sugarman. Newcastle: Cambridge Scholars, 2007.
3–10.

Mifflin, Margot. *Bodies of Subversion: A Secret History
of Women and Tattoo.* New York: Juno, 1997. Print.

"Miss Zittella Flynn." *New York Times* 17 May 1938:
23. *Proquest Historical Newspapers.* Web. 27 May
2011.

Mitchell, Michael. *Monsters of the Gilded Age: The Photographs of Charles Eisenmann.* Toronto: Gage, 1979.

"Mollie Bailey, Circus Owner, 1844–1918." Great Texas Women. The University of Texas at Austin. Web. 12 August 2011.

"The Mollie Bailey Texas Top." *White Tops* November 1929: 1+. Print.

Montgomery, L.M. *Anne of Green Gables.* New York: Grosset & Dunlap, 1908. Print.

Montgomery, Richard R. *Barnum's Hunters, or, Trapping Wild Animals for the Greatest Show on Earth.* New York: Tousey, 1887. Print.

Morello, Karen. *The Invisible Bar: The Woman Lawyer in America, 1638–1986.* New York: Random House, 1986.

Morton, Timothy. *Ecology without Nature: Rethinking Environmental Aesthetics.* Cambridge: Harvard University Press, 2007.

Moy, James S. "Entertainments at John B. Ricketts's Circus, 1793–1800." *Educational Theatre Journal* 30. 2 (1978): 186–202. Print.

"Mrs. Ella Bradna Dies." *Sarasota Journal.* 12 November 1957: 2.

"Mrs. Lake-Hickock Dead." *New York Times* 23 August 1907: 7. *Proquest Historical Newspapers.* Web. 10 April 2011.

Mulvey, Laura. "Visual Pleasure and Narrative Cinema." *Film Theory and Criticism: Introductory Readings.* 7th ed. Ed. Leo Braudy and Marshall Cohen. New York: Oxford University Press, 2009: 711–22. Print.

Munsterberg, Marjorie. "Ekphrasis." *Writing About Art.* Web. 30 November 2011.

Murray, Charles Theodore. *A Modern Gypsy: A Romance of Circus Life.* New York: American Technical Book, 1897. Print.

"Myrtle Corbin, the Four-Legged Woman of Blount County." ALBLOUNT-L Archives. Web. 6 August 2011.

"New, Bigger Circus Thrills Garden Crowd." *New York Times* 24 March 1905: 6. *Proquest Historical Newspapers.* Web. 10 March 2011.

*1917 Courier.* Ringling Bros. Circus. CHS: Circus Historical Society. Web. 12 August 2011.

Niven, Penelope. *Carl Sandburg: Adventures of a Poet.* New York: Harcourt Children's Editions, 2003. Print.

"Noted Woman Midget Ends Life by Hanging." *New York Times* 9 November 1940: 32. *Proquest Historical Newspapers.* Web. 19 July 2011.

"Old Circus Clown Tinks Modern Show Too Elaborate." *New York Times* 20 April 1924: X15. *Proquest Historical Newspapers.* Web. 2 April 2011.

"Olive Oatman." *Tattoo History from A to Z. Tattoo Archive.* Web. 22 December 2010.

"One Circus Afternoon." *New York Times* 29 March 1903: 8. *Proquest Historical Newspapers.* Web. 27 May 2011.

Orr, Gertrude. *The Tiger Lady: The Life of Mabel Stark, Noted Animal Trainer.* Akron, OH: Saalfield, 1935. Print.

Otis, James. *Toby Tyler, or Ten Weeks with a Circus.* New York: Harper, 1881. Print.

Palmer, Virginia. "Rose Holland, Circus Queen." *Exclusively Yours* 1 June 1966: 7–11. Vertical File, Rose Holland. Parkinson Library. Print.

*Panorama of Circus Train Unloading Horses.* S. Lubin, 1903, Film.

Paquet, Laura Byrne. "Those Daring Young Girls." *Victorian Decorating and Lifestyle.* April-May 1996: 30–32+. Print.

Parkinson, Greg. "Poster Princess — Victoria Condona." *Bandwagon* July/August 1980: 11–14. Print.

Parry, Albert. *Tattoo: Secrets of a Strange Art as Practiced among the Natives of the United States.* New York: Simon & Schuster, 1933. Print.

"The Passing of the Once Popular Sideshow Freak." *New York Times* 26 February 1911: SM12. *Proquest Historical Newspapers.* Web. 4 August 2011.

Peacock, Louise. *Serious Play: Modern Clown Performance.* Bristol: Intellect Books, 2009. Print.

Peck, George Wilbur. *Peck's Bad Boy with the Circus.* Chicago: Stanton and Van Vliet, 1905. Print.

*Peck's Bad Boy with the Circus.* Dir. Edward F. Cline. Perf. Tommy Kelly, Ann Gillis, and Edgar Kennedy. Sol Lesser, 1938. Film.

Pednaud, J. Tithonus. "Sandwina: Woman of Steel." The Human Marvels: Presenting Peculiar People. Web. 4 September 2011.

"Peep behind the Scenes." *New York Times* 22 April 1896: 10. *Proquest Historical Newspapers.* Web. 7 March 2011.

"The People of the South Pacific." *Chicago Tribune* 8 September 1895: 38. Print.

Perlmann, Joel, and Robert A. Margo. *Women's Work?: American Schoolteachers, 1650–1920.* Chicago: University of Chicago Press, 2001.

Perz, Bunni Bartok. *Black Bras Don't Show the Dirt, or Life on a Mudshow.* Sarasota: ValJan, 1984. Print.

Pfening, Fred D., Jr. "Human Cannonballs." *Bandwagon* November/December 1976: 4. Print.

———. "Spec-ology of the Circus." *Bandwagon* November/December 2003: 4–20.

———. "The Strobridge Lithographing Company, the Ringling Brothers, and Their Circuses." *The Amazing Circus Poster: The Strobridge Lithographing Company.* Eds. Kristin L. Spangenberg and Deborah W. Walk. Cincinnati: Cincinnati Art Museum, 2011. 36–42.

Pfening, Fred D., III. "The Circus in Fiction: An Interpretation." *Bandwagon* May 1972: 14. Vertical Files, Fiction, Parkinson. Print.

Phillips, David Graham. *Susan Lenox: Her Fall and Rise.* 2 vols. New York: Appleton, 1917. Print.

*Pink Tights.* Dir. B. Reeves Eason. Perf. Gladys Walton, Jack Perrin, and Dave Dyas. Universal, 1920. Film.

"The Play: 'Jumbo' Finally Gets under Way at the Hippodrome, with Actors, Acrobats, and Animals." *New York Times* 18 November 1935: 20. *Proquest Historical Newspapers.* Web. 17 March 2011.

"Pretty Rose Wentworth: A Remarkable Woman Who Does Many Things at the Circus." *New York Times* 28 April 1895: 16. *Proquest Historical Newspapers.* Web. 18 January 2011.

"Race Issue at a Circus." *New York Times* 9 October 1904: 5. *Proquest Historical Newspapers.* Web. 18 March 2011.

*Rebecca of Sunnybrook Farm.* Dir. Marshall Neilan. Perf: Mary Pickford, Eugene O'Brien. Mary Pickford Company, 1917. Film.

Revell, Nellie. *Right off the Chest.* New York: Doran, 1923. Print.

_____. *Spangles.* New York: Grosset and Dunlap, 1926. Print.

Riley, Glenda. *The Life and Legacy of Annie Oakley.* Norman: University of Oklahoma Press, 2002. Print."

Riley, James Whitcomb. "The Circus Parade." *Poems and Prose Sketches of James Whitcomb Riley.* New York: Scribner's, 1898. 141–42.

Ringling, Alfred T. *Life Story of the Ringling Brothers.* Chicago: Donnelley, 1900. Print.

*Ringling Bros. and Barnum & Bailey Route Book,* 1922 and 1941. CHS: Circus Historical Society. Web. 14 September 2011.

"Ringling Bros. Help Wisconsin: Wives Are Members of Suffrage Society — Allow Campaigning on Circus Grounds." *Woman's Journal* 13 July 1912: 2. Print.

*Ringling Bros. Official Program.* 1893. CHS: Circus Historical Society. Web. 1 Oct. 2012.

*Ringling Bros. Route Book,* 1890 and 1903. CHS: Circus Historical Society. Web. 14 August 2011.

Roach, Joyce Gibson. *The Cowgirls.* Denton: University of North Texas Press, 1990. Print.

Robbins, Tod. "Spurs." *Who Wants a Green Bottle? And Other Uneasy Tales.* London: Allan, 1926.

Roberts, Phil. "Agnes Thatcher Lake: Equestrian Rider, Circus Performer, and Wild Bill's Wife." Web. 11 October 2011.

Robie, Frank. "The Real Bird Millman." *Bandwagon* November/December 1998: 44–46.

Rossi, Victoria B. Christiani. *Spangles, Elephants, Violets and Me: The Circus Inside Out, a Memoir.* New York: iUniverse, 2007. Print.

Roth, Hy, and Robert Cromie. *The Little People.* New York: Everest House, 1980. Print.

Row, E.W. "Nominating Nellie Revell." *New York Times* 28 June 1922: 11. *Proquest Historical Newspapers.* Web. 19 February 2011.

Ruben, Marina Koestler. "Alice Ramsey's Historic Cross-Country Drive." 5 June 2009. *Smithsonian. com.* Smithsonian Institution, n.d. Web. 22 May 2010.

Rule Sheet, 1912, Ringling Bros. Vertical File, Circus Women. Parkinson. Print.

Rules Concerning Ballet Girls Supplementary in Contract, October 1912 to March 1913, Ringling Bros. Vertical File, Circus Women. Parkinson. Print.

St. Leon, Mark. "An Unbelievable Lady Bareback Rider, May Wirth." *Bandwagon* May/June 1990: 4–13. Print.

Savarese, Nicola, and Richard Fowler. "1931: Antonin Artaud Sees Balinese Theatre at the Paris Colonial Exposition." *TDR* 45. 3 (2001): 51–77. Print.

Saxon, A.H. *P.T. Barnum: The Legend and the Man.* New York: Columbia UP, 1989. Print.

Scharff, Virginia. *Taking the Wheel: Women and the Coming of the Motor Age.* New York: Free, 1991. Print.

"Seats Fall at a Circus." *New York Times* 30 April 1907: 1. *Proquest Historical Newspapers.* Web. 6 July 2011.

Sherwood, Bob. *Hold Yer Hosses! The Elephants Are Coming.* New York: Macmillan, 1932.

"Shots Kill Mrs. Codona." *Los Angeles Times* 1 August 1937: I.3. Print.

Shteir, Rachel. *Striptease: The Untold History of the Girlie Show.* New York: Oxford University Press, 2004. Print.

"Slapstick as an Art," *New York Times Magazine* 10 April 1938: 9+. *Proquest Historical Newspapers.* Web. 6 October 2011.

Smith, A. Morton. "Circus Stars of Yesteryears, VII. Bessie Castello." *Hobbies — The Magazine for Collectors* February 1951: 28–29.

_____. "Circus Stars of Yesteryears, VI. Elizabeth Hanneford Clarke." Part I. *Hobbies — The Magazine for Collectors* December 1950: 26–27. Print.

_____. "Circus Stars of Yesteryears, VI. Elizabeth Hanneford Clarke." Part II. *Hobbies — The Magazine for Collectors* January 1951: 28–29. Print.

_____. "Circus Stars of Yesteryears, Eugenie Silbon." *Hobbies — The Magazine for Collectors* July 1950: 24–25. Print.

_____. "Circus Stars of Yesteryears: Ma Belle Chipman." *Hobbies — The Magazine for Collectors* April 1951: 26–27. Print.

_____. "Spec-ology of the Circus." *Billboard* 31 July 1943: 51+. Print.

Smith, Bill, and Jerry Naunheim. "Gorin's Gentle Giant: Miss Ella." *St. Louis Post Dispatch Magazine* 22 January 1995: 7–10. Print.

Sobel, Bernard. *A Pictorial History of the Burlesque.* New York: Bonanza, 1956. Print.

*Spangles.* Dir. Frank O'Connor. Perf. Marian Nixon and Pat O'Malley. Universal, 1926.

Spencer, Balinda (Estella) Merriam. *Diary of a Circus Lady.* John Robinson's Ten Big Shows Combined Season 1889. MS. Parkinson Library.

Spyri, Johanna. *Heidi, Her Years of Wandering and Learning: A Story for Children and Those Who Love Children.* New York: Platt & Peck, 1884. Print.

Standish, Hal. *Fred Fearnot and the Snake-Charmer; or, Out with the Circus Fakirs.* New York: Tousey, 1906. Print.

_____. *Fred Fearnot's Wild West Show, or, The Biggest Thing on Earth.* New York: Tousey, 1900. Print.

Stanton, Jeffrey. "Coney Island — Dreamland." Web. 12 August 2011.

Stark, Mabel. Letters to Earl Chapin May, 1933–34. MS. Earl Chapin May Collection. Parkinson Library.

Stark, Mabel, and Gertrude Orr. *Hold That Tiger.* Caldwell, ID: Caxton, 1938. Print.

Steegmuller, Francis. "Onward and Upward with the Arts: An Angel, a Flower, a Bird." *New Yorker* 27 September 1969: 130–43.

Steinmeyer, Jim. *Hiding the Elephant: How Magicians Invented the Impossible and Learned to Disappear.* New York: Carroll and Graf, 2003. Print.

Stencell, A.W. *Girl Show: Into the Canvas World of Bump and Grind.* Toronto: ECW Press, 1999.

Stoddart, Helen. *Rings of Desire: Circus History and Representation.* Manchester: Manchester University Press, 2000. Print.

"Storm Hits Circus: Audience in a Panic." *New York Times* 19 June 1910: 20. *Proquest Historical Newspapers.* Web. 21 October 2011.

"A Study in Concentration as Circus Opened in Garden." *New York Times* 9 April 1937: 23. *Proquest Historical Newspapers.* Web. 18 November 2011.

"Suffrage Movement and Women's History." *Jessie Jack Hooper Collection.* Oshkosh Public Museum Virtual Exhibit. n.d. Web. 11 December 2009. Print.

"Suffragists at Tea with Circus Women." *New York Times* 8 April 1912: 7. *Proquest Historical Newspapers.* Web. 20 March 2011.

*Susan Lenox: Her Fall and Rise.* Dir. Leon Gordon. Perf. Greta Garbo and Clark Gable. MGM, 1931. Film.

Sutherland, Donald E. *The Expansion of Everyday Life, 1860–1876.* New York: Harper, 1989. Print.

"Suggested Comments by Celeste Atayde: An Interview." 1/25/96. MS. Vertical File, Tosca Canistrelli. Parkinson Library.

Sweet, Robert C., and Robert W. Habenstein. "Some Perspectives on the Circus in Transition." *Journal of Popular Culture* (Winter 1972): 583–90. Print.

"Sword-Swallower X-Rayed." *Popular Science* August 1938: 29. Print.

Taber, Bob. "Olga Celeste." *White Tops* July-August 1962: 33–34. Print.

Tait, Peta. *Circus Bodies: Cultural Identity in Aerial Performance.* New York: Routledge, 2005. Print.

"Tall Miss Ella Ewing." *New York Times* 18 April 1897: 14. *Proquest Historical Newspapers.* Web. 23 February 2011.

"The Tank's the Thing. *New York Times* 29 March 1895: 3. *Proquest Historical Newspapers.* Web. 5 March 2011.

Taylor, Robert Lewis. *Center Ring: The People of the Circus.* New York: Doubleday, 1956. Print.

"10,000 See Woman Die in Fall in Detroit Circus Trapeze Act." *New York Times* 3 February 1931: 22. *Proquest Historical Newspapers.* Web. 30 September 2011.

Thayer, Stuart. *Annals of the Early American Circus, 1830–1847.* Vol. II. Seattle: Peanut Butter, 1986. Print.

_____. "C. E. Webb's Russell Brothers Circus." *Bandwagon* March-April 1969: 13–19. CHS: Circus Historical Society. Bandwagon. Web. 16 September 2011.

"Tody Hamilton, Circus Agent, Dies." *New York Times* 17 August 1916: 11. *Proquest Historical Newspapers.* Web. 20 August 2011.

Toossi, Mitra. "A Century of Change: The U.S. Labor Force, 1950–2050." *Monthly Labor Review* (May 2002): 15–28.

"Trainer Reaches Top: Pallenberg Makes Name Mean Best in Bear Acts." *Billboard* 25 June 1955: 86.

"Trainer Seriously Hurt by Lion." *New York Times* 29 January 1932: 19. *Proquest Historical Newspapers.* Web. 2 September 2011.

Truzzi, Marcello. "Introduction: Circuses, Carnivals and Fairs." *Journal of Popular Culture* (Winter 1972): 531–33. Print.

Tully, Jim. *Circus Parade.* New York: Boni, 1927. Print.

Twain, Mark. *The Adventures of Huckleberry Finn.* London: Chatto and Windus, 1884. Print.

"Under the Marquee." *Billboard* 27 February 1943: 37+.

*United States Census of 1900: A Series of Tables Compiled from the Official Returns Giving the Distribution of Population according to the Twelfth Census.* New York: Appleton, 1901. Print.

"Variety, Minstrel and Circus." *New York Clipper* 12 October 1889: 519 and 4 Jan 1890: 713. Print.

"Very New Woman Is Josephine Mathews, Acrobat and Clown." June 1896. Vertical File, Women Clowns. Parkinson Library.

"Vessel Type EC2: The Liberty Ship." *Troopships of World War II.* Web. 27 July 2011.

"Wages, Hours and Speed in the Missouri Boot and Shoe Factories." *The Survey: A Journal of Constructive Philanthropy* 25.2 (1910): 96–97. Print.

Walk, Deborah W. "The Gilded Legacy of the Circus Kings." *The Amazing American Circus Poster: The Strobridge Lithography Company.* Cincinnati: Cincinnati Art Museum and the Ringling Museum of Art, 2011. 15–19.

Wallis, Michael. *The Real Wild West: The 101 Ranch and the Creation of the American West.* New York: St. Martin's Press, 1999. Print.

Weir, Hugh C. "The Women of the Circus." *Hampton's Broadway Magazine* (June 1909): 797–805. Vertical File, Circus Women. Parkinson Library.

Wertheimer, Barbara M. *We Were There: The Story of Working Women in America.* New York: Pantheon, 1977.

West, Mae. *Goodness Had Nothing to Do with It.* New York: Avon, 1959. Print.

"Why Miss Williams Is a Clown." *New York Times* 31 Mar 1895: 27. *Proquest Historical Newspapers.* Web. 20 May 2011.

"Why They Go to the Circus." *New York Times* 13 April 1900: 9. *Proquest Historical Newspapers.* Web. 3 May 2011.

Wiggin, Kate Douglas. *Rebecca of Sunnybrook Farm.* Boston: Houghton, 1902. Print.

"With the Ladies of the Circus." *New York Times* 1 April 1906: SM3. *Proquest Historical Newspapers.* Web. 4 September 2011.

*The Woman Always Pays.* Dir. Urban Gad. Perf. *Asta Nielsen, Robert Dinesen,* and *Poul Reumert.* Kosmorama, 1910. Film.

"Woman Circus Star, 90, Dies in Poverty." *New York Times* 4 July 1932: 13. *Proquest Historical Newspapers.* Web. 4 December 2011.

"Woman, Undeterred by Fall off Trapeze, to Appear Here Again with Circus Soon." *New York Times* 22 March 1936: N7. *Proquest Historical Newspapers.* Web. 4 January 2011.

"Women Hear How to Train." *New York Times* 30 March 1917: 20. *Proquest Historical Newspapers.* Web. 4 September 2011.

"WPA Circus Performance Given for 150 Children at Bellevue." *New York Times* 9 November 1935: 17. *Proquest Historical Newspapers.* Web. 11 April 2011.

Yates, L.B. "The Circus Girl." *Saturday Evening Post* 17 July 1920: 30–34+. Print.

_____. "Troupin' with the Tents." *Saturday Evening Post* 22 April 1922: 20–22. Print.

"You Can't Mix Husbands with Tigers, Trainer Says." *Minneapolis Star* 2 July 1934: 1. Vertical File, Mabel Stark. Parkinson Library. Print.

Zora, Lucia. *Sawdust and Solitude.* Ed. Courtney Ryley Cooper. Boston: Little, Brown, 1928. Print.

# Index

Numbers in **bold italics** indicate pages with photographs.